The Polish Prince

Zbigniew Janczewski

THE POLISH PRINCE

WWII Memoirs of Zbigniew Janczewski

DISCLAIMERS

This story is intended to be an accurate depiction of historical events from the perspective of Zbigniew Janczewski. Opinions in the memoirs are his own and are unchanged to maintain complete authenticity.
In some cases, names have been changed to protect individuals' privacy.
All statements in annotations are intended to supplement the story. Sources of information are listed in the Bibliography at the end of the book.
All illustrations within this book are based on authentic data from their respective times and places. To the best of the copyright owner's knowledge, all sources have been approved for use, and every effort has been made to contact any copyright holders.

Copyright © 2022 owned by Polo Altynski-Ross

All rights reserved. No part of this book may be reproduced or used in any manner without written permission of the copyright owner except for the use of quotations in a book review. For more information, contact: polo@thepolishprince.info.

First paperback edition June 2022
First ebook edition June 2022

Paperback ISBN: 979-8-9860624-0-2
Ebook ISBN: 979-8-9860624-1-9

thepolishprince.info

*Since wars begin in the minds of men,
it is in the minds of men that
the defenses of peace must be constructed.*

– *Preamble to the Constitution of UNESCO, 1945*

Contents

INTRODUCTION
    Foreword xi
    Preface xiii

THE STORY
    Confession 1

PART I: The Pre-War Years
    Childhood 7
    Those Years – Równe 13

PART II: The War Years
    September Memories 19
    Russian Occupation 28
    1941 32
    Russki Chase 46
    November 7 53
    Winter Escapade 62
    The Final Solution 71
    Dumka Saves Lives 82
    The "Trial" Against Poles 99
    Eve 103
    In Germany 107
    Escape from Hell 117
    Victory Day 134

PART III: The Post-War Situation
    The Long Return 143
    Ursul 165
    The Asylum Route 173

PART IV: Life in the Eastern Bloc
　The Post-War Concentration Camp 189
　Masuria 206
PART V: Summation
　Prince Czetwertyński 223
CONCLUSION
　Epilogue 230
　Additional Photographs 231
　Bibliography 238

Foreword

On February 24, 2022, the aggression of the Russian Federation against Independent Ukraine began, opening another brutal and bloody chapter in world history. Vladimir Putin's reason for starting the war was morbid ambition and sentiment for a great imperial Russia, the dream of creating a third Russian empire (after the Romanovs and the Soviet Union). Unfortunately, despite the experiences and atrocities of the Second World War, it has once again become clear that military action is still a means of conducting politics.

Moreover, the war in Ukraine is taking place in the mass media, hence it is happening before our eyes. The images passing through public space of brutal acts of murder committed by Russian troops against the civilian population elicit feelings of rage and pain, as well as raise questions about the fate of the victims' families and loved ones.

How do the dynamics of this type of conflict shape reality? That is the subject of this book assembled on the initiative of Polo Altynski-Ross, who was inspired by his late great-grandfather Zbigniew (Zbyszek) Janczewski's memoirs. Zbyszek, growing up in the multicultural melting pot of the city of Rivne, now in Ukraine, was an eyewitness to the atrocities of war, losing many friends and loved ones in the process. His fate is a story of wandering through militarily occupied territories, while developing interpersonal and international relationships on both sides of the equation, escaping death on many accounts. Along the way, he endures a wide variety of emotions caused by objective events and the experience of war. Unfortunately, it is a story that will be retold, in many of its elements, by current sufferers of Russian aggression.

Therefore, while walking with Zbyszek, let us not forget those currently in Ukraine. Let us recognize these experiences so that we can only read about them as lessons for life. A young writer, by taking his inspiring actions of analyzing historical facts, co-translating, and editing the written content of memoirs, shows respect for his ancestor and gives hope that war will no longer have space to decide and influence our fate.

—Bartosz Grodecki
Polish Deputy Minister
Ministry of the Interior
April 24, 2022

Preface

At the age of eleven, I was informed that my Polish *pradziadek* (great-grandfather) had written memoirs of his experiences through and after the Second World War. I was told that he had written them in the early 1990s but never managed to publish them. The following summer, my family traveled to eastern Poland to visit our relatives. When I told my great-grandfather about my newfound interest in his writing, he gave me his full blessing to do as I wished with his story.

After translating the original memoirs during my summers in England (with the help of my fluently Polish-speaking mother), I was incredibly entranced. How could one individual go through so many interesting, tragic, and unbelievably exhilarating moments? The volume of experiences is like that of no other memoir I had ever read. The coincidences, the occurrences are on that level of a wholly imagined narrative—or in fact, like that of a movie.

Besides its thoroughly entertaining aspect, I also believe that this book ought to be a piece of history. Every verifiable event has been fact-checked, many parts have been supplemented with additional information, and there are informative illustrations to help you grasp the experiences that my great-grandfather has done his best to convey. Even though many of the places mentioned in this book may have changed names—or, in the case of many small villages, were completely wiped off the map—they are actual locations. I will also state that all viewpoints and opinions are original and unchanged to keep his story ultimately authentic.

For a majority of the Second World War, my great-grandfather lived in what is today western Ukraine. Then within Polish borders, the region was a melting pot of many nationalities: Poles, Ukrainians, Germans, and eventually Russians, who each proclaimed, in varying degrees, for the destiny of that region to be under their own nation's rule. Even though this violent "scourge of nationalism" (as my great-grandfather phrased it) was ultimately destroyed by the goodwill of humanity, he predicted that at any moment, winds may rekindle this blight. His premonitions seem to be a direct reflection of what is springing up at this very moment with the 2022 Russian invasion of Ukraine.

The value of this story is timeless: it educates today's world about the relevance of historic events in Eastern Europe, through a thrilling, inspirational telling of survival against all odds, intertwined with poetic, teenage love. Bringing this awareness to the world is one way to break the pattern of history, and that is what I hope my great-grandfather's story will ultimately achieve.

—Polo Altynski-Ross
Great-grandson

THE POLISH PRINCE

Confession

An age-old Chinese proverb says, "May you live in interesting times." This proverb is a curse: seemingly innocent, although containing an ominous, camouflaged content, like almost all of the ancient wisdom of the East. I wish only for an enemy life in "interesting times." I'm curious who gave me this wish.

Almost half a century has passed since the war. I lie in an intensive care unit bandaged like a doll, plastered from head to toe. From time to time, the duty nurse creaks the door open unobtrusively, and then again silence ensues, with only footsteps sometimes heard in the corridor. I am now familiarized with this ward of the hospital very well. It's a vestibule to eternity. Not everyone comes back from here—it's the closest a living being can reach to hell, paradise, or non-existence.

Sometimes I fall into unconsciousness, and when I return, my head swells with thoughts. I become encircled with memories of my younger years like a swarm of enraged bees. I become reminiscent of a time when a childhood friend, Sławik, and I attempted to steal honey from an apiary. Only good legs saved our lives then. For the next three days, my upset mother would apply a soothing compress to my stings. Only after a week could I see God's world through swollen eyes.

A cracked spinal column, concussion, a broken leg and ribs, result from my car driving into a tree by the road. After surgery, I awake and spot the surgeon. When he notices I have stirred, a half-grin appears upon his face.

He asks, "Did you rally your car? At your age? Everyone was very surprised when they heard you had survived: the car went to scrap."

I gaze at the surgeon's young face and become entranced in deep thought—man, what do you know about life? Maybe someday, when your hair goes gray, you will understand that there are two greatest passions and adventures in life: the first and last love. The first is a juvenile disease in which courses of events are quite easily blurred in the memory. The second is a severe and incurable disease that can only culminate bitterly.

Hell! I have become sentimental, but have I been like this since my youth? Raised on the works of Polish novelist Sienkiewicz, I believe in beautiful, pure, selfless love. I've been looking my whole life and maybe even come upon it—but it has passed by me unnoticed. In spite of the saying "third time lucky," I had my luck many more times than that, but every time I thought I had found that true love, it would fall apart like a house of cards. And now I end up in the hospital room, all alone.

I'm looking for happiness, but what is happiness truly? Money, power, or success with relationships? I had abundant money and acquaintances, and I was not interested in climbing the power ladder, as the higher up, the greater the fall. I was looking for something that you get only once in a lifetime. This pursuit of unconditional love is how I reached into my sixties, a time when I finally caught sight of the golden meadow, which according to Stefan Żeromski, human eyes see only once in a lifetime.

An attractive young nurse leans over me, wielding a syringe. I sense a feeling of hatred towards me; perhaps I am seeking too much attention. The nurse inserts the needle and leaves without uttering a word. I return to my thoughts about women, love, and happiness, then fall into a slumber.

Time passes. My restless pondering is, at a point, interrupted by the head of the ward and a younger doctor. These craftsmen of medicine do not speak a word to me as they join me in my "apartment." They exchange a few words in a low voice, and again quiet ensues as they close the door. Only echoing steps in the corridor and a bird's song can be heard: I am reminded of the melody of last spring, a wonderful, sunny spring, after which I had promised myself so much.

An acute chest pain interrupts my meditations. I push the bell button, and another nurse comes up. This time it is an older, gray lady whose gentle, kind smile and quiet voice allow me for a moment to forget my discomfort. Soon after another injection, I fall back into the darkness of unsettled sleep.

After some time, consciousness comes back—and with it, the pain—until another nurse inserts an anesthetic into my skin.

I peer at the ceiling. Although my body is covered with numbness, I still have my brain consciousness. My mind continues to revolve around the days that have passed and will never come back: "Never enter twice into the same river."

My thoughts persistently return to those younger childhood years. I start a journey in time and space.

PART I
The Pre-War Years

— 1 —
Childhood

Masha hopped over the towering fence, effortlessly, with the skill of a nimble deer. I rushed after her. After climbing a nearby tree, I stuffed apples beneath my jacket, when suddenly the sounds of the rustling of leaves in the almost motionless orchard were replaced by the noises of barking dogs and very loud cursing.

"*Zejdź na dół, cholerne dzieci!* (Get down, damn children!)"

A scowling, elderly man stood underneath the tree, angrily waving a stick, with two large dogs encircling. Masha and I climbed to the highest branches, but the situation was desperate—there was no way of slipping by. The barbed wire at the top of the fence near the tree made it impossible to escape. Without the sharp fencing, we could risk breaking out of the trap, but with it there? Our hands were numb from holding the branches already. The owner patiently waited for the siege to end, but the dogs raised a furious shriek.

"*Zejdź na dół!*"

Masha's father arrived, informed by someone from the neighbor's house, and rescued us from oppression by handing over five silver zlotych.[1] With my head lowered, I was accompanied by the girl and her father. A crowd had gathered at the noise of the dogs. I recognized a belittling tone from a friend in the yard: "What a fool, he got caught."

Masha wasn't allowed to leave home for two weeks, whereas my enraged father punished me with a belt. My parents had higher

---

1 *Polish currency*

expectations for me, which, on an obscure level, seemed to strangely uphold the speculations of my true origins.

* * *

My grandparents from both sides came along to the region of Wołyń[2] in the second half of the 19th century. A land flowing with "milk and honey" (containing the most fertile chernozem in Europe), it accommodated the largest agricultural estates, which attracted many people from crowded areas in post-divided Poland and the surrounding European countries.

My father's grandparents were settlers of Wołyń from Poznań, in western Poland. My father's parents successfully managed land tenancy and were raising a large family when the First World War broke out, and as a so-called "Prussian subject," my grandfather was sent to Siberia and no one ever heard of him again. Grandma Josepha stayed alone with a large number of growing children, somehow managing to tend to their needs.

My father, Ignacy, the oldest of her sons, was recruited to the Tsar's army in 1916. Being involved with the Tsar did not benefit him greatly since the imperialist regime soon imploded, falling apart when the Soviet revolution began. Right after, he came home to marry Wladyslawa, the daughter of an administrator of a manor owned by Prince Michał Czetwertyński,[3] in Obarów. Obarów was merely a few kilometers from Równe, our hometown with approximately forty thousand inhabitants.[4]

---

2 *Today, the historical region is known as Volhynia. It is in present-day west Ukraine.*
3 *I have so far been unable to find this member of the Czetwertyński family.*
4 *During Polish administration, the town was called Równe, but during German and Soviet occupation, it was named Rovno or Rivne (today's name).*

EASTERN EUROPEAN BORDERS, PRE-NAZI ERA

After the Treaty of Versailles (1919), which ended the First World War, and the Treaty of Riga (1920), which ended the Polish–Soviet War, central Europe was carved as illustrated below. It stayed this way until the rise of Hitler in the 1930s. In this map, "Równe" is highlighted in Poland's darkened region of "Wołyń."

My mother Wladyslawa's side obtained a much richer biography. The son of a noble farm man, my mother's father was well known for his many abilities and masculine beauty. During the reign of Tsar Alexander III, the Soviet Army recruited him to the Leib Guard in Saint Petersburg. After a ten-year-long period of service, he remained a non-commissioned officer—it was only his Polish origin that did not allow him further promotion. "In four non-commissioned officers, three of them are Poles," his Russian captain used to recite humorously.

After those ten years of duty, my maternal grandfather returned home and married a nobleman's daughter. Later, they moved together to Wołyń, where Prince Czetwertyński offered him a position as a mansion administrator. Grandfather managed the Prince's fortune mainly in Obarów until the Polish border partition in the 1920s. It was there that he gave his daughter, Wladyslawa, away to marry a young apprentice: my father.

My mother Wladyslawa was well known among people from a young age. In the summer of 1919, as a spy in the Polish–Russian war, she warned about approaching Bolshevik cavalry. The message reached the top, and the Polish squadron managed to organize a defense and retreat to a nearby town—but my mother came very close to paying for this stunt with her own life. An informant had told the Russians that a "traitor" had warned the Polish Army, resulting in the commander calling for a search. Wladyslawa was caught and locked in a cottage near the Bolshevik camp. Waiting for execution, my mother managed to bypass the guards on duty, escaping through the window.

After ten years of marriage to my father, at the end of 1926, Wladyslawa gave birth to me, a healthy boy. They named me Zbyszek. My parents' neighbors, who were the same age, had long since begun raising several children, so as a late-life first child I became an object of gossip and speculation as the youngest around. This is why, for many, many years, people nicknamed me "Prince." It made me angry and unhappy at the time as I didn't understand what they were truly insinuating; however, I learned to live with it. This seemingly insignificant nickname had a surprising epilogue, which was not revealed to me until years later.

After the war, Polish authorities acknowledged my mother's contribution, and she received a diploma of honor and a monetary award.

My father received an offer to work as a director of the "Soldiers' Home" cinema in Równe and was given a business apartment in one of the many army buildings, which had been converted into accommodations.

It is difficult to remember my childhood now—half a century feels like, and is, a long time. I'm extracting the events and facts from the abyss of my past like a bucket of water from a bottomless well.

Looking through the windows of the apartment in Równe where I lived the first years of my life, you could see a significant military training ground. When the soldiers weren't practicing, all you could hear were the little ones playing just over a fence. I was among them.

Few other events from that period stick in my memory. Sometimes my mother had a visitor—the colonel's wife. She was a beautiful, elegant woman, always asking my mother the same question: "Do you mind if I take Zbyszek for a walk today?"

My mother was usually happy with that. Of course, the colonel's wife had two kids of her own, but even so, she must have thought that my curly blond hair and dark eyes more likely matched her beauty.

She would grab my hand and walk with me to the bakery near the Empire Cinema. Over there, we were entertained by elderly gentlemen with gallant manners. They greeted the colonel's wife and kissed her hands, then shook my hand and stroked my hair. While they chatted, I enjoyed a giant ice cream in the summer or cookies in the winter, which several times made me sick. Still, my mother didn't dare refuse the colonel's wife whenever she asked to take me out as it might've been considered impolite.

At the age of seven, my father allowed me to go to the cinema with him. During those days, sound in the theater was non-existent. A pianist sat in the corner of the projection room, playing music according to the action on the screen.

We were most amused when the tunes would not match the action of the movie, such as when dashing army marches accompanied tragic scenes or vice versa: when romantic and touching melodies made the background for comedic moments on the screen. It was all an excellent experience for the audience at the time, especially for us youngsters.

Some of the most popular films were Western movies, which often induced animated reactions from the viewers. A typical setting included a brave cowboy on a prairie after a fight with indigenous opposition, cooking over a fire. Suddenly, another man would crouch behind the cowboy's back, intending to stab him ferociously with a knife. The whole audience would stand up and shout unanimously, "Watch out!" The "hero" must have heard our yelling because he managed to evade the consequences.

The audience's reaction to tragic movies was also very lively. All of the films such as *Ben Hur*, *God of His Fathers*, or *The Lepers* were lived through very deeply and sorrowfully. Only crying women disrupted public silence. However, our eyes were also pretty wet, despite the number one rule of those times: "Boys don't cry."

Although now obsolete, this societal standard proved good advice for the years to follow, which brought unimaginable challenges to every person, no matter age, nationality, or denomination, in Europe.

— 2 —
Those Years – Równe

Some time in the early 1930s, my parents and I moved out of our flat to Auntie Maria's house, near Równe. Auntie's husband, Gaj, was the manager of Prince Janusz Radziwiłł's[5] nearby fortune in Ołyka and later his estate in Szpanów. The home was a large manor, with over a thousand acres of fertile wheat and beetroot planted grounds, even having its own sugar factory. Father used to do all kinds of repairs on that property. Those repair jobs led him to set up a small locksmith business and eventually accommodate us in house number 74 within the city, also owned by Uncle Gaj.

In the autumn, I began school. It was an exclusive primary school under the name of Henryk Sienkiewicz. My mother's ambition was to send me to this international institution as I would learn multiple languages, which later saved my life on numerous occasions during the war. All of the pupils were a mixture of Polish (Catholic), Ukrainian (Orthodox), German (Evangelist), and Jews from many nationalities—the whole mosaic of Wołyń then.

All lessons began and ended with a Christian prayer. While we were praying, children with other beliefs had to stand and wait until we finished. Every Sunday morning at nine o'clock, all Polish-Catholic pupils gathered in the courtyard, minded by a teacher at the local church. The school was a long, one-floor building with a gymnasium built into

---

5 *Prince Janusz Radziwiłł (b. 1880, d. 1967) was a Polish nobleman and politician. He owned two palaces in Warsaw, as well as estates like those in Szpanów and Ołyka, although unfortunately all of his major belongings were confiscated after the war by Communist authorities. Interestingly, his great-grandmother was Princess Louise of Prussia, the niece of Adolf Hitler's idol, Frederick the Great.*

the main edifice, divided into two parts: female and male. In the middle of the massive courtyard was an invisible border between the girls and the boys. No one ever dared to cross this line.

Like my school, the entire city of Równe was also diverse; inhabited by Poles, Ukrainians, Germans, and Jews. In the pre-war years, it was the largest in Wołyń. Vibrant with people, it was also the location of a grand railway junction.

What is left in my memory of Równe in those pre-war years? There was a main road that flowed into the city from the west of the town of Klewań, crossing the poor neighborhood of Cegielnia. Flowing directly through the obtrusive military barracks, it spread further down a steep street, crossing the railroad tracks and the Ujście River. Upon reaching downtown, it passed a great two-story Catholic church made of red bricks on the right side of the waterway. A little further, the road ran past a smaller Orthodox church, then it stretched along with single and double story homes and ended up behind another church where the street rose, crossing Grabnik.

Grabnik was a district of officials' and officers' workspaces upon a hill located by the divine Park Moscicki. Behind it, the street turned into a road again, and eventually disappeared somewhere among the wheat fields in the east until it reached the town of Korzec at the Soviet-Russian border. The border was not far, only sixty kilometers away. For the inhabitants of Równe, the country behind that border was as remote as if located somewhere in Midwest America.

Beyond the magnificently built main street, the smaller roads branched out perpendicularly to a one-story building lot, among which from time to time staggered two-story houses. Further down, one such smaller road, Legionów Street, led into Biała Street, which reached a high fence. On the other side of that tall fence were military units and railway station platforms.

House number 74 was no different from the others on Legionów street: brick, plastered, appearing as one-story from the road, and two-story from the small, cozy backyard. Before number 74, another brick twin house stood beside a great orchard with a high fence of train track underlays that separated the railway and the yard. In return for accommodation in a humble apartment within the building, owned by my uncle, my father repaired the fence, swept the street, and completed other maintenance work.

Our house, like the whole town, was international. The biggest and most luxurious apartment was occupied by a court official, Mr. Dobrowolski, and his family. A Russian family lived in the front, and the center contained two rooms inhabited by Jewish women: Sonja Meier, a dressmaker, with her two sisters Henje and Manje, all old maidens (the girl without a dowry had no chance of marriage with other Jews).

We lived on the ground floor, on the right side of the corridor. The apartment on the opposite side was inhabited by a widow named Dejko, with three children: two adolescent daughters and a younger son Sławik, a close friend of mine. The nationality of this family was difficult to recognize—the mother spoke some strange Polish-Ukrainian-Russian mixture. It was only during the German occupation that she revealed their true Ukrainian nationality.

Two Polish families occupied the neighboring home, and on the opposite side of the street, there was a one-story red-brick house with two wealthy Jewish families. Mr. Bardas—a director of the Hebrew grammar school in Równe, a nobleman well respected in the city—lived in that house. I developed an unusual friendship with him, as I was a Christian child and he was a well-educated Orthodox Jew.

Mr. Bardas would meet me on our street, and we would engage in a typical conversation: I would say, "Good morning, sir," then he would politely ask, "Have you done your homework? Do you have time for a chat and a cup of hot chocolate?"

I always said I was done, but my designated homework time suffered the consequences as I never refused when Professor Bardas invited me for a steaming mug of hot chocolate. I would enter his richly decorated apartment, especially interested in the large shelves set neatly with leather books, including gilded spines inscribed with foreign languages. Mr. Bardas, seeing my interest, would sit down, and sipping his coffee, explain to me patiently the importance of these letters and words, as well as the history of his nation. I enjoyed hearing about them until I realized that I had gone past my homework time, which detracted me from the casual chat.

A wealthy fur merchant, Mr. Zylber, with his wife and daughter, Masha (who was one year younger than me), occupied the second wing of that house. We became close acquaintances, although it was difficult for us to meet often; the girl was under the strict surveillance of a governess who would follow her every step like a mother hen. Only Masha knew how to occasionally evade her. Whenever I communicated to her with a quiet whistle, she would lose the governess and appear at our agreed meeting point in shallow breaths.

After reaching the orchard owned by a man named Mr. Borodie, I would take over the education: shooting with a sling, slipping through fences, climbing on tall trees, and even stealing sour apples guarded by noisy dogs, the most delicious treat. Masha would lose respect for all of the sweets given by her mother in favor of these sour vinegar-like apples.

Mr. Borodie's orchard often mesmerized Masha to such an extent that no force could tear her off. When the call of her mother and governess—later desperate roaring all over the street—finally reached our sober ears, Masha would possess an innocent face, claiming she hadn't heard them. Without any fuss, she would distract her parents from her bruised knee, scratched face, and torn dress. It was her art. Masha promised an improvement of her behavior—until the next whistle.

So it was inevitable that Masha and I got caught red-handed in the orchard at that time, resulting in myself being punished with a belt, and Masha being grounded for two weeks. Instead, I was left to carry on the escapades with my dear friend Sławik, our neighboring widow's son.

At first, Sławik and Masha were just friends who I kicked a ball with, but during wartime misery, they became my companions whom I went on more expeditions with, fetching wood during freezing days or picking up potatoes when cold and hunger stared us in the eyes as the dreadful years of war arrived.

Those years came in 1939, along with the arrival of the Red Army into Wołyń.

PART II

The War Years

— 3 —
September Memories

Many rumors circulate among people about the number thirteen and its day in the calendar. For some, it's an unlucky day, while others believe it to be favorable. September 13, 1939, was a day in my life that signified the truth in such speculations. It was the end of the happy, sunny days of childhood and a brutal awakening to the nightmarish world of adults.

During my carefree childhood years, on the second or third day of the summer holidays, my father or mother took me twenty kilometers by train from Równe to Klewań. Then, for another seven kilometers, we walked along the road of the Radziwiłł princes and through to the path winding among the hills. Some of these were actually burial mounds, the graves from ancient times. It was at this point we would reach the village of Hołyszew. I spent my summer holidays in this village, near another home of Uncle Gaj, located in the beautiful hilly lands on the border of Wołyń and Polesie, the former Eastern Borderlands of Poland.

Uncle leased his own twelve-hectare farm in this area, which was the place of an old military settlement, divided among former Polish soldiers who fought in the struggle for independence in 1918-1920. Composed of scattered farms, the area was occupied loosely.

There was a turn into a field trail just beyond the village, where a forest would appear on the horizon. Further down, you could spy an avenue planted with cherries, which led from the road to my uncle's residence. The days passed while in the woods, on the river, or in the field, with peers from the neighborhood.

In the summer of 1939, the faces of adults became sad and thoughtful; even the chuckles of young, usually giggling aunts were not too merry.

In July, Father's youngest brother, Antoni, joined the army. The air smelled of war. War, a mysterious, unknown word, was heard from adult stories for a twelve-year-old as some great adventure. At the end of August, when a message arrived declaring the holidays had been extended, I knew that this "adventure" would not pass me by.

On September first, a neighbor with a radio informed us that war had begun—German troops were attacking Poland. Instead of hacking through meadows and exploring in the woods, I now sat with adults at the radio apparatus more and more often. The speakers spilled unfamiliar, unintelligible words: "Koma-five is coming, Dora-six is coming," and finally, the message of "Westerplatte is in defense" repeated every hour. Where Westerplatte was, I did not know, but I strangely regretted that I was not there.

The faces of adults became more and more sad and thoughtful as more and more city names came from the loudspeaker: Kraków, Poznań, Gniezno, Bydgoszcz... Heavy fighting continued on these fronts.

Suddenly, Father arrived from the city with the message of a call to return to school. This made me concerned—not at the thought of returning to the school bench, but instead that the war would pass me by.

Uncle drove us by cart to the station. After a long wait for a train, finally, a red-capped stationmaster appeared, announcing to the waiting: "Ladies and Gentlemen, do not stay, I do not know if the train will come at all."

This was something new. Before the war, the PKP[6] was known to be reliable and punctual to such an extent that you could adjust your watch with the arrival of each train. This was an extreme sign something terrible was happening. It was necessary to return all the way home on foot. Dense traffic on the road bustled, as cars and trucks of troops rode both ways.

In the city, a lot had changed. Many neighbors proudly walked the streets with inscribed, bi-colored armbands of the LOPP[7] on their shoulders. A

---

6   *Polskie Koleje Państwowe (Polish National Railway)*
7   *Liga Obrony Powietrznej i Przeciwgazowej (Anti-Aircraft and Anti-Gas Defense League)*

valid blackout had begun: all windows were cross-taped with stripes of paper. Anxiety grew among the population, and every household stored as much food as possible until the shops were completely bought out. The traffic of convoys of people and equipment at the nearby station grew day by day—wagons constantly filled the tracks. Now, two refugees from Pruszków inhabited our apartment.

School was exciting: instead of sitting in the pews, we dug shelters in the school garden along with the soldiers. I felt that the day of great adventure was close. Since there were no regular classes, I often spent my time with Sławik near the railway station, a place of many interesting events.

One day, on the sizable station ramp, we noticed soldiers unloading cannons. They were heavy, thick as trees, and their protruding noses were masked with branches. It was apparent they had arrived straight from the factory because their huge barrels were red—there had not been time to paint them a protective green color. We heard strange conversations among the people working on the ramp: France and England had declared war on Germany, and alarming news that the Germans were already near Warsaw. Eager to inform my parents of what I had seen and heard at the station, I decided to return home.

Suddenly, as I scrambled back into my yard, I heard a distressing scream.

"Airplanes are coming!"

A few steps more, and a continuous whir reached my ears. I gazed up, and from the west, squadrons with black crosses on their wings emerged. Mesmerized, I was frozen with my head tilted to the sky when a sudden high-pitched sound, piercing deep into my heart, tore through the air.

A massive explosion shook the houses, windows shattered, and an enormous mushroom of smoke and dust rose over the station. Scampering under the nearest tree, I saw my mother running out of the house and locking the door out of the corner of my eye. An enormous piece of plaster peeled off the wall and fell down. A wide cloud of dust reached the ground all around.

The roof of the outhouse, on which the plaster fell, saved my mother's life. Covered in white powder like a miller, she ran to me and covered me with her body. A moment later, we stood up and shook off the dust. I inspected my surroundings—from the landscape of the railroad station, the tall railway pressure tower had disappeared entirely.

The sinister roar of the engines in the sky made the area around seem momentarily mute. For a second longer, we stood quiet, not knowing what to do, until a loud shout broke our mutual helplessness: "To the shelter!"

In the garden of our neighbors, we came across a shelter of open, zigzagged excavations. Nearby, only a few dozen meters away, the high fence separated us from the military warehouses.

"This is a dangerous place," my mother decided.

There was no living soul in the shelter. Man, the creator of civilizations, feels safer in a more social environment, and this apparently prompted my mother to seek a better location.

We made our way towards the city center. Exhausted, we came upon a trench full of people when hell broke loose once again. With a shrill whistle and a bang, bombs rained from the sky and exploded nearby. The houses close by were starting to burn. Smoke, sparks, fire, and dust blasts covered everything. It was dark in the trench, and people huddled together, coughing and praying loudly. Embraced tightly by my mother, I shook like an aspen in the wind—there was not much left of the war hero. That's not how I imagined this great adventure.

It may be that everything lasted a few minutes or an hour; I cannot say for certain to this day. The fire crackled terribly, and the noise of the explosions did not stop.

Waiting for the worst, we remained curled up until a voice from the street called out: "People, the air raid is over! This noise is the sound of an explosion of ammunition wagons!"

The commanding voices of police filled the air. Fire trucks arrived following the howling of sirens, and water hoses started to unravel, pumping out gallons of water. Stepping out of the trench, we peered around carefully—several houses were still in flames.

On the sidewalk, firefighters were laying the wounded and dead in a row. Among them, I recognized, with horror, the faces of friends from our street. Death had passed us by so close.

"Do not look." Mother took my hand and began leading me home. "We have to escape from here," she declared, pointing to the ruined station.

Our apartment was windowless and demolished.

"Ignac, stay and secure the windows," my mother yelled to my father, who had just appeared. "I am running away with our child; we will meet with relatives in Oleksyn. Here, it can be hell again in only a moment."

The station was still burning and crumbling from explosions as we entered the yard. Dud missiles had landed in a few nearby gardens, which luckily had not exploded—the reliability of bombs was still to be questioned.

During this bombardment, trains of equipment and ammunition completely clogged the station. Even so, the worst scenario did not result: it was the courage and determination of a Polish officer that saved the city's life in the end. This officer, threatening with a weapon, forced the railwaymen to detach and pull the wagons somewhere to a safer location.

We swiftly left the city, and the sky grew dark. Stopping at a friend's village, I gaped with horror at the great fire, a blood-colored glow flooding the sky over my hometown. For the first time in my life, I had peered at the cruel face of war. Even though this was only the first of the terrors I witnessed, this first one remains etched deep in my memory forever.

I laid awake all night. Finally, when Father awoke, he announced that it would be safest for me near Dęby at Michal's, where we had come back from just days ago. It was not nearly so easy to travel this time, as refugees flowing east had flooded the road from Łuck to Równe. Cars, carts, bikes, and walkers were the booty of an avalanche of panicking, fearful people constantly glancing up at the sky. Resisting the current wave to travel east seemed impossible.

My parents decided that it would probably be better to hike by the railway, which was not the safest option, but at least there were not so many crowds. We traveled along a path next to the railroad in the burning sun, which an occasional locomotive rode through.

Half a kilometer from the railway line, the path led us around Prince Radziwiłł's mansion of Szpanów, when a freight train, full of refugees, suddenly screeched and began to brake rapidly. The railcar whistled, and before it even stopped, people began to spill out of the wagons. Promptly, in the sky above the train, German bomber aircraft with strange, as if broken, wings dove at hellish speeds.[8] Following the terrifying signature whistles, the bombs descended, and amid the thud of explosions, I could hear long blasts from machine guns.

Luckily, we were able to scramble into a nearby ditch.

"Bastards," my father furiously spat. "They murder civilians, bloody heroes."

That was something new. In the war that my father fought, only the soldiers and weaponized civilians died, but not innocent, defenseless civilians, including women and children. Here, the cold-blooded, intentional crime was obvious.

In the end, the murderers with black crosses on their wings flew north. The survivors of the massacre began to gather the bodies of the dead and wounded, laying them along the tracks. Carts from the direction of Szpanów appeared, on which they placed the bodies.

We continued our journey.

"There was not one soldier on that train," father repeated, still unable to reconcile with what he had seen before. "Did those bandits up in the sky not see it—or did they not care to see it?"

Late at night, terribly tired, we reached our destination. It was quite safe here; the farms scattered across the fields were not a target of attacks.

A car and several carts of refugees stood in the yard of the house—until the sound of the engines above (which were showing up in the sky evermore) made them scatter like chickens.

During one air raid, someone saw red stars on the wings of one of the planes. The men wondered what that could possibly mean—was there help coming, or just another enemy?

The news was getting worse: Polish cities were falling, Warsaw was besieged, and the German troops had crossed the Vistula. Now those airplanes with stars on their wings were seen in the sky more frequently, but that situation was still unclear.

---

8 *These were German "Stuka" dive-bombers. The horrifying whistles referred to here are the wailing sirens installed on those aircraft—which were used not only to provide audible feedback of speed to the pilot, but to inflict terror in the minds of the people below.*

One day, the clatter of caterpillar treads and the resounding hum of tank engines came to our ears from behind the forest. Friend or enemy? Everyone was asking. A neighbor who had a radio explained the case.

"Soviet troops have entered Poland!"

Dead silence. The faces of the adults were very pale.

NAZI AND SOVIET INVASION OF POLAND, SEPT. 1939

On the first of September, The Second Polish Republic was invaded by Nazi-German forces, with the Soviets following sixteen days later. As per the Molotov-Ribbentrop Pact—which established temporary Eastern European borders—eastern Poland, including Równe (labeled as "Rivne") and most of Wołyń, was a part of the Russians' spoils, and became a part of the Ukrainian Soviet Socialist Republic.

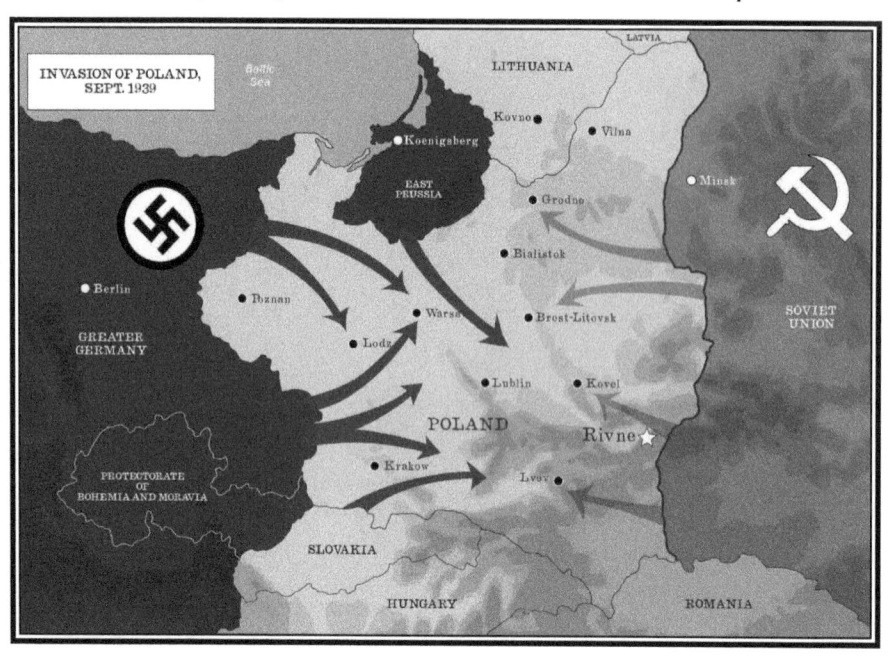

From the direction of the setting sun, several Polish soldiers appeared. They had traversed through the fields, a shortcut to Uncle's estate. One of them was my father's little brother, Antoni, whom we warmly welcomed. The soldiers told us all the truth: the invading Soviet army was not a friend who comes to the rescue, but an enemy who murders and captures Polish soldiers.

"This is the fourth partition of Poland," someone mumbled quietly, with tears in his eyes.

My father's brother changed into civilian clothes, then stashed the weapons and ammunition. As he stripped the embroidered white eagle from his hat, tears the size of peas ran down his face. A man does not cry, but no one questioned those tears. Our world, our homeland, was falling into rubble.

The situation was finally clarified late in the evening when we heard a sudden loud bang from the butts of rifles on the door. After someone opened it, a handful of soldiers with gray cloaks and red stars on their pointed caps fell into the room. The bayonet rifles glittered sharply in the light of the oil lamp.

"*Ruki vverkh!* (Hands in the air!)" the order fell.

Everyone gathered obediently and raised their hands.

"*Yyest li Pol'skiye soldaty?* (Are there any Polish soldiers?)" asked an officer, who then cautiously inspected the house, clasping his weapon.

The Red Army men sat on the benches and chairs and soon after demanded food and drink. From outside, you could hear traditional melodies played on the Russians' harmonicas.

— 4 —
Russian Occupation

Back in the city, there was joy and bliss on the wartime posters, while the people staring at them were sad and hungry. The deserted shops had only sweet vodka on all the shelves, bread was rarely available, and once every week or two, you would be lucky to purchase a bag of sugar. The waiting line for that sugar would be a kilometer long.

Poles, Ukrainians, Russians, and Jews each had their own school, lectured in different languages. Located in an older school building, the majority of teachers in the Polish section were Jewish intellectuals, university lecturers who had fled from western to eastern Poland to choose Russian occupation over the Germans.

Difficulties in learning appeared in the first days of my new school, in October 1939. The teachers were the best of the best, but the curriculum was not compatible with the previous program of my Polish institution; since the Soviets controlled the school system in Wołyń at this time, they based our education on their traditional methods. Polish education was traditionally much longer. As a result, after six years of primary school, I found myself in the seventh grade of the ten-year Russian system, and therefore more or less in the second, instead of the first, year of Polish junior high school.

It was a jump into deep water with classes in four languages—Polish, Russian, Ukrainian, and German—yet somehow, I managed. However, I did struggle with the secrets of mathematics; algebra and trigonometry became almost as confusing for my friends and me as black magic.

Masha, my childhood friend with whom I used to steal apples, attended a Jewish school, and Sławik a Ukrainian one. Each of us, after our classes, would join the endless food queues unless we shared a common goal—an expedition for fuel.

Winter 1939 was cruel, and apparently, such harsh winters seemed to only happen in the war years. Temperatures reached negative thirty degrees Celsius, yet the Soviet governing body didn't deliver any heating supplies, and coal was simply unavailable. Therefore, wood was the only source of heat and needed to be collected with our own hands. That job fell on us older children as the adults could be severely punished for this procedure.

Sławik, Masha, and I tried as hard as possible to ensure our families didn't freeze. First, we took the wood from private fences around houses, and when we ran out of that, we took tall fencing built from railway supplies that separated individual allotments from the train station.

We created a special tactic. At about eight o'clock in the evening when the railway guard would change, we would sneak up to the fence, and while one watched for danger, the others would slug the underpinning right at the soil, drag the wood together, tie them to a rope and take them to a safe place. Masha would stay on the lookout. The hard labor belonged to Sławik and I: cutting and collecting the wood. We would then equally divide our loot among ourselves.

Within two days, the stoves had eaten our booty, and we were expecting another expedition. It was never safe as the railroad guards fired guns without hesitation. The bullets often whistled and whooshed around the ears, but they never caught on flesh. We hid in the shadows, and good legs would save us once again.

Eventually, we did get caught.

It was a rather bright night, and a watchman crept up on us unnoticed. While Sławik and I were in the middle of the procedure with Masha looking out, the shadows screamed in Russian.

"*Ruki vverkh!*"

We couldn't escape by the usual route, and after a quick evaluation of the situation, all we could do was helplessly raise our hands.

"*Stupay!* (March!)" he commanded.

The guard escorted us obediently to the security department at the railway station. He then shut the door and left without a word. It was a bitterly freezing, ill-lit room. We looked at each other helplessly.

"What will they do with us?" Masha whispered. "Will they take us to Siberia?"

"Siberia" was a taboo pronounced in a whispered horror because everyone believed the place to be hell on earth. With the onset of frost, the Soviet authorities had begun to export Polish soldiers, policemen, and officials there. Typically around midnight, a truck-full of NKVD[9] soldiers would appear at a location. Among the cries of women and children, unfortunate families would be escorted, then loaded onto freight wagons in an extremely cramped fashion. Some would stay in that place for a couple of days before all the wagons were full. Children died from the cold, and their bodies were thrown out each morning before all the carriages were loaded. Fear fell on the whole town about the taboo of Siberia.[10]

Suddenly, the bolt slammed, and the door opened widely. Soon we came close to the officer's rugged face. He mentioned the word sabotage, so we expected the worst punishment—until Masha saved the situation: she whimpered quietly at first, then her sobs turned into loud wailing, and the two of us started to join her. The officer covered his ears, and something must have twitched in his heart. His posture suddenly slumped.

He scratched his head, then shouted, "*Idi k chertu!* (Go to hell!)" and pushed us out the door.

We ran home, a little stunned.

Our mothers' faces were red with tears. After this incident, we still did not suspend our activities because the idea of an even colder winter was haunting. We only managed to double our vigilance. Even before the winter ended, a whole kilometer of the mighty railway's fence ceased to exist.

Then came the long-anticipated spring. The expeditions for fuel had finished, and studying was the priority. Sometimes on the way to school, we would meet Masha. She grew up and matured into a beautiful young lady; girls of her nationality ripened early. I would gaze at her with admiration. When we walked together in places where no one could see, we

---

9   *The People's Commissariat of Internal Affairs ('Naródnyy Komissariát Vnútrennikh Del' or NKVD), was the brutal Russian secret police that saw action in WWII, primarily focused on repression, expulsion and the murdering of "undesirables."*
10 *In fact, it is estimated that as many as 1.7 million Poles of Soviet-annexed Poland were deported to the east between September 1939 and June 1941.*

held hands—something in our hearts woke up when we were together, making it difficult to part.

In the summer of 1940, we heard about the advancing of the Germans into France, as well as the evacuation from Dunkirk. Yet, life stood still in the east, as Soviet occupation guaranteed momentary peace.

I continued with my studies and listened to the radio about the battles in the west. I completed exams for the next year happily; thanks to the superhuman patience of my teachers, during the school year of 1940, we had caught up to the standards of the foreign system of education.

Pulling the bucket from the memory well gets easier when I recall the events that take place soon after that.

The year 1941.

— 5 —
1941

One could say this was a year that... using the poet Adam Mickiewicz's words from the *Pan Tadeusz*... an enemy jumped into another enemy's throat.

Just like the prior winter, there was no fuel for the fire. The rest of the surviving fences from the previous winter had also disappeared. For a few days school was suspended.

After the severe frosts of the beginning of the year, an exceptionally early and warm spring came. However, the faces of older people did not show any joy. In addition to the problems of everyday life, there continued to be a lack of basic articles in stores—getting just half a kilogram of sugar required an all-night stand in the queue, even though the chimney of the sugar factory in Szpanów was visible just beyond a hill. New worries arose; more and more people talked about war again.

At the beginning of March, we had just left school when news spread that a German plane had crashed-landed over the city. It fell somewhere near the small village of Tiutkiewicz, a few kilometers away. Not paying attention to the distance, some of us rushed to get there.

In the field behind the village lay the machine's remains with a black cross on the wing. The guards, however, did not let us come closer.

At home, when I told my mother where I was and what I saw, she only sighed heavily.

"The war is here again. What is a German plane doing several hundred kilometers from the border placed as far as on the River Bug?" She paused for a moment in deep thought. "It's a reconnaissance plane," she added.

Various rumors circulated about this incident, and although city officials stated that the German plane had gone astray, no one believed it.

My mother's premonition of war soon began to meet reality. The station was loud at night as soldiers unloaded heavy military equipment, cannons, and tanks. The occasional rumble of caterpillar treads brushing against the street pavement would wake us up in the early twilight.

The school year was coming to an end. The celebration of labor, honoring May 1st, was to be especially festive this year. As the best Russian language student in my class, I was appointed by Ivan Ivanovich, our Russianist, to the academy's inauguration.

I was supposed to deliver the poem "*Ja, syn trudnego naroda pod krasnoje znamia staju* (I, a son of the working people under the red banner of labor)." After that, there was going to be singing, band declamations, and other festivities. The ceremony was to be attended by the city authorities and a general of the Red Army.

The poem was not complex. I learned it in an hour, and I remember it to this day. Yet, I felt a strange reluctance to recite this poem—I do not know, did my mother infect me with her premonitions, or did my guardian angel whisper something in my ear? It was enough that the case ended with a scandal, and she exposed my favorite teacher to big trouble.

On the first of May, I came to school for the celebration.

Upon meeting Ivan Ivanovich, he questioned me, "*Ty vyuchil stikhotvoreniye?* (Did you learn the poem?)"

I have never failed in these matters, but this time, with a squeezed throat, I whispered, "*Nyet.*"

Ivan Ivanovich fell into a frenzy. "*Au, k chertu tebya!* (Oh, to hell with you!)" he roared at the top of his voice, slapping me over the ear.

I sprinted as if I was washed away from the class, chased by a furious bunch of flowery Russian curses. I knew that I had brewed myself some beer,[11] as the order of the ceremony was interrupted, and I had created havoc for a really kind, respectable man.

Until the end of school classes (and these ended in mid-May), I could not look him in the eye—but maybe this "nyet" saved my life: only two months later, when the Germans turned on the Russians, those who

---

11 *Polish saying: to cause himself some trouble*

publicly declared their sympathies for the Soviet authorities were taken to Biala Street and executed. I saw it with my own eyes.

* * *

I met Ivan Ivanovich a couple of years later on my street. He greeted me warmly, and we exchanged a few words about the dreadful events which had unfolded then. It was the time of Poles' slaughter in Wołyń unleashed by the Ukrainian nationalists.

Ivan Ivanovich, a Ukrainian himself, had tears in his eyes. "God, dear God, what are the bandits doing, murdering our brothers?" he sighed heavily.

* * *

In mid-June, after the exam, we were given the testimony of completion of eight grades of the ten-year system, which corresponded more or less to the Polish junior-high graduation. The certificate was beautiful, on chalk paper, displaying the coat of arms of the Ukrainian Soviet Socialist Republic in two languages: Polish and Ukrainian.

My classmates and I were expecting another exam to qualify for the ninth year after the holidays. I had good social and language grades, although mathematics and physics were not so great. I decided to make use of the holidays to sit down and fill in the gaps. Meanwhile, the development of events ultimately thwarted my plans: the airplanes with a crescent cross on their wings appeared once again in the clouds and bombed the cities.

One night, I was sleeping well and innocently when my mother's alarmed voice appeared in my sleep: "Ignac, hey! You have to wake up the boy! Let him flee from here: at any moment, hell will break loose."

Father shook me and spoke loudly over my ear: "Get up, get dressed quickly and go to your aunt in Grabnik."

Rubbing my sleepy eyes, the splendor of a beautiful, sunny morning blinded me. Opposing this peaceful atmosphere, I could hear a loud cannonade in the distance.

As I entered the yard, a lone plane passed by in the sky above. Anti-aircraft artillery, set up around the city, threw all ammunition into it until dark clouds of bullet explosions obscured it completely.

"Run away to Aunt Franka's in Grabnik!" Mother ordered in a trembling, raised voice. "Look how many trains are standing at the station; German bombers will come here soon!"

I started running, forgetting to take a piece of bread. Infinite columns of the Russian Army marched across the nearby streets. I went hurriedly towards the town center.

In order to reach Grabnik, you had to get to the bridge and travel across to the other side of the river—which turned out to be a most difficult task. The military post stopped me, forcing me to turn back. Standing on the street, I wondered how to make it to Grabnik. In the end, I decided I would sneak down the meadows and shrubbery by the waterway bank.

From the riverside bushes, a Red Army soldier jumped with a rifle and shouted, "*Ty kuda, pacan?!* (What are you doing here, boy?!)"

I stood motionless and looked around—they must have thought I was heading for the camouflaged branches, which revealed several peeking barrels of anti-aircraft guns pointing towards the sky. They allowed me to continue my way. However, I still had to adjust my course a few times before I finally got to Aunt Franka at midday.

She had just put a plate of soup on the table when a cry went out.

"They're flying!"

I peered out the window. Slowly, rows of a flying squadron approached the city with their signature Balkenkreuz cross. Old friends from 1939, I thought. Soon the bombs rained down.

Grabnik, a district located on the hills, towered over the city. You could see every explosion like they were on the palm of your hand. Fire and smoke of the blasts soon enveloped the crowded train sets at the railway station and the adjacent district of the city, burning all night like a torch. Nobody could extinguish the fires. It was June 22, 1941, only the first day of the greatest war in Eastern Europe—Operation Barbarossa.[12]

---

12 *The codename of the initial German invasion of the Soviet Union (June 22 - December 5, 1941). Consisting of about 150 German and thirty Finnish and Romanian divisions, which totalled almost four million men, with close to four thousand tanks, three to five thousand aircraft and as many as twenty thousand artillery pieces, this was the largest invasion campaign in the history of mankind. Even though the Soviet numbers were somewhat larger than the German forces, they lacked preparedness and many of their*

GERMAN ADVANCEMENTS IN EUROPE DURING OPERATION BARBAROSSA

By the summer of 1941, the German Reich, with its Italian allies, had taken over almost the entire European continent. France had fallen, Britain was (temporarily) at bay, and now Germany's Führer, Adolf Hitler, turned to the east: the Soviet Union. This map shows the height of advancements over an 1,800-mile front into Russian territory through the rest of 1941.

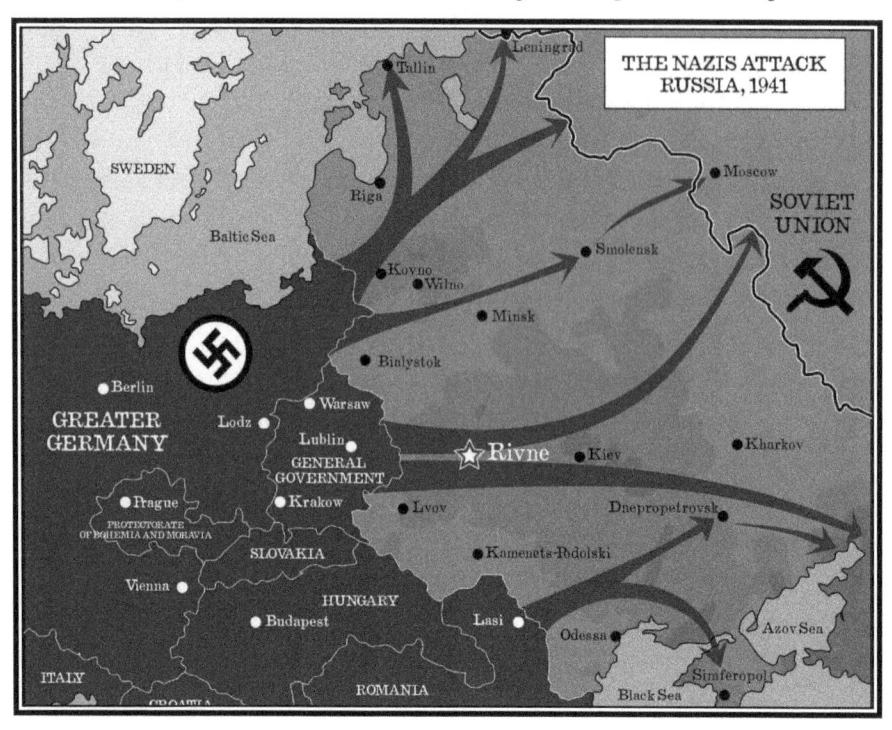

aircraft were obsolete, which contributed to initial German success.

In the evening, my mother and father arrived in Grabnik.

Father bemoaned, "Again, the windows collapsed from the frame, damn it, just like in 1939."

The glow shone all night long over the station and the burning district of the city.

Before dawn, I was on my feet again.

"We will run away from the city," Mother said to Aunt Franka. "It will be safer there."

We went by road to Szpanów. Silence prevailed among the fields; only somewhere high could we hear the harmonious chorus of the larks.

I was happy with this trip to Szpanów, where Uncle Gaj was the manager of the agricultural estate and sugar factory, which before the war was owned by Prince Radziwiłł from his lineage in Ołyka. So companionship for the days of war would not be lacking as my two cousin brothers, Leszek and Danek, lived there.

My uncle was a good-natured man. He ruled the estate before the war, and the Soviet authorities also left him alone. Old trees surrounded the manor house. The gardens behind the gentle slope of the house fell to a giant pond, overgrown with some marsh. An island stood in its center, among which a dozen or so ancient trees grew, also scattered with bits of bricks. Supposedly a fortress once stood there, but wars and uncertain times had washed it away from the face of the earth.

I had stayed with my uncle's family a few times right before the war, and I knew my cousins to be riotous, playful boys who didn't do well in school. Aunt Maria invited me to bring order to them, as I was considered the kinder, older, and well-educated cousin. It was challenging to do, though, as studying was not in their minds at all; it was only a game of prancing about, fussing, fighting. This usually meant my pedagogical career would end. My disappointed aunt would send me back to Równe with a blessing: "Better go home, boy!"

Aunt Maria had one ugly vice—she was morbidly stingy. My uncle's family was very wealthy in those days: in Równe, they had two tenement houses, and my uncle, as the manager of the large estate, made good money. The manor house was an official residence accommodation, with six cows (which brought an abundance of milk) cared for by the servants in the Prince's barns and a maid who completed all domestic work. The pantry was full of cheese, butter, and ham, which would be thrown away from time to time if they lost their freshness. Despite my aunt's constant abundance of food, she was very frugal when serving her visitors—counting almost every bite of food per plate. How would my aunt accept us now?

A familiar rumble in the west woke me up from my pondering. Above the distant horizon, a squadron of bombers emerged, flying eastward.

My aunt welcomed us with a sour face.

"What's going on in town?" she questioned. "Are the houses still standing?"

"They are," my mother answered, "But half of the city is burning, and those…" here she pointed with her thumb up into the sky, "…fly and fly."

The rumble of engines in the sky lasted, with short breaks, until the evening. The Soviet anti-aircraft weapons carried thick fire. Black clouds of bullet explosions often intercepted the flying squadrons, yet that did not seem to deter them. Sometimes a few Soviet fighter aircraft with short hulls, nicknamed Rata, showed up. German fighters chased them or knocked them down without much effort.

Shortly after, Father arrived. Even him my aunt welcomed without enthusiasm; one more mouth to feed—you could see her thoughts on her face. However, both cousins, Leszek and Danek, were delighted by his arrival.

In the afternoon, already wading belt-deep in the swampy pond, we trudged to the island, our favorite, exceptional place to bathe. On the second day, we went there again. The days were beautiful, warm, sunny, and peaceful as the bomber squadrons flew east. From further or closer, we could hear the rumbling of explosions, and still, we were as carefree as if the war was going on at the end of the world. This ignorance was hardly a feat—one of the miraculous privileges of youth.

On the fourth day of battles, the traffic in the air revived to such an extent that our necks hurt from looking up at the sky. Finally, it seemed like the Soviet air forces had woken up from the shock. The planes with a red star and a black cross fought intensely, although the advantage of the Germans—their experience and better equipment—could be seen now and then. Eventually, the heavy streaks of smoke in a clear sky signified the tragic end of the fighting in the air.

It was foreseeable that we wouldn't stay a long time with my aunt. A couple of days later, we decided to pack our belongings, and all three of us traveled to the village of Oleksyn. Here, the Danilczuks—our friends from earlier times of wandering and fishing—welcomed us with great hospitality, plenty of food, and a nice place to sleep. The Danilczuks were Ukrainians, but they treated us as their own, people in need.

In the night, a distant thunder reached our ears for the first time. Everyone woke up and jumped outside.

"A storm is coming," someone remarked.

My father—who had been a soldier of three armies and had experience to draw from—listened for a moment, then murmured, "It's the army front; in two or three days we'll have guests here."

Silence returned in the morning, and a beautiful sun rose. After breakfast, somehow nobody was in a hurry to work—people felt the coming threat.

Finally, Wołodek, the eldest son of our hosts, pulled out a triangular bandura from behind the fireplace and winked at me: "*Chody pośpiwajesz* (Come, let's sing)."

In the simpler days, during our wanderings with a fishing rod, we would often stay at the Danilczuks, and Wołodek always played the bandura as I sang old Ukrainian dumkas. So, it was this time again. Wołodek played and I sang, only this time the distant echo of the approaching front accompanied us.

After the usual repertoire of old songs and dumkas, I unexpectedly started singing new, recently overheard partisan, Bolshevik, and other Russian songs: "*Po wojennej dorogie* (Along the war road)," "*Tuczy nad gorodom stali* (The cloud standing above town)," and "*Po dolinam i po wzgoriam* (Over the hills and valleys)."

As we were sitting by the house near the hedges, quite a crowd of people surrounded us, consisting of close and distant neighbors together. Eventually my tunes became croaks, and the growing thud of engines above our heads doused my desire to sing.

The day passed fairly calmly. We had gotten used to the continuous whir of the machines up above.

Suddenly, during the evening, someone brought a message: "The Russians are running!"

One of the two main roads that the Germans pushed east was the Brest-Łuck-Równe-Zhytomyr-Kiev highway, which ran only a few kilometers from Oleksyn.

When darkness fell, the village became quiet, as if extinct, and even the dog did not bark, while there was an increasingly loud rumble on the side near that road. The Soviets had fled.

In the morning, the noise outside halted, although soon artillery thundered in the west and north. Explosions were only heard from time to time, but as the day progressed, the thunder began to grow in strength.

"Sit at home!" repeated mother, with her ears pointed out, constantly alert.

But who will keep a fourteen-year-old in the apartment during these interesting times? Under any trivial excuse, I managed to get out of the house, yet as I walked out onto the village street, I instantly stepped back, frightened. Singularly and in groups, it appeared that ghosts were running along the road. They were panicked Soviet soldiers from divided units who ran in underwear only, barefoot, and without weapons.

"*Rovno, tuda?* (Równe, this way?)"

"*Da*," I nodded, and they were gone.

The artillery gunfire continued to grow, and finally, I spotted the explosions of the cannons in the meadows behind the river.

The blasts shot a row of several dozen shells at a time, each time closer and closer, creating a grand impression—yet, at the same time, my legs were rooted into the ground with fear. Then, the next salvo of shells roared right onto the village's bank of the river. I held my breath until the moment when I heard a scream just above my ear. It was my mother.

"Run away, into the field!"

Jumping up as if someone had whipped me, I ran as far ahead as I could from these explosions. First, I rushed down a country street, then I turned to a path in between barns, and finally into a field of grain. All of a sudden, as I was panting heavily, a loud German shout came to my ears.

"*Halt!*"

A thought flashed quickly through my head—do I run into the grain? Do I stop? Deciding to stop, I turned slowly. Behind me stood a group of soldiers wearing heavy helmets with rolled-up sleeves and weapons at their faces. As they were watching me curiously, I slowly, as if with soft clay legs, stepped towards them. On their dirty faces, you could perceive a sense of scary and combative excitement. I glared into the barrels of their rifles and at their fingers on the trigger.

One of them finally growled, "*Wohin?* (Where to?)"

With a fierce larynx, I blurted out in German, "*Die artillerie schießt* (The artillery shoots)."

These three words unloaded the tension. God bless Mr. Hrabal, who used to push German on us, I thought. These three words possibly saved my life.

"*Geh nach ninten* (Go to the back)," said one of the soldiers.

"*Aha, hast du die Russen geschehen?* (Aha, have you seen the Russians?)" he then asked.

"*Nein, keine Russen* (No, I have not seen Russians)," I replied and then almost fainted, as fear escaped me like air from a punctured inner tube.

They seemed satisfied with that answer. Even so, from the soldiers' conversation, I understood that they found my clothes to be questionable and that I was dressed strangely. Just before the war, my mother bought me a Polish soldier uniform from the market. I didn't have other appropriate clothing, so Mother cut the sleeves and made sure it fit like a glove—but she forgot that although the cut of my uniform was different, the khaki color was the same as the Soviet uniforms. You could not see the cut design in the distance, so the Germans could have taken me for a Soviet fighter and shot me like a sitting duck. Evidently, my guardian angel was watching over me. She was watching over me many times during the war.

I returned to the Danilczuk hut. My mother was giving me something to eat when my father abruptly entered the house, out of breath.

"We're running!" he shouted and threw himself towards the door.

Without disputing, I rushed after him.

We ran across the dirt road and went as far as we could behind the village until we were completely out of breath. Father stopped, glared at me reproachfully while gasping for air, and finally asked: "What songs were you singing, fool?"

"The usual thing," I said uncertainly.

"For your singing, the Germans could have put us against the wall: you sang Bolshevik songs! For things like that, they would kill us, idiot. They would take us as Communists. I overheard, thankfully, the conversation of several Ukrainians who decided to let the Germans know about you," Father added.

We did not return to the village that day. We decided to spend the night in a lineman's shed near the railway tracks.

A powerful explosion shook the area in the early evening. The earth swayed underfoot. A gigantic mushroom of smoke rose above the forest beyond the village, reaching the clouds. In the middle, you could catch sight of the regular violet circle. A dozen or so minutes later, a similar explosion shook the ground.

"Russians are blowing up their ammunition sets," explained the linemen to my father. "There, in the early summer, were huge warehouses and trains full of ammunition."

"And who builds such ammunition stores so close to the border?" asked my father. "It's the fault of the Russian generals," he added.

But it was not the generals' fault. Many years after the war, I read that the Soviet war doctrine, according to Stalin's guidelines, was based around the idea "*budem bit' vraga na yego territorii* (we will beat our enemy on their territory)." This strategy did not take into account a defensive war—therefore, the ammunition warehouses located so close to the frontline in case of retreat had to be destroyed.

In the late evening, the shooting and explosions were silenced. We slept on straw for the night, and in the morning, my father was wondering what to do next. You could still feel the rumbling in the east and south, but after a few hours, it subsided.

Father decided: "We're going back home!"

In the suburbs, passing by the big food depots, we noticed an unexpected movement: the local people were smashing the doors of the storehouses and taking as many supplies as possible. We managed to take our own souvenir, a sack of sugar, which allowed us to survive the first hungry days of German occupation.

Our home survived, but it was difficult to recognize the suburb well known to us. Our apartment was completely robbed. The windows were completely demolished. We started our renovation—we replaced the frames and the glass with cardboard and plywood.

By the evening, almost all of our neighbors returned from wandering. When the dusk fell, they gathered in front of the house and wondered what the next step was, when again a new terror arose: a German military transport had reached the station. The street flooded with marching booted German soldiers wearing feldgrau-colored uniforms. Two of them entered our yard.

Examining us carefully, they questioned, "*Sind Juden da?* (Are any Jews here?)"

Our Jewish neighbors, Sonja, Manje, and Henje, instinctively crumpled.

Nevertheless, our neighbors jointly declared, "*Nein, keine Juden da* (There are no Jews here)."

The soldiers left after a moment.

We understood then that the new authorities did not like Jews. We felt this strongly in the forthcoming days.

"What will happen to us?" asked Masha in a fearful voice when we met at the store where bread was sold, after a very long time of not seeing each other. "I cannot even buy food because I'm a Jew."

"Leave it to me," I replied and joined the line.

I found Sławik in the same shop, and we shared our bread with Masha. A couple of other Jews noticed.

"Zbyszek, buy some bread for me too, please?" whispered the little voice of Jankielek—the son of a poor tailor from our street—from behind the fence.

I bought some bread for him too, and then Mrs. Katz appeared with the same request.

When I got in the queue again, a Ukrainian came to me and snarled: "Are you buying bread for Jews? I will tell the Germans."

This was no joke. In the multinational cauldron which Wołyń was then, you had to keep your eyes wide open; for every humane impulse you could pay a high price. I retired from the queue and returned the money to an upset Mrs. Katz, turning my ashamed face away.

"What am I going to give to my hungry children?" Mrs. Katz whispered, with eyes full of glistening tears.

Each day, the Jews would be restricted further with new, dreadful rules.

Another day, I met with Masha, and I noticed she was wearing a white band with the star of David on her shoulder. We stood facing each other as thick tears poured over our cheeks. Suddenly, I heard a rumble. A noise was coming from a hand-operated platform, used typically to handle luggage at the station, which four young Jews were rolling onto the pavement by the street. On the platform sat a German railwayman smiling mockingly. From time to time, he waved a whip in the air and struck upon the laboring Jews. I gritted my teeth. Why do they let themselves be so humiliated? Why don't they run into forests where, despite the ruthless terror, the first acts of guerilla sabotage—caused by war prisoners who had managed to escape from the camps and form partisan units—had begun to appear?

The situation of the Jews in Wołyń was especially difficult. The nations, which over centuries had developed a neo-sympathetic relationship, began to glower at each other with a new hatred: a black plague of nationalism had sprung up—neighbors were afraid of neighbors, as for any help to the Jews they could pay with their head.

And how true it is that the severity of this situation has mostly gone away from my memory, but some of these memories are still stuck today in my head like rusted nails.

It was the beginning of July 1941, a week or two after the Germans had entered. A group of boys and I were playing with a ragged ball on the large railway track, at the Wodokaczce pumping station, near a meadow that stretched broadly at the fork of Legionów Street. On the other side of the street, a tall, daring fence surrounded the military barracks. A couple of dozen meters from the barrier, you could see a pitched high cliff. Gunshots fired there often—the soldiers used the gorge as a shooting range.

Tired of playing with the ball, we rested. Then, we heard a new noise from the ravine: a regular series of continuous fire. It was the rattle of automatic machine guns.

"What's going on there?" one boy asked, and we froze in silence.

From the gate of the fence, we noticed trucks full of people—prisoners of war. Those people got off the truck platforms, set up near the pits in rows, and the soldiers opened fire. There was a constant supply of trucks coming every minute. Moments later, newly spewn bodies of people unknown to us were setting over the pits. We watched, mesmerized but petrified, until the executions came to an end.

Running through the gardens, afraid to be seen on the streets, we scurried back home. All over the town, we found posters advertising those executions.

Ukrainian police troops in black uniforms, who had allied with the Germans, were often seen marching the streets, singing a dark song: "*Smert Lacham i Żidiwsko—i Moskowskoj Komuni* (Death to Poles and Jews—and Moscow Communists)." Old resentments and disapprovals intensified with a hundredfold force from the anguish of the war. There was zero civil communication between nationalities.

The cruel Nazi military occupation decided to eradicate the population with hunger ever further, and, by this point, Jews were not even allowed to utter a single word on the street. Complaints about this rule would end badly for anyone. Workers who were shipped to Germany received miserable helpings of food weekly that could be eaten in a single sitting: a kilo of barley-flour bread, twenty decagrams of beetroot marmalade, and twenty decagrams of meat, which even a dog would sniff long before eating.

Star-banded beggars occupied the streets. In silence, they pulled out their hands, but no sane person could help them. It was only possible to occasionally buy half a loaf of bread if you were lucky and not a Jew. The rich and fertile land of Wołyń had become a place of famine and poverty.

Masha would sneak into our apartment in the evening and bring a variety of items my mother would exchange for food at the market. Money was of no value; instead, the exchange trade was flourishing. This form of assistance was also forbidden for the Jews, although until the "black plague" came to our area, our neighbors were still helping each other.

— 6 —
Russki Chase

Red posters from the German Reich hung on the streets, threatening death for any help to Jews and Soviet prisoners of war.

"Go to Grabnik, again," my mother decided. "There, it should be calmer. The Soviet Army may bombard the city at any moment." She gazed anxiously towards the station.

I obediently went. On the way, I spotted a few of my colleagues.

"Go to the jail," one hollered. "You'll see what happened there!"

Crowds of people were walking towards the prison. I joined them. A German gendarme was standing by the gate, and people were coming in and out freely. At the entrance to the building, I was struck by a terrible stench as swarms of black flies circled the air. I glimpsed into the first of the cells, and a horrific view hit my eyes: the prisoner's bodies were twisted on the floor, splattered with blood, and covered in fragments of the damaged walls as a result of explosions. The same was visible in the second, third, and further cells of the prison. On the next floor, they were identical in their contents—massacred corpses, a stench, and flies.

Many of the people, pale and shocked, had come to find their loved ones' bodies.

"These bastards," someone was speaking Polish towards the Soviet NKVD.[13] "They were throwing hand grenades into the cells—the injured did not have a chance to survive!"

---

13 *The 1941 NKVD Prison Massacres were ten to forty thousand murders that the Russian secret police carried out within a week or so of the German invasion of the Soviet Union, to avoid handing the prisoners over to the Germans.*

An elderly lady cried loudly in front of the entrance, and someone stated she had recognized her husband's body. Soon, the German military police ordered several dozen Soviet prisoners of war to take the dead out. After being thrown into the ladder carts like wood, they took the bodies out of town into the old Jewish cemetery. Who actually died there would probably remain a mystery forever. The prison was needed for the new perpetrators.

It was an emotional day for me. On the main street, German soldiers were escorting an endless column of Soviet prisoners of war west from Korzec. Thousands of them walked, exhausted, thirsty, hungry, many wounded and sick. They dragged along, with their heads down, like people already condemned to death. They weren't exactly wrong, as waiting for them, from behind the fenced-off war prisoner camps, was the most terrible of death: starvation.

It was not the end of the events of this long July day. In Grabnik, my aunt had just given me a piece of bread with lard when someone outside yelled out.

"Tanks!"

I leaped out into the yard. On the side of the suburban village of Tiutkiewicze, five tanks with a star on each turret steered towards us on the steep hill. It was most likely the rest of a splintered armored unit, attempting to break free from the surrounding enemy forces.

With a few other boys, I stepped back into the house—from the attic window, the view was much better. We spied an anti-tank cannon, operated by curled-up German soldiers, in the bushes on the other side of a nearby street. A shot from this cannon banged. The first of the tanks spun around in a circle, and when another shot hit, it tumbled down the steep slope. The second tank, firing from the machine gun barrels, paraded fearlessly uphill—until the next accurate projectile of the cannon hit it, and the armored dragon stood in flames. The other three were in a deadly trap. Visible from above as if on the palm of our hands, they began maneuvering to break away, under the fire of the enemy. Unluckily, any retreat was out of the question. One burning vehicle terraced the center of the road; a sharply falling slope was visible on the left, and a steep upward slope was on the right.

At last, one of the desperate tanks pushed the burning machine down. It did not help much—the German shooters, using the temporary turmoil, hit the third tank, and shortly after, the fourth tank. The fifth dashed forward courageously, and it seemed that a miserable fate awaited the ambushing Germans until a final striking shot from their cannon halted the advancing machine. The armor-piercing projectile exploded inside, and the tank then rolled a dozen or so meters as if a drunk man was operating. No one escaped from the standing machines—the crews died on the spot. The whole clash lasted just a few minutes.

German soldiers came out of the lilac bush and approached the smashed, charred, smoking machine. One of them pulled a bottle of vodka out of his backpack, and everyone in turn took a few sips from it.

On that day, I had viewed enough of war and death. I fell into a deep sleep, and a powerful explosion that snatched many from their bedding in the middle of the night did not bother to wake me up. It was clearly not safe in Grabnik.

The next day I came home. My mother began to think of another place to send me, so I used the moment of freedom to explore with my friends, as there were so many stimulating things happening everywhere.

One of my colleagues reported: "In the barracks, there are a lot of Soviet tanks."

And we ran there immediately.

The Germans had not managed to occupy the vast barracks yet, which had housed the Thirteenth Infantry Regiment, the Uhlan Regiment, a large artillery unit, and several other Polish Home Army divisions in the pre-war period.

We had no trouble in finding a gigantic tank parking lot. There were several dozen brand new machines, which for unknown reasons were not used to fight (Father spoke later, saying that apparently some of the parts for them were missing).

It was a real paradise for teenagers. We were sitting behind the steering device of combat machines, turning the towers, aiming at barrels with cannons, and trying to hit the drum with a machine gun. The fun would probably have lasted longer if one of our older colleagues had not found actual machine gun cartridges. He released a series of shots, which crashed into some of the other armored tanks. The gunfire, unsurprisingly, alerted some nearby German soldiers. We jumped out of the hatches and ran away like hares as bullets whistled over our heads.

Mother, who was constantly looking for a location out of harm's way for her only child, stated: "Tomorrow you will go to your cousin Olga in Zdolbunów. It is a smaller place; it will be safer there."

So, the next day, I went to Zdołbunów. It was a small town of several thousand, unfortunately also with a large railway junction. In addition to Olga and her husband, my mother's brother Stasiek lived in Zdołbunów with his family. He was an invalid from World War I. His small family did not guarantee many merry days. Fortunately, Olga's sister Jadźka and brother Zygmunt happened to be there too, with whom I could have more fun. And during the war, it never took long to be entertained.

I could not sleep that night. The hens from nearby farms were repeatedly clucking, when all of a sudden, a deafening explosion shook the sleeping world. I opened my eyes, and outside of the window, it was as clear as broad daylight. I reached for my clothes and shoes—which should be within easy reach according to Father's instructions—dressed quickly and set foot into the garden. The glare of a vast fire blinded me. A train, with a dozen or so wagons of fuel, was burning. Its fire thrashed into the heavens and spilled over the earth. There was no time to lose: the crowds on board—and they were prisoners of war—were let loose and escaping from the wagons standing in the station. I was swept away by the masses.

We scampered blindly through the gardens, towards the giant swampy pond, as far away as possible from this hell, until the morass blocked our escape route. Some ran on blindly, wading deeper into the swamp, and the rest of the refugees stopped at the edge and peered around for another path.

"Help! Help! I'm drowning!" a female voice called.

I threw myself in that direction, and, in the glow of the fire, I spied a white figure immersed above the waist in the swamp. As I trudged through the mud, I approached the person step by step and began to recognize that it was a woman. I offered my hand and pulled her out of danger into the dry land. To my heavenly amazement, I knew the would-be morass victim: it was Olga, my cousin! She was only in her shirt—she had not even managed to pull on her bathrobe in panic.

Walking along the marshland, we reached the bridge on the river and the nearby road. Here a large crowd of refugees gathered. Many of them were fearfully chattering their jaws after having a cold bath in the swamp.

We waited for a while until the early summer dawn lightened the sky, and the flames on the station began to settle. The crowd moved slowly. Trudging, with deep fear in our hearts, we wondered if the house would be in ruins. Amazingly, Olga's wooden house was intact! The burning fuel that spilled over the station did not pass further, and so the fire had stopped at the track that ran a dozen or so meters from the house.

We breathed a sigh of relief. The house was standing, and Jadzka, my cousin's sister—who miraculously sat all night in the wooden outhouse—greeted us in the doorway. My other cousin, Zygmunt, had the most peaceful experience of all during this horrible night. We found him sleeping like a gopher in a hay shed when we returned from the overnight escape. Awoken, he looked around and wondered why there was a lot of shouting: the Germans had already brought in heavy equipment and hundreds of people to clean up the track.

What was the cause of the fire? Probably sabotage. In the afternoon, red posters with a long list of murdered suspects, primarily residents of the small town, were already on the walls of the nearby houses. There is nothing here for me, I thought, and traveled home the same day. There were no safe places during the war.

In the middle of July, the news of the "Russki[14] chase" spread through the city. An endless river of Soviet soldiers-taken-prisoners, escorted by German enforcers, marched along the main street from the east to the west. They walked and walked all day, all night, and even another day without a break. They were tired, hungry, exhausted. They carried the wounded, weakened by hunger and thirst. They begged for a sip of water, for a piece of bread. We could not help much—we barely had enough bread for one of us, and giving even a cup of water was quite dangerous.

---

14 *A term used to refer to Russians*

The escorts grievously snapped the locks of their rifles and kicked out any pitiful observers.

The prisoners awaited a tragic fate. Great warehouses and the huge training ground behind the high fence on our street rapidly filled with people. Soon, the captives had eaten the grass to the last straw. Emaciated figures at the barrier stood and shouted to the passing crowds. Some of them took off their robes and threw them over the fence, asking for bread in return. I had now seen what bread could be for a man.

In a shop where, from time to time, several hundred loaves of black bread were brought, a crowd of people constantly roamed. Jews lurked in the alleys, and every time someone passed by with food, they would also desperately attempt to trade their clothing for it.

One exceptionally dark August night, I decided to walk Masha home.

We stood on the pavement, and suddenly Masha wrapped her arms around me, squeezed me, and whimpered, "Zbyszek, dear God, what are they going to do with us?"

I hugged her and kissed her on the forehead. I embraced her even more intensely to stop myself from crying—despite the fact that I was taught at a young age that a man does not cry, and I was almost fifteen years old. I wanted to say some nice, comforting words. Unfortunately, I did not say anything because rage and helpless anger towards the Nazi torturers suffocated my throat.

Behind the fence of barbed wire, the captive prisoners were dying of hunger. The war was revealing its cruel, battle-hardened, savage face. A few boys from our street and I pulled out carrots and cabbages in the local gardens and threw them across the fence. We did this for a long time, until an enraged sentry shot warning bullets in our direction.

"Why are they not fighting? Why are so many people taken prisoner?" Father wondered after I made it home. The answer came soon.

At the station, several dozen Soviet prisoners of war were working to unload some equipment. At some point, the door of our house opened, and a young, maybe eighteen-or nineteen-year-old, Russian prisoner stood in the doorway.

"*Matushka, day mne kusochek khleba* (Mother, give me a piece of bread)," he pleaded.

Mother sighed deeply, "They would kill us for it, it says on the posters; for any help to the Soviet prisoners and Jews, there is a death penalty."

When the prisoner saw our horror, he reassured, "*Ne boysya Matushk, Nemets pozvolil mne* (Do not fear Mother, a German allowed me)."

Mother peered out the window. A group of working prisoners stood by a merciful, elderly guard, who was allowing the young prisoners to leave and ask for food from the civilians. She put a plate of barley soup and a slice of bread on the table. He ate greedily.

My mother looked at his youthful yet miserable face for a long time and finally asked in Russian: "*Ty mnogo ssorilsya v molodom vozraste, Synok?* (Have you fought much in your young age, Son?)"

Tears leaked from his eyes as he peered at her and replied, "*Matushka, za chto mne drat'sya?* (Mother, what was I supposed to fight for?) *Moya sobstvennaya mat' zarabatyvala v kolkhoze tol'ko kilogramm zerna za rabochiy den'* (All my own mother ever earned was one kilo of grain per working day in the kolkhoz)."

I remember these words to this day, as well as the scene before my eyes, of the carts loaded with corpses of deceased prisoners who were dragged to the Jewish cemetery by their exhausted, barely alive colleagues.

November 7

Autumn approached fast. At home we slept on straw mattresses; my mother had long ago exchanged the bedding on the market for food, even though another nasty, freezing winter was awaiting us. Every time I saw Masha, her beautiful face became more and more saddened. When we had to part, she would often wait for me to wave my hand or show me a full-of-sorrow smile. I would share my poor food supply with her, even though I was starving myself already. On the streets in the mornings, the Jews would pile the hand-operated platforms with bodies of those who died in their homes from hunger.

When the Germans took over in the summer, they created "Reichskommissariat Ukraine." The local Ukrainian authorities reorganized schooling, and my mother, who spoke perfect Ukrainian, managed to register me in a technical institution—the only school in the city—by some unknown miracle.

GERMAN-OCCUPIED GOVERNANCE OF EUROPEAN REGIONS, END OF 1941

At the extent of Operation Barbarossa, almost the entirety of the European continent and even a significant portion of North Africa was under German influence. This map illustrates the governance of all occupied regions, and "Równe (Rivne)" is highlighted in the country of "Reichskommissariat Ukraine." Note that Italy, Finland, and a number of other Southeastern European states were not directly under German control, but their governments were either supported by, allied with, or oppressed by the Wehrmacht.

The only Pole among Ukrainians in the school, I was a constant object of derision and provocation: any dislikes expressed between the inhabitants of Wołyń, which were already present in the Polish Republic era, exploded with a full flame under the influence of German fascism. The Germans—the demigods, the masters of Europe—stood at the top of this social ladder. In their shadow, Ukrainian nationalism grew stronger and stronger, and Poles became sub-men of that second category, although in many cases Germans hired them for lack of specialists in different positions.

As I only swallowed saliva and my bowels twisted in hunger, I watched jealously while my colleagues ate sausages during the breaks; they were mostly farmers' sons. Luckily, some good people among them occasionally gave me a piece of bread with lard, which allowed me to focus during my classes. Nevertheless, I was alone—except for one half-Polish, half-Latvian girl named Wierą, who hid her origins carefully from the Ukrainians. It was her that half the school unsuccessfully sighed at, as from what I knew, after a few words from these admirers, Wierą would turn away from my fellow "friends." The courtship of my colleagues was generally primitive and boorish, and it was in this field that I saw a window of opportunity and an occasion for revenge.

My simple idea played out smoothly: I smiled, said a few nice words, and arranged a date with the girl, under the pretext of help with technical drawings, which was my forte. Wierą invited me to her house, where she lived with her aunt. Soon, the first youthful feeling of love enveloped me like a flame. I thought about her during the day and at night. We went to school together and we returned together—we spent every free moment together.

Her aunt, who had lived in the city for a long time, was not ill-disposed towards Poles, and she always looked at us together with a smile, often offering tea with cherry preserves. The months passed, and every time we looked at each other, it was as if we saw a rainbow.

Sometimes I wandered with Wierą to the Orthodox church. One meeting is stuck in my memory: the holiday of Jordan. The church was full of people, and when we went to the river for the procession, a man was bathing in the ice for the memory of St. John's baptism. Although the assembly took a few hours, I was content with the girl by my side.

When I came back home, my mother spent a long time warming my bone-cold legs after being in the snow.

My sweetheart naturally caught the attention of my colleagues. "*Proklatyj Lach* (Damn Pole)," they insulted. "He picked up the prettiest girl at school."

The times were more and more restless. Robberies, murders, and attacks towards Poles were multiplying. During one particular lesson, the school's headmaster, an avid Ukrainian nationalist, glared directly at me while stating a testimony that the time had come for "solving the problem" of the Poles, and a shudder passed down my spine. There is nothing good for me here, I thought.

My father and mother worked all day. Father, as a locksmith, was permitted to run a mechanical workshop, which sometimes brushed against danger. My father's clients were a mixture: the inhabitants of our district asked for minor repairs, and at other times unknown strangers brought ironworks, strangely resembling parts of firearms. My father did his best to hide this, but the teenager's eye can see everything.

One distinct event sticks in my memory. A sudden pounding at our door woke us in the middle of the night. Mother opened the door and instinctively froze: a group of German gendarmerie stood in the entrance with service plates on their chests, armed to the teeth with machine guns.

"Dress up. You will go with us," one of them ordered my father in Polish. He began to clothe himself with trembling hands.

"Ignac," my mother whispered, "I'll give you a change of underwear."

"You do not need it," the gendarme assured. "Your husband will come back in an hour," he added.

We sighed with relief. A visit in the night from the German military police did not usually bode well—but this time, in fact, my father did return after an hour. All they wanted him for was to open a secret military document case, from which the keys were stolen or lost.

The rumble of trains rushing with equipment and supplies to the east did not stop day and night. The life of the city's inhabitants became more miserable and more difficult. Every day when walking to school past the city center, triumphant German military marches blasted from the speakers, and the German Army Commander would often communicate:

"*Oberkommando der Wehrmacht gibt bekannt Deutselland siegt an allen fronten* (High Command of the Wehrmacht announces Germans are winning on all fronts)." These triumphant reports of victories on the Eastern Front and the number of sunken enemy ships would sound from all sides.

A cold autumn rain was a sign of the beginning of winter—another enemy of humanity's poverty and suffering. At the beginning of November, red envelopes were distributed to Jewish houses, ordering them all to arrive on the 7th to an *Umschlagplatz*[15] at the big city square where in times of peace and prosperity, the town's market was held. They said it was for resettlement of the Jews, but nearly everyone could sniff the lie. Three older Jewish girls from our neighborhood came to my mother for advice.

"What to do? Go or not? Where will they move us to and what for?"

For a long part of the night, I heard petrified whispers. Failure to attend was punishable by death. The following evening, Masha came running.

"I want to say goodbye to you. Tomorrow we will have to go."

For a long moment, we squeezed our hands in the silence of the dark.

The Jews from nearby towns were escorted by Ukrainian policemen for the whole day preceding November 7th for resettlement. Old, sick or wounded people were taken on stretchers. The rest of the population looked at this picture in despair—where would they go?

In the town at the market square, there was an ever-growing crowd of poorly clothed, starving people, and ahead of them was a long November night under the naked sky surrounded only by German Gestapo. It was still dark the next morning when our Jewish friends joined them. I spotted Masha in the crowd, and she stared back at me.

"I will write to you!" she shouted as her silhouette disappeared into the darkness.

From the early twilight hours, wind was accompanied by dreadful snow and rain—it was a day in which you wouldn't even shove the dog outside. The whole morning we waited in fear. What will they do with

---

15 *German meaning: collection point. This term was used during the Holocaust to denote where Jews from ghettos were supposed to group together for so-called "relocation."*

the Jews? Where will they take them? Finally, a neighbor brought the bad news.

"The Germans and Ukrainians are murdering the Jews in the clay pit outside of the city."

"Impossible," whispered my mother in horror. "Are they going to murder them all?"

Each neighbor passed the news to another, and very soon, the entire street was in a state of shock. The proclamation was so hard to comprehend that no one could believe it. Thirty thousand Jews occupied the city, and if they were all executed, the entire population would be cut in half!

The door to our home opened, and Sławik's head appeared.

"Come on, Zbyszek, let us go and play," he winked at me.

"Whatever you do, do not leave the street," my mother warned.

Sławik was clearly excited. As soon as we got out of earshot, he voiced in a hushed tone: "The Germans are murdering the Jews right now in the clay pits. Let's go!"

We managed to borrow a bike from an old friend named Antek. He worked in the German post office as a messenger and had a bicycle license, an extremely rare privilege.

The clay pits where the killing was supposedly happening were about one kilometer southeast of the city, behind Grabnik, the most beautiful and affluent area now entirely overtaken by Germans. Erich Koch,[16] the Reichskommissar of Ukraine from 1941 to 1944, one of the most ruthless leaders of Eastern Prussia, was based in Grabnik, too.

Sławik and I alternated the bike—one pedaling, once sitting on the frame—passing the nearby districts, which seemed frozen in dread. We then had to bypass the most strictly guarded region by riding along the river and fields. In the end, we rode through the wet meadows to the hill of the old Jewish cemetery. Despite a cold, gusty wind and the downpouring snow and rain, we managed to reach it without complications. We knew the area well; it was a secluded place, excellent for skiing downhill every winter. It was also hidden from most angles unless you came the same way we arrived.

---

16 *Erich Koch (b. June 1896, d. November 1986) was the Nazi Gauleiter of East Prussia. He later died as a war criminal in the Polish prison of Barczewo.*

We left the bicycle in the bushes, and as slowly as the Amerindians (like in Western films), from bush to bush, from rock to rock, we climbed to the top of the hill. At the top, tall spruces were growing on one side of the slope. We crossed them and looked carefully onto the opposite side. The wind on top of the hill blew right through my bones, and I began to quiver.

On the road below us, a chain of Ukrainian police officers in black uniforms, armed with shotguns, diligently watched the area. From this position, we could spy the horrors of the clay pit. We moved a little closer and instantly heard the unmistakable rattle of machine guns combined with a horrible inhuman scream.

With the naked eye, all you could see was a muffled human crowd. I was stone cold in shock, and my heartbeat seemed to pause indefinitely. From a combination of the cold and dread, my teeth started chattering uncontrollably. It was hell on earth. Somewhere in this crowd of unfortunate people was Masha, and all I could do was search hopelessly for her face.

Sławik took out a cannon scope, which he had salvaged from the Soviets' neglected weapon tools, and handed it to me. Through the glass, you could spy everything as clear as your own hand. German Gestapo and SS men surrounded the crowd of helpless people. The process was extremely methodical: every moment, a couple of the Jews would be separated from the main group and get told to undress. Then, the guards threw their clothes and belongings on a large pile, and the naked, petrified victims were pushed into the clay pit by the butt of rifles, where machine guns worked without interruption. There were several of those pits, and the people would melt in your eyes. It was diabolical.

"Come, let's run—they might spot us," Sławik shook me frantically. His face was pale, too.

We went down the same road through the cemetery, back through the meadows, then Sławik put me on the frame, and we rode back into the city. We dropped Antek's bike off and parted, rushing to our homes.

My mother was tearing her hair in worry.

"Where were you? What were you doing? Take off your clothes and go to bed!" she shouted, seeing how badly I was trembling, like a leaf in the wind.

I spent three days in bed with a fever. A doctor diagnosed pneumonia, but my young body won the battle, and I recovered in no time. I told my mother everything I saw.

"You know what they would do if you fell into their hands? Germans do not like living witnesses of their crimes, and so they would kill you without a thought!"

* * *

This first Holocaust[17] was one of many, and today, after all these years, I am still reminded occasionally of it in my nightmares. Some of those events are embedded in my memory as if I lived them yesterday. None of our neighbors came back, and I never saw Masha again.

Soon, it turned out that not all the Jews were murdered on that day, and some of the young and healthy the Nazis spared, which became a workforce that they used to the end.

A ghetto was set up for the remaining Jews, and we were ordered to resettle to another district of the city. Our quarter, located in the trilateral between the railway station and the barracks, was considered by the occupier as the best area for the ghetto. The Jews who escaped from the November massacre settled in this easy-to-guard triangle. Their fate was dreadfully miserable. They were completely cut off from the local population, and the entrance to the ghetto was forbidden under the death penalty. A Jew outside the ghetto was ruled the same punishment. Help from Poles under the watchful eye of Ukrainian nationalists was also impossible. Surrounded by a large barbed wire fence, that ghetto existed until July 1942, when the "ultimate solution of the Jewish problem" was operated: all Jews were exterminated. A tragic glow entrapped Wołyń.

The German garrison stationed in the city guaranteed relative peace for the time being. Even with this assurance, towards the end of 1941, anxiety increased. There was even a death penalty for having and listening

---

17 *On Nov. 6-7, 1941, the Sosenki Forest near Równe was the place where fifteen to eighteen thousand Jewish adults and another six thousand Jewish children were brutally murdered, a massacre coordinated by the German Einsatzgruppe Fifth Division. Some Ukrainian auxiliary forces assisted in this effort, and this was one prime example of how they used those massacres to practice the techniques of efficient genocide, allowing them to efficiently do the same to the remaining eastern Polish population later in the war.*

to a radio. People were asking themselves the same question over and over again—what will happen next?

The war was taking place somewhere in the east and the west. However, the news of these battles that reached us was contradictory and unbelievable—the German loudspeakers, which used to announce the upcoming collapse of Moscow in a triumphal tone, would now just report heavy fighting in the east. And so the German road-roller of war, which flattened everything in its path, was stopped somewhere in its tracks.

Soon after, the school was closed down. The authorities sent some of the young people to work, and the students from the villages returned to their families. I had to say farewell to Wierą—it was uncertain whether we would ever see each other again. In tears, we both vowed sorrowfully, promising ourselves that we would find each other again when everything calmed down.

— 8 —

Winter Escapade

Winter began in the middle of November. Sharp frosts covered everything, and yet the days were sunny and quiet. The winter school holidays continued. On one such sunny, beautifully cool day, a foolish idea came to my mind, which I almost paid for with my life.

"I will go to Grandma's," I informed my mother.

A startled look appeared on her face. "That far? It's twenty-five kilometers away, it's frosty, and it's already late," she remarked.

The clock had just struck mid-day.

"He will go a few kilometers, his legs will hurt, and he'll come back," my father interjected.

That comment awakened my ambition. Everything seems easy and straightforward when you are fifteen, so I had no trouble deciding to prove my point. I dressed quickly, and despite the protests of my mother, started on my journey. I was drawn to go to my grandmother's. Usually at this time, near the New Year, it was a busy and merry place. Young aunts, neighbors, and distant cousins usually provided a few cheerful days.

I left town by the road to Klewań and Łuck. I surveyed around carefully, hoping for a ride. Unfortunately, the street, as far as the distant horizon, was deserted. I walked briskly because the sun seemed to move ever faster along the cloudless winter sky.

When I reached the place where I had to turn into the field, near the village of Michałówka, the bright ball of the sun was hidden behind me. A dark winter night was falling. Stars glistened brightly in the cloudless sky, and in their reflection, you could just about see the road in front—if I were to get lost, the trip would end tragically for me. At about halfway,

I unfortunately began to understand the pain in the legs that my father had predicted.

I accelerated my pace: I ran downhill and trudged uphill. The ice creaked underneath my feet. Sometimes, deep snowdrifts blocked the road, and at other times it was hard to walk in places where the winter winds were blowing the snow into the air. And the pathway itself spiraled like a ribbon across the fields, forests, and ravines—it seemed to lead to nowhere.

In the valleys between the hills, faint lights flickered from time to time in the windows of low huts, as if inviting: "Come in, rest, warm yourself." However, my voice of reason was telling me something different, and my fantasy was overcome by fear—after all, they were Ukrainian villages, and I therefore could not count on a welcome party. Relations between Ukrainians and Poles had been especially terrible since the Germans appeared, which I had already personally experienced at school. I passed as quickly as possible through these villages while squeezing a stick in my hand that I had broken off somewhere in the forest.

The frost had completely solidified. A strange silence prevailed in the air—the well pump handle did not creak, the dog did not bark, and even the cock did not crow. The ritual of feeding animals must have taken place earlier in the day, and now the villagers must be sitting in warm rooms, slurping soup and eating dumplings. At the thought of this, I began to feel a twinge of hunger in my stomach.

I did not come across one living soul on the trail. At one point, when I felt the smoke from a chimney and the smell of hot soup, I almost opened the gate of a yard of a hut, only stepping back at the last second. My Ukrainian was not very fluent, so the hosts would realize that I was not their countryman.

I clenched my teeth and walked on. The footpath now led through an old pine forest. It was almost pitch-black, but eventually, my eyes got used to it. To detect any form of the trail, I had to look for signs of sleds between the trees.

Far away, something flashed in the darkness, and a shudder passed through my head. Fairy tales of wolves that appear during the winter in these parts of Polesie came to my mind. My hair bristled in fear. I was totally alone, with only a stick in hand, when what seemed to be a wolf's glistening eyes, glaring right towards me, appeared far in front.

    I slowed my pace and strained my eyes. The lights did not move, so they definitely were not animals. As I approached closer, with careful footsteps to avoid any noise, the gleaming dots became clearer. Attempting to squint even more, I finally saw that they were only two dim lights in the windows of two cottages, standing at the edge of the forest. So there are people here! My first instinct told me to knock on the door, come in, and ask for a sip of water—but with the last of my willpower, I held back: what awaits me in this hut? It was a time when unknown people should be feared more than a wild animal. The encouraging news was that I knew this place well from holiday wandering; hence, I was only a few kilometers from my grandmother's house. Although my legs were so sore that I could barely drag myself along, this discovery gave me strength.

    The road, covered up with snow, had vanished entirely from my eyes. It now led between bare hills. The wind had blown the snow into the valleys, and so only Venus glowing in the winter sky pointed out my direction.

    The remainder of my energy began to dissipate, and then I spotted a village near a hill on the right. It was Hołyszew, a known Ukrainian settlement. I avoided it with a wide arc and trudged to the edge of the forest. It was only three more kilometers from the road, running along the edge of the woods, when my grandmother's cottage emerged from behind a hill. A profound feeling of relief entered my heart, yet my legs refused to obey. The temptation to sit next to a tree trunk and rest indefinitely was so intense that it was only with the greatest difficulty that I managed to overcome it: I understood that if I were to sit down, I would immediately fall asleep and freeze to death. This was undoubtedly one of the most challenging temptations that I had to overcome in my life. Fortunately, I managed to resist it. It was hardly another half hour of walking until I caught sight of a long, cherry-tree alley, and soon after, my grandmother's hut. Alas, her windows were dark!

    I knocked on the door and stood for a long while before someone answered. Grandma, Uncle Gaj, and my aunt were incredibly shaken and surprised by my arrival—a knock at the door at night in those times did not bode well.

In such times, some rumors went around about the attacks of Ukrainian nationalist gangs on single Polish settlements located far from the villages. Uncle Gaj, my father's brother, lived happily with Ukrainian neighbors, married a Ukrainian and had two children with her, yet later in the war, even that was not enough to save him from martyrdom at the hands of those nationalists.

"Did you come from Równe?" asked Grandma Józefa. "It is such a long way, and the frost is very sharp." She shook her head in disbelief as she looked at me, adding, "We huddle quietly like a mouse under a broom, and we do not use lights because there is a lack of kerosene, and the light in the windows can lure uninvited guests. Ukrainians look at us the same way an angry bull would, and we expect the worst."

Soon I had the opportunity to learn the truth of these words.

"I am going to Klewań," Uncle Gaj announced two days later. "Are you coming with me, Zbyszek? Maybe I will trade or buy something in town," he added. "We do not have soap nor oil, and the worst is that we do not have salt—food without salt hardly goes down the throat."

I stepped up on the cart, and the horses stirred. I was willing to travel with Uncle Gaj since it was the holidays. As I remember him, my uncle was a handsome, talkative man who could deal with any situation. I always spent a part of my summer holidays with Grandmother Józefa in Dęby, so my father's brother and I knew each other like bald horses.[18]

"Uncle, what happens if they attack us?" I asked, a sudden fear squeezing me by the throat.

He smiled and opened the hem of a blanket covering the bundle of hay we were sitting on. I looked down, and from the grass protruded a rifle butt and a few magazines.

Uncle arranged his affairs in the deserted, empty town of Klewań, and before dark, we were on the way back. At the edge of the city, we passed the old castle of the Radziwiłł's princes on the high embankment.

---

18 *Polish saying: to know one another extremely well*

The hooves of the horses rumbled on the bridge over the river and then on a trylinka-designed road built just before the war.

We entered an unknown village. My uncle did not come back the same way we went to Klewań. He obviously had a specific goal; nevertheless, I felt strange anxiety in my heart.

The flat road soon ended and was replaced by a gravel surface leading to yet another village. The cart was rolling slowly over the potholes when a strange sight emerged from behind the corner of a country street. There was a magnificent brick building with brightly lit windows, with many people standing in the yard and even on the road in front of the gate.

"What the hell?" remarked my uncle. "A wedding, or what? But today is not Sunday? You," he turned towards me, "hold firmly onto your seat. There is something I do not like about this!"

As we drew near the front of the building, one of the men standing in front of the gate approached the wagon and commanded, "*Stij pan, dal'she ne poyidesz* (Stay back, you will not go any further)," and then he grabbed the horse's bridle.

In an instant, Uncle Gaj stepped up and whipped one horse and then the other, with all his might. Both horses climbed and jumped accordingly. The attacker did not have time to hop on. The wagon crashed and banged on the bumpy gravel, and moments later, after the momentary surprise, a group of peasants followed us in pursuit.

I could feel the panting breath of the pursuers, and their hands were already gripping the wagon's ladders—until Uncle's weapon gave them something to think about: a whip. The thick, flexible, oak stick roared over my head once, twice, and again on the right side, and the attackers began to drop like ripe pears from a tree as Uncle's efficient hand struck them in the head.

Shrunken, I clung to the side, praying that the cart would endure the tumultuous ride. The pursuit slowly crumbled, and in the end, only two or three men chased us persistently, yet they dared not approach the wagon too closely.

"Be careful. I will have to shoot!" Uncle shouted.

And indeed, in the dark, a shot blasted, and shortly after, a second followed. Bullets in response whistled somewhere overhead, but only for a second, as the attackers decided that picking off the cart in the night was a waste of ammunition. The chasing of the pursuers finally stopped.

Uncle Gaj urged the horses a moment longer, then slowed down, wiped his sweaty forehead with his sleeve, glanced back at me, and sighed with relief.

"Well, we broke out of the devil's mouth. Do you know what they would do with us? They would break us with stanchions! It's good that the horses and the wagon are sturdy."

My uncle pulled his rifle from the bundle of hay, switched on the safety lock, and put it next to him again.

"*Psiakrew!* (Damn it!) In this situation I could use an automatic," he groaned.

The raw frost glistened in the light of the blinking sparkly stars on the navy-blue winter sky. We drove for a long time, and Uncle turned on only familiar dirt roads until finally, the cart stopped.

He jumped off the wagon, put his ear to the ground, listened for a moment, then declared: "Silence, they are probably not chasing us."

I jumped out of the cart, straightened my numb legs, and with my hand stroked the neck of one horse. My hand slid off its damp skin. Sweat was dripping from both horses. For the second time in just a few days, I had gotten to know about the feeling of deep, unshakable fear.

We arrived home late in the evening. My uncle repeatedly stepped out into the courtyard with his rifle and listened for movement the rest of the night.

Finally, he told us in the morning, "It seems like those devils did not recognize us because we would undoubtedly have a visit."

We did have a visit that same day; however, it was from a different side. Around noon, a gorgeous black Mercedes rolled up, and from it came out a tall, striking man in a brown Nazi uniform, sporting a red band with a swastika on its sleeve.

"What the hell?" Uncle murmured. "I have not invited anyone like that."

We threw ourselves under the windows until finally, someone shouted, "It's Hans Friedman. What's he doing here?"

Friedman was the leaseholder and Uncle's neighbor. I knew his German family. Before the war, I played with his daughters Hilda and

Irma whenever I was on holiday at my grandmother's. In the fall of 1939, Friedman and his family left for Germany.

We settled in the yard. Friedman shook our hands; he recognized me instantly.

"What are you doing here, Zbyszek?" he asked politely, then he talked to Gaj.

From what I overheard of the conversation, Nazi authorities appointed Friedman to be the foreman of our district.

We invited him inside for a glass of lime tea. After drinking, the German began to gather for departure—and then I had a crazy idea.

I asked the unwelcome guest: "Are you going to Klewań? Can I come with you, sir?"

The starosta,[19] taken aback by the request, raised his eyebrows.

He considered it for a moment, then graciously replied: "Yes, I am going to Klewań, and I have a place in the car so you can go."

We opened the car doors.

"Sit in the back so that no one can see you," he added.

A moment later, we were racing away from the house as I curled up in the backseat of the beautiful car, glancing surreptitiously at the passing winter landscape.

At the market in the town, I got out of the vehicle, and instantly a strange emptiness struck me. The market was usually a bustling and noisy place. I looked around carefully and clearly understood the situation: the Orthodox church stood intact, but the Jewish synagogue illuminated my eyes with its broken door and empty eye sockets of torn windows. The population of Klewań before the war consisted of Jews, Poles, and a few Ukrainians. Now half of the inhabitants were lying in clay pits.

A suspicious passer-by occasionally crossed the deserted town. The Klewań railway station and the summer resort located around it were three kilometers from the city, so it only took half an hour to reach. The housing estate located in the forest, south of the Łuck railway track, was a favorite of Jews and Poles from the cities of Wołyń. To the north of the railroad, an old, towering pine forest grew, stretching tens of kilometers, until somewhere far away in the vast swamps of Polesie. Many of my

---

19 *The chief administrator of a Polish district or region*

relatives, aunts, close and distant cousins lived here. During my stays in the summers before, time passed carefree, and I dreamt of the days when I rested at an open window, with the soft swaying of the old trees putting me to sleep.

I was welcomed this time with open arms. Cousins, especially the female cousins, were as happy as children whenever a relative appeared from the large city of Równe, the largest in Wołyń.

The days passed untroubled, wonderful, and cheerful like we were in a perfect fairy tale—until the moment when a man, masked in snow from head to toe, stood in the doorway during a raging snowstorm. It was my father. I could hardly recognize him.

"You're here, and yet there is a third call from the *Arbeitsamt*[20] waiting for you at home," my father was gasping heavily.

With the Arbeitsamt, there were no jokes, so the next day, despite the raging snowstorm, we headed east to Równe. The wind would close our mouths, the snow stuck in our eyes, but we carried on stubbornly until the afternoon when my father finally succumbed to fatigue. From a hill, we spied a village in the valley.

Father looked closely and said: "It's Obarów, your family village. I have good friends here. Let's stop by and rest."

"But they're Ukrainians," I warned my father.

"It does not matter," he replied. "They are decent people; nothing threatens us."

And our old friends received us as guests. A familiar guest from the outside world was usually very welcome. Fresh-baked dumplings with beans and poppy seeds rushed onto the table, and some home-brewed samogon immediately warmed us up.

The men got into conversation and memories when they both fought against the Bolsheviks during the Ukrainian uprising of 1918—which was suppressed and resulted in my father and his neighbors starving for many days.

After the first bottle of Russian samogon, our hosts brought the next one in, and as the winter evening fell early, they invited us to spend the night, which we gladly agreed to. We slept in an honorary place in a

---

20 *Labor Office*

Ukrainian cottage—on the stove. It was hot as hell. The whole night we kept turning over because the heat was unmerciful, and when the late winter morning shone in the windows of the hut, we rose. Right after breakfast, we bid our farewells and went on our way. As the village was only a few kilometers from the city, home was only an hour away.

Here a fourth call to the Arbeitsamt was waiting for me. So, of course, I went there immediately. An unpleasant surprise met me here. For disobedience of the ruling power, I was sentenced to two weeks of forced labor to help with the demolition of ruins. Each day I worked for twelve hours under the watchful eye of Ukrainian policemen who did not allow a moment of rest, and each of anyone's smallest attempts to do so resulted in merciless punishment. It left me with a few black stripes on my back and respect for authority. Such was the sad end of my winter holidays, and the new year of 1942 did not look good.

— 9 —
The Final Solution

After the authorities suspended school, they directed me with my former colleagues to work. This was probably the most beautiful and peaceful time for me during the German occupation, yet every native of the city was starving. Food ration cards were so small that despite my mother's efforts, I was still constantly hungry, until suddenly, like manna from heaven, I had received work in a place called "Packetaction." This "land of plenty" was made up of a few wooden barracks near the railway station, where we assembled food packages for German soldiers returning from the front.

Long wooden tables stood in the barracks. One by one, we placed a kilo packet of sugar, two kilos of flour, a kilo cube of butter, a kilo of dry sausage, a pack of sweets, a liter of sunflower oil, and two packages of Juno cigarettes in cardboard boxes. We were naturally never hungry with this kind of work; breaking a piece of sausage or clump of butter or a handful of sugar into my mouth only took an instant, although it was associated with significant risk. The boards in German and Ukrainian warned about stealing food, and several colleagues who did not believe in these warnings became convinced of the prohibition extremely painfully—fifty strokes from a wooden board on the bare bottom was the lowest punishment for theft. Even so, as our German overseers watched diligently for our movements and beat us mercilessly with thin sticks on the back or the head in the event of being caught, we came to such a skill of this practice that we avoided these threats with ease.

A fence of barbed wire divided our land of plenty from the starving ghetto. Some of the Jews who survived the November massacre lived there (those who did not go to the Umschlagplatz or hid well were saved and used for labor). The Germans employed professionals in workshops that produced for the needs of the Wehrmacht. It was a poor existence. Admission to the ghetto was forbidden under the death penalty, and only the daring ones risked their lives, smuggling food through the barbed wires—even though there was not much to smuggle, as the whole city was hungry. The measly weekly allowance at that time for a working person had been reduced to a one-kilogram loaf of white barley bread (which was fresh and tasty one day, then the next day was fragile and bitter), twenty decagrams of beetroot marmalade, and a small amount of meat that the dog still sniffed for a long time before eating.

Three months of work in that land of abundance allowed me to survive another winter of occupation. Despite the severe food shortages at home, my mother did not let me bring anything home to eat. I remember her words, "I want you to survive this war," to this day.

A day's shift lasted ten hours, with short breaks. During one such break, a carol was coming from somewhere outside. Entranced by the melody, we scuttled out into the front of the encampment. One of the Soviet POWs, who delivered products from railway wagons to our barracks, was situated on a ramp, performing a series of songs. We stood as if we were rooted into the ground, and so did the escorting German soldiers. The prisoner sang in a deep, euphonious voice—as it turned out later, he was a tenor of the Kiev Opera. His repertoire of Russian tunes was exceptionally rich: *Wołga, Karobuszka, Brodiaga, Suliko, Simieńki Skromnyj Płatoczok* (Blue Headkerchief). These melodies sound in my ears even today. It was a wonderful concert. One song flowed to another, and the crowd of prisoners, German soldiers, and ourselves listened in an incredibly peaceful awe.

We became the aristocracy when we packed the parcels since we had direct access to food. Auxiliary work, like the transport of food from wagons to barracks, was carried out by Soviet prisoners under the strict supervision of German soldiers. These hungry captives had no way of taking anything from the goods they were transporting, but as we were the ones who fortunately handled the supplies, whenever we stole food, the prisoners would blink at us, expecting us to give them something.

A very unpleasant event sticks in my memory. After a lengthy freight train drove into one of the many station tracks next to my workplace, convoy soldiers opened the doors of the wagons, out of which Russian

POWs began to emerge. From each of the carriages, they were removing and stacking rag-wrapped items on the railway ramp. As I stood, I scrutinized the rags further, and upon a dark realization, began to shiver—they were people! Dead bodies of Soviet soldiers, which seemed to be dismembered in many places.

As tragically awful as the view was, I continued to stand, petrified, gaping at the horrific sight. My eyes were only pulled away when a prisoner, ignoring the menacing shouts and barrels of the rifles aimed at him, approached me and pleaded for food.

"Will you give me a piece of bread?"

I flinched and stared at him intently. He had a healthy and intelligent face, but his eyes reflected a saddening, terrible hunger, and this was enough for me to take out a piece of bread from my pocket without hesitation, which I often took with me because it was impossible to eat only sausage, butter, and sugar.

When the prisoner snatched my bread greedily, I questioned him: "*Otkuda vy i gde popali v plen?* (Where are you from and where were you taken prisoner?)"

"*Ya iz Moskvy* (I am from Moscow)," he answered, "*Ya sidel v Khar'kove; vosem' dney nesli nas bez khleba i vody—v nashey povozke my'yeli troikh tovarishchey* (I was imprisoned in Kharkiv; for eight days they carried us without bread and water—in our wagon we ate three comrades)."

We were still for a few more moments until one convoy soldier slammed the butt of a rifle into the back of my interlocutor and chased him away.

I already had seen the horrors of hundreds of murdered prisoners in cells, killed by the NKVD with grenades in June 1941, the extermination of Jews in the clay pits, and piles of Soviets who had died of hunger and cold in the freezing warehouses, then transported by carts to the Jewish cemetery—and even so, this view specifically rattled me severely. I did not know that the war would show me its sickening face this many times. Even after half a century, I recall many of these distressing sights as if I saw them yesterday.

From the windows of the barrack where I worked, I could recognize the house where I spent my childhood, as well as the garden and orchard, which I missed so dearly now. When the German authorities turned this area of the city into the ghetto for the survivors of the first massacre of Jews, they relocated us to Chmielna Street, where the yard was the size of a large room, with no garden or orchard. The garden in those times of famine was often a salvation for many people.

Until the spring of 1942, I worked in the land of plenty. Around that time, we noticed the soldier's packaged food allotments were getting smaller—there was no longer any butter, and the ration of sugar, flour, and sausages were halved. Not long later, we were told: "Tomorrow you shall report to the Arbeitsamt, there they will assign you to another job."

So the days of satiation and abundance of food were over. As I was leaving, I ate so many sausages that I was sick for three days.

I went and applied to the Arbeitsamt. They directed me to work as an apprentice in the *Deutsche Post* mechanical workshop (the militarized German post). The work was interesting. Here I came into contact with the automotive industry; the workshop overhauled Renault-type trucks, which the German army had captured thousands of in the Battle of France. My bosses—and there were three of them, all excellent specialists—were older gentlemen: one from Berlin, another from Kassel, the third from somewhere in northern Germany. They treated me like a son and taught me a lot. At under sixteen years of age, I was given the opportunity to sit behind the wheel of a car. Repaired cars were allowed to be tested in the massive backyard of the workshop, and this privilege almost ended badly for me.

Once, my younger cousin Rysiek came to visit me. I wanted to impress him, so I put him in the passenger seat, made a few rounds around the square in front of the workshop, and ventured out into the street. I drove from one street to another until I arrived at the city's main road. It was here that I pressed the accelerator until the meter showed one hundred kilometers per hour. We cruised through the town, and it was only when we passed the military barracks that the roar of a siren reached my ears, and in the rearview mirror, I spotted a German military police car behind, blinking its lights.

There were no jokes with these men. Two German gendarmerie, in helmets with metal plates on their chests and pistols in their hands, jumped out of the car behind me.

"*Hände hoch!*" one of them shouted and ran to us.

Their surprise was sky-high when they caught sight of two puppies, arms raised, with one of them behind the wheel.

"*Was machst du?* (What are you doing?)" the other roared, aiming at me with a pistol.

"*Probefahrt* (Test drive)," I answered in a shaky voice.

The gendarme put the pistol in the holster, sat behind the wheel, and drove us back to the workshop. Here he handed us over to one of my bosses—Dżupa from Berlin. Rysiek was in no danger, as he was just a candidate for an apprentice, but the hairs on my neck pricked up in dreadful anticipation. Dżupa peered at me sternly, took a rubber hose in his hand, and came over to me.

Yet, to my surprise, when the gendarmerie left, he threw the hose in the corner and only took me lightly by the ear.

"*Du dumme kerl* (Stupid boy)," he scorned in German. "You know how it could end for you? In prison or a punishment camp. You are lucky," he pointed his finger at me, "that he did not suspect you of stealing a car."

I enjoyed working in the car workshop. There was only one drawback: although my bosses gave me a piece of bread and butter from time to time, I was constantly unsatisfied. I could eat the pitiful weekly allocation in one day, and Mother had already taken all of the items at home that we could exchange at the bazaar for food.

It was relatively safe at this time in the city since Równe inhabited the "*Reichskommissariat*[21] *für die Ukraine*," ruled by Erich Koch. Even so, his governing was tragic and ruthless. Every few days, posters announced the execution of a dozen or so people for helping Jews or partisans, or other "crimes that threatened the security of the Reich."

One day when I was on the street, meeting with a school friend, I mentioned my hunger troubles.

"Come to us, to the network brigade," he advised me. "Partisans are destroying telephone lines, and we go and repair them all the time all over Wołyń, so you can always buy or steal something in the countryside," he added.

Driven by my extreme hunger, the idea appealed to me. I told my bosses about it reluctantly, and they agreed. The following Monday, I

---

21 *German Board of Ukraine*

came to my new workplace. The labor was demanding and treacherous: we carried and placed telephone poles, climbing on them at great heights, as guerrilla warfare was getting more and more active outside of the city. It was not easy and pleasant, but at least it was possible to get a loaf of bread or steal a chicken.

It was now summer. A few of us unloaded telegraph poles from a train wagon onto the railway ramp and then into the truck. On a scorchingly sunny day, sweat dripped from our foreheads as we carried heavy pillars when a passenger train squeaked its brakes two rail tracks away. German gendarmerie and SS men jumped out of the car doors and quickly positioned themselves every few meters along the locomotive. The locks on the machine guns clicked open.

"Look," my friend nudged my side. "It's Hitler," he uttered in a whisper.

I glanced toward the train. In the open window of one of the wagons, I spotted a face with the characteristic mustache, sporting a high military cap with a brown rim that shielded his other features. Even in the split second that I caught sight of his silhouette, I could sense his authoritative demeanor.

He stood for a moment, glanced at us, and we dared not look at him again.

Our foreman Kraska, a German from Silesia, also saw the Führer and shouted at us loudly: "*Schneller, schneller, arbeiten!* (Faster, faster, work!)"

The railwaymen quickly changed the locomotive and the passenger train moved on.

In the late summer of 1942, the Germans decided to "finally resolve the Jewish problem." From the morning, we could hear shots in the direction of the city ghetto.

Someone announced, "The Germans are finishing the Jews!"

This time the Jews were not driven out of the city to the pits but were executed at the crag near our former home. Ukrainian police in black uniforms pulled out the unfortunate ghetto inhabitants from their homes and led them to the bluff, from which I could distinguish a series of machine gun blasts. German military police heavily surrounded the entire ghetto. That day, as I was coming back from work on the city's main street, I noticed German gendarmerie standing with weapons ready to fire every few meters on the right side of the road. The shots in the ghetto thundered without interruption. It seemed that the soldiers were in a hurry to finish their work by evening.

Danger hung in the air. I ambled down the main street, eyes wide open, observing what was going on—and a lot was happening. Two gendarmerie led a civilian with outstretched arms, hung with women's underwear—bras, shirts, panties.

Every few steps, they gave him a stout kick in the buttocks, and he screamed: "*Ein moment, ein moment!*"

It was a "rat" who had sneaked into the ghetto to hunt for the victims' property. The incident was so tragically comical that passers-by burst out laughing. And I did too for a split second, until the laughter froze on my face: a military policeman standing nearby had taken a rifle off his shoulder and fired it across the street.

Opposite, from the side of the ghetto, an eleven-or twelve-year-old boy was scurrying away. The gendarme aimed and fired a second and third time. Apparently he missed because the boy managed to kneel between the houses. Enraged by this, the guard grabbed his rifle by the barrel, ran a dozen steps toward the boy, and with all of his impetus, bashed the child with the stock of the weapon. The boy's brain spurted on the wall of the house.

I felt weak, and darkness appeared in front of my eyes. I clenched my teeth and quickened my pace. When I made it home, I had already developed a fever, and my mother put me to bed.

War is a brutal time of violence and crime, and even the massacre of Jews in the clay pits outside the city I had watched from afar, but this time, right before my eyes, a child was murdered.

The next day I went to work, still feverish. We heard blasts in the ghetto from time to time—this time, they were aimed at the last Jews who had managed to hide through the first day.

At work, a dozen trucks and a convoy of about thirty German soldiers were already standing in the square. Uh-oh, a long trip is waiting for us today, I thought, and was not mistaken. Soon we headed towards the direction of Zdołbunów. We passed that town, then a few completely charred settlements, and finally arrived at our destination—the village of Pinczańwka—empty and deserted.

A kilometer in front of Pinczańwka lay banged down telegraph poles. The soldiers surrounded the settlement efficiently, but there was no living spirit in it. The population had apparently all escaped to a nearby forest. We started putting up the fallen poles. Some of them were next to a prosperous farm, which had also been deserted, and right in the yard sat several fat hens. A young German soldier stood with the rifle in his hands on the side.

I pointed at the fat chickens and spoke: "*Die huhner* (The chickens)."

"*Gut*," he nodded, then opened the barn door and drove the whole herd inside.

I threw a rod accurately and cornered three of the chickens. We caught them soon, although they clucked so loudly that they could be heard at the other end of the village. We had to kill them immediately because it was forbidden to take anything in abandoned villages.

"*Haben sie messer?* (Do you have knives?)" I asked the soldier.

He pulled a pocket knife from his pocket and pressed it into my hand.

"*Schlachten sie!* (Slaughter them!)" he directed, "*Ich kann nicht* (I can't)." He was shivering like he had a fever. This unexpected reaction from the soldier almost made me roar with laughter.

Time was pressing. I heard a patter of heavy shoes—someone was approaching us. I immediately pulled a bayonet hanging at the soldier's side and efficiently cut off the hens' heads. I gave the German one hen, threw two in the bag, and we both hid in nearby hemp three meters high. Finally, an NCO[22] ran into the yard, looked into the barn, swore a few ugly words and left. That day I did not return home empty-handed; the prey allowed me to survive several gloomy, hungry, occupation days.

Every day when I returned home, the loudspeakers placed on electric poles continued to broadcast confusingly triumphant messages from the front, always ending in a proud, perky march—until the autumn of 1942, when the communications said something about the heavy fighting at Stalingrad, and then they completely died down.

---

22 *Non-Commissioned Officer*

HIGH TIDE OF GERMAN CONQUEST, AUTUMN 1942

The German war machine reached its pinnacle at the height of the summer 1942 offensive (Operation Case Blue) into the Russian Caucasus region. Note that even though the Nazis occupied vast territories, resistance behind their lines as deep as Rivne was quickly growing, and the overextended fuel and food supply lines were gradually dissipating. The defeats that followed on the Eastern Front, starting at Stalingrad, and the forced retreat from North Africa after the Americans landed, began to spell a contraction of Nazi power and prestige. The map illustrates the height of occupation and changes to the landscape below.

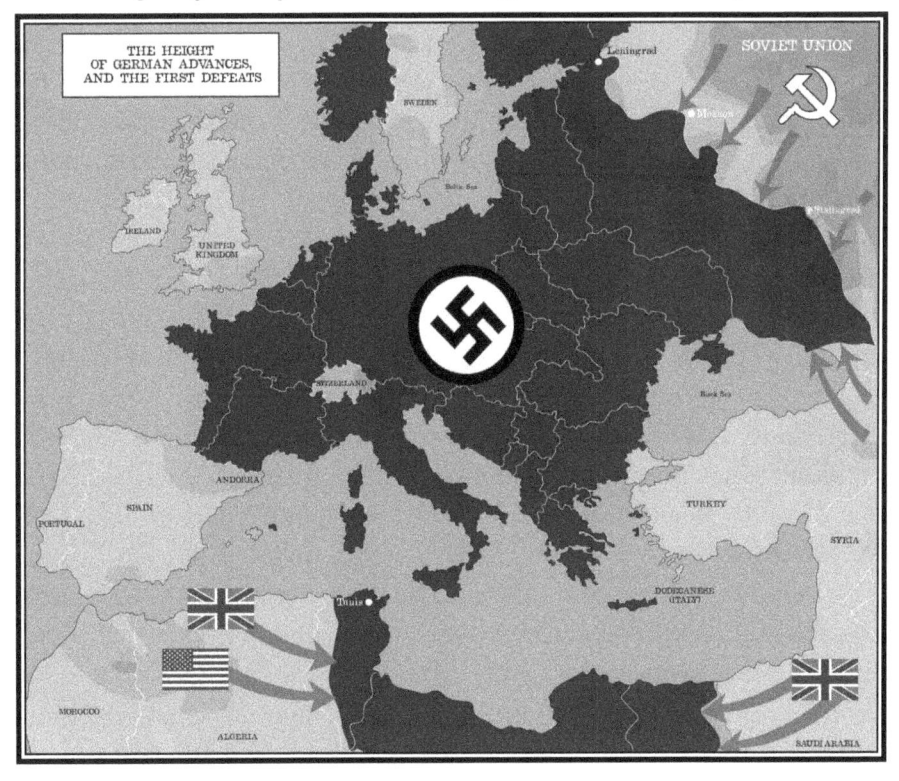

Note: flags of the Allies and their forces do not necessarily correlate with the exact positions of the arrows.

Almost every day, we went under the protection of a convoy to the fields, erected new poles, and connected broken telephone wires cut off by partisans. It also was becoming increasingly difficult to buy or steal food. Our service became more and more dangerous and pointless. One day the poles were erected; the next they were again cut down. Several times bullets whistled over our heads, and despite the "safety zone"—the Germans cut the forest three hundred meters wide on both sides of the tracks and road leading to our workplace—which slightly helped, it was still not safe. Driving through the forest, we had to lay on the truck's floor so as not to be a target for partisans.

In the spring of 1943, when the news of the German defeats on the Eastern Front arrived and the actions of guerrillas grew stronger, the situation in Wołyń became tragic. At the call of the UPA,[23] the Ukrainian police, who previously served the Germans, went into the woods with arms and supplied already established guerilla troops. A final resolution towards all Poles in the region had begun. Every night the glow of fires brightened the sky. Units of the insurgent army invaded Polish villages and farms, brutally murdering the inhabitants, plundering their farms, lighting them aflame, and letting them smoke.

It was not peaceful in the city now either, as Soviet partisans were also on the prowl. The sizable German garrison could hardly control the situation during the day, and various guerilla groups ruled the night. In broad daylight, in the guarded German district, a general was kidnapped in his own car, and a shootout exploded nearly every night. Once again, once closer, and even so close as next to our house, that in the morning we found the corpse of an unknown man lying on the roof of our shed. On another spring night, a powerful explosion shook the house, and we rushed to the windows. Only a hundred meters from our home, a steam engine lay derailed on the track, blown up by the partisans—in the middle of the city. You can only begin to imagine what was happening in the entire province.

None of us were certain about the course of a day or even an hour. Now, field trips of work were getting further, and they lasted for two and

---

23 *Ukrayins'ka Povstans'ka Armiya, also known as the Ukrainian Insurgent Army*

three days. There were no Sundays or holidays. I was coming home so exhausted that I had no strength to undress.

I was only sixteen years old. It was also at this time that I found myself in the hands of the "Banderites," which was what the Ukrainian insurgents called themselves after their chief, Stephan Bandera.

— 10 —

Dumka Saves Lives

I stood stiffly, tied by my arms and legs to the trunk of a pine tree, and peered all around at what was going on in the forest camp of the UPA sotnia[24] led by General Łastiwka (who was surprisingly of Polish descent) in Horynia. It seemed to be a normal camp life: in the evening there was a buzz of talks and commands, and then someone hung a boiler far above a fire, in which they were apparently cooking dinner because the tasty smell of smoked meat reached my nose, teasing my famished stomach which had been fasting for several days.

I knew this area, this forest. During long wanderings with my father, an avid angler, I got to know these parts of Wołyń's Polesie well. While he soaked his stick and stared at the still water for hours, I was easily bored, so I explored the area around Horynia, the river of my childhood. The river would meander among the high, precipitous banks and cut here and there through wooded ravines, whose bottoms were covered with crystal clear pools. The burial mounds, the high graves erected hundreds or thousands of years ago, were visible on the distant horizon. Further on, the north banks of the river became lowered, and the region was covered by an undivided forest, which stretched all the way to the estuary by the swampy banks of Prypeci.

I looked at the forest I knew, but my thoughts were conflicted. What is waiting for me? What will they do with me? Shuddering thoughts stung my head. Get away, but how? Tied by my arms and legs, I had no way of escaping, and the Banderites were wandering around the camp, from time to time giving me ominous looks.

---

24 *A military unit of approximately one hundred soldiers*

Someone threw branches to the fire, and it burst forth, illuminating a wide circle. The armed people gathered at the campfire, all wearing caps with signs of tridents. They were dressed in various uniforms: black, Ukrainian police of their time under German command, standard German feldgrau uniforms, Hungarian, brick-colored garments, and even the khaki green attire of the pre-war Polish Army. There were also many weapons: Polish and German Mausers, Soviet Mosins, and even short Italian Carabiners.

At the campfire, it became more crowded and bustling. After supper, among the seated circle of men were dense scatterings of moonshine bottles. The buzz of conversations drowned out my contemplation.

At some point, the conversation came to me. I set my ears.

"What does the commander want to do with him, with this *Laszek*[25]?" they were wondering.

"We probably will play with him," others guessed.

As I overheard this, a shiver shot down my spine. I had seen the results of these Banderites' dalliance in the burned Polish villages and settlements of Wołyń. The devil himself would not come up with a crueler death than one from UPA hands. Once, I saw people who were chopped, burned, and torn apart with the aid of two bent trees. What was to await me? And I got caught so stupidly…

* * *

As the Germans dismantled all schools in 1941, the youth were subsequently employed where the occupants of the war machine demanded. After numerous jobs, I worked with the German mail and telegraph teams. The number of destructions of the telephone poles increased each day, and now weeks had come when my mother rarely saw me at home.

It was a hot summer in 1943. The Germans only had power in the city. In the provinces, the UPA, Soviet, and Polish guerillas dominated indivisibly, and sabotages on a large scale occurred on a daily basis. So our next job did not surprise us: a kilometer behind the city, along the Równe–Kiwerce railway line, were collapsed telephone poles. Under the

---

25 *Term used to refer to Poles*

cover of German gendarmerie, we put up the columns and connected the wires from dawn to dusk.

When the German commander arrived at night, he decided that we were to sleep in a fortified station, where a dozen or so military crew at night did not even feel safe extending their nose anywhere beyond the palisade and the surrounding minefield.

The night passed peacefully, and from dawn we returned to work. We were hungry. The day before, we all had eaten the bread we had taken with us, so we started the morning with a fast, making it difficult to work. I asked our German *vorarbeiter*,[26] Heinz Kraska from Upper Silesia, when we were going to get something to eat. He answered my question in silence—he also had swallowed his last bite the day before. We worked all day hungrily, and when evening came in the next fortified station, we were given a mug of tea and went to sleep. Dreams are heavy when your stomach is empty; you can't fall asleep easily, and the pangs wake you up frequently.

On the third day, the same. We were given a cup of hot water and were sent to work. Feeling that I was weakening, I clenched my teeth, and dark patches alternating with bright ones flew before my eyes. The German gendarmerie looking after us were famished too—I heard them cursing those who could not or forgot to provide them with food.

Around noon we completely stopped.

No one had any strength when Kraska turned to us: "Are we far from a village?"

"Not a kilometer away, maybe one and a half," I answered.

It was Horodyszcze, a village by the River Horyń, where many Równe vacationers flocked to before the war.

After slowly driving several kilometers through the high-growing forest, we approached the railway bridge over the river. We got out of the truck.

Kraska thought for a moment, scratched his head, glimpsed at us, and asked: "Maybe we will get something to eat there? Who will volunteer and come with me?"

---

26 *German word for foreman*

We glanced at each other. There were no volunteers; extensive forests were the favorite area for partisans, and they were stationed in the villages. I would not wish even the worst enemy to be in their hands.

A silence lasted a long while as hunger twisted our bowels. He waited patiently, and finally asked again: "Well, who is going?"

I raised my hand, and another desperate person joined me in a moment.

"Well, let's go," muttered our boss, "in the car and drive."

We sharply rushed from the spot, but when the truck pulled deeper into the forest, we slowed to a stop. Kraska turned off the engine and called us to the front.

"You know what these fireworks do?" he asked, showing us German hand grenades with long wooden stems, like a so-called "pestle."

"We know it!" we replied in accordance.

"Well, look at it, rascals," he added. "If necessary, unscrew the cap, pull the ring on the string, count to five and throw. You each get two."

By hiding the pestles behind the belt of my trousers, I felt a little more confident, and my fears flew away somehow—I was armed after all.

The car began to move, and we rushed along the forest trail, clutching the handles in the cabin. After a while, we reached our destination, and the car halted violently on a wide road on the edge of the village. Kraska stayed in the car, not switching off the engine. I ran one way, my colleague the other, and we rushed to nearby cottages.

I came to a house, opened the door sharply, and came upon an older man sitting at a table, smoking a pipe. On top, there was a huge loaf of bread. I grabbed it, and before the man managed to open his mouth, I rushed out of the hut, tearing a large chunk out of the bread and pushing it into my mouth. I could hear screams in the village, but I didn't pay attention to them until I reached the road and froze. Kraska was gone. I saw only the dust and his disappearing car on the bend. He had driven away when he heard the voices of command in the village, leaving me at the mercy of fate.

Shots rang out—there was no time to lose. I looked right out of the corner of my eyes: a dozen or so armed men were running toward me in the rural street. The bread fell out of my hand.

I sprinted in full swing, hearing from behind the wheezing of the running men and repeated screams: "*Stij! Stij!*"

The bullets whistled over my head. I ran with great effort—the three-day fast let me know what a weak person I was—and then I reminded myself of the grenades.

I pulled the ring from the pestle, and without turning, I threw it down the road behind me. The explosion, the whirlwinds of the shards, and the moment of hesitation in the pursuers gave me a second of advantage, so I continued to run like a hare. Then, I suddenly noticed that in the fever of escape, I had made a big mistake. I had run away from the village, to the forest—a partisan's favorite territory.

Backup was coming, as I could hear the patter of legs and crackling of twigs in the woods under the pursuers. Those who decided to surround me spread through the forest, their voices coming from several directions. I ran with the last of my strength, squeezing the second pestle in my hand, and then I finally stood and threw it with a flourish, in the direction from where I heard the most voices.

I kept going, with my last remaining stamina, as red patches of effort flew before my eyes. It was only at the moment when I thought I had lost the voices of the hunters that I stumbled on a large, protruding tree root and fell flat with my face in the sandy earth. I began to get up when the butt of a rifle grounded my face once again.

I lost consciousness, and when after a while I tried to get up, a strong kick to the side knocked me back to the ground again for the third time.

A moment of silence, followed by roaring in Ukrainian: "*Vstavay!* (Get up!)"

This made me aware of whose power was in control of me. I slowly rose from the ground, quivering in pain. I glanced up; a group of armed men in black uniforms with gray collars and a trident sign on their forage caps. So I had gotten the worst; I was in the hands of the Ukrainian nationalists: either the Banderites[27] or the Bulbas.[28] As long as they do not torture me—ran through my head—so long as they do not torture me.

---

27 *The most radical, right-wing nationalists, named after their leader Stepan Bandera*
28 *Another nationalist group, from the legendary leader of the Zaporozhian Cossacks, Taras Bulba*

The Banderites stood, watching for a moment. Two of them tied my arms tightly to the back, and one of them nudged me in my back with the barreled rifle and roared: "*Stupaj!*"

We marched for a long time along the road in the high-growing pine forest, until we reached a shining ribbon of water. It seemed to me that I recognized this place from times when fishing and wandering with my father. Soon we reached the river bank, where, among century-old pine trees, tents of their camp were spread out. A tall man in black uniform, with a German machine weapon hanging on his belt, stepped out of one of them.

He studied me carefully and asked in Ukrainian, "*Ty chto?* (Who are you?)" I didn't even manage to open my mouth before a voice came from the side.

"*To Lach, ja jeho znaju* (It's a Pole, I know him)."

I looked at the speaker and recognized him. It was Charczuk, a boy from my street with whom I once kicked a rag ball in the fields. So they knew who I was. I would not have any chances.

The tall man—he was clearly the commander of the squad—thought and finally questioned, "Do you know German?"

When I told him yes, he brought some papers from the tent and ordered: "Translate!"

I looked through the papers with some commands and orders written in German, from the garrison commander in Równe to the regiment in Kopostopol, which was nothing important. I knew both languages, German and Ukrainian, well, so I translated fluently. The commander stroked his chin, took a pencil and a notebook from his pocket, and wrote down some sentences from what I stated. When I finished, he ordered to have me tied to a thick pine in the middle of the camp. The men completed the order eagerly and tied me tightly to the tree.

It was a clear summer afternoon. Along the blue sky, clouds floated like white lambs as the familiar river shimmered down below. In the late afternoon, the forest became still, and only the sweet buzz of insects disturbed the silence. Movement ceased in the camp. Two squadrons of Banderas marched in opposite directions to rest. The camp guards were also napping, and only the sentry seated in front of the commander's tent was peeking at me suspiciously from time to time with a droopy eye, threateningly rattling the rifle's lock. I stayed tied up on this idyllic summer afternoon as contrastingly nightmarish thoughts swirled under my skull.

They recognized me, so I have no chance, no lie will convince them, so all that is left is death, so long as they do not torture me before... At the moment when black thoughts had already led me to the brink of madness, my mother's religious words suddenly flashed through my head: "Son, when death looks in your eyes, when you doubt it all, sigh to God, he will not abandon you in times of need."

I felt a slight relief at this comforting idea, and finally tired of hunger and the pain in my wounded head, I fell into a half-asleep, half-dazed state. I did not hear what was happening around, waking up only when the smell of cooked meat hit my nostrils. The fire burned; its golden shimmer reflected onto pine tree trunks. Now and again, a person would come up and stare into my eyes, and a shiver passed down my back when I saw the eyes of someone else I recognized. What the hell! Two familiar Banderites in one single branch are a bit too much—I thought with humor. The tragedy of my situation was unenviable.

By the fire, the buzz was getting livelier. Someone brought a Ukrainian bandura and began to strum it, then finally play. I heard a familiar tune, a familiar dumka—I knew hundreds of them as when I was with my father on the shores of Horynia, I listened to them in Ukrainian villages where my father had many acquaintances. The bandura was playing louder and louder, and someone attempted to sing in an out-of-tune, drunken voice, but his companions quickly hushed him. The longing melody of the dumka sounded throughout the camp until it was muffled somewhere deep in the forest and dissipated in coastal bulrush.

I stood there enchanted, forgot about the pain and hunger, and when a new dumka flowed over the fire, I sang in a full voice: "*Tam, de krutyt'sya richka Yatran', z-pid kamenyu pidnimayet'sya voda... Tam diva bere vodu, chornobrova i moloda...* (Where the Yatran river twirls, water rises from under the stone... There, the maiden takes water, black-eyebrowed and young...)"

Conversations by the fire subsided and were replaced by absolute silence. It was as if a thunderbolt had struck the camp.

One of the Banderites broke off, ran to me, slapped me in the face, and roared: "*Mowczy, proklatyj Lasze!* (Quiet, bloody Pole!)"

I went quiet, and silence fell again by the fire, until finally the commander reprimanded, "*Ty durnyj Ivan, czaj śpiwaje* (You idiot Ivan, let him sing)."

Someone came up to me and unraveled the cords. I fell down on the ground, numbed. I was brought up and taken to the fire, seated and told to sing.

"*Isty?* (Food?)" I asked. "*Ya holodnyy* (I'm hungry)."

Someone put a slice of bread in front of me, somebody else a piece of pork fat and some moonshine from a canteen, and the audience waited patiently for me to eat and drink. I wiped my mouth with the back of my hand. I glanced at the sitting bandura player, whose face was brightly lit by the fire, when the soul escaped into my heels: it was Wołodek! I gaped at him intently. Yes, it was Wołodek, the son of my father's friends from the village of Oleksyn, where we stayed during our wandering. When we showed up in their hut, after a satisfying dinner, our host's son would take a bandura from the wall and play while I sang. Half of the village would come down to listen to our performances.

Did he recognize me, or did he not recognize me? I was thinking frantically. Fate has happened in the strangest way; we've come together in such unusual circumstances, I thought.

At the bonfire, a dispute began about what I was to sing until the commander decided, "*Spivay pro richku Yantru ta divchynu* (Sing about the Yantra River and the girl)."

And so I sang dumkas about Sahajdaczny, a Cossack who went to war, then about a Chumak from Crimea who transported salt around Ukraine and who suddenly died in an open field, as well as about a white birch, weeping above a Cossack's grave—and so on until I lost my voice.

"*Dayte yomu kovtok samohonu* (Give him a sip of moonshine)," ordered a Banderite.

Someone gave me a canteen, I took a big swig, which blissfully warmed up my body, and the world seemed to cheer up a little. The threatening faces of the murderers softened slightly; they did not look as hostile to me as they had before.

And when I took a break, the commander looked at me and asked: "*Chy znayete vy virshi?* (Do you know poems?)"

"*Znayu* (I do)," I responded and began to recite poems by Shevchenko: "*Yakshcho ya pomru, pokhovayte mene v mohyli na shyrokomu stepu u kokhaniy Ukrayini...* (If I die, bury me in the grave on the wide steppe in beloved Ukraine...)"

And then I recited some other Ukrainian poems by Łesi Ukrainka, Ivan Franko, and other lesser-known poets. The companions stared at me and listened thoughtfully—"What is this *Lach*[29] capable of?" they must have been thinking. I was an absolute mystery to them. Was I a Lach or not a Lach? The devil must only know.

The hens cackled somewhere in a distant village, announcing midnight, and I kept reciting and cantillating poems to the audience, seeing in the eyes of these ruthless murderers the glow of melancholy and nostalgia, when finally the commander rose and decided: "*Idemo spaty* (We must go to sleep)."

The camp fell silent and I was attached to the tree again, but not as hard and painfully as before. I stood a moment in thought, and when the dawn in the east announced the coming end of the night, I fell asleep. I had won the first round of the fight for my life.

The camp woke up early. The normal bustle began: the weapons were cleaned, breakfast was eaten, and the partisans bathed in the river—while I stood numb, forgotten by God and people.

Banderite Wołodek brought me a piece of bread and a cup of water.

He winked at me knowingly and put his finger on his mouth, whispering in Ukrainian: "*Malchi* (Stay quiet)."

So, at least there was one kind soul in this hostile camp—I felt a little lighter in my heart.

After breakfast, the commander ordered a drill. A short, bulky officer from a subdivision taught gunners the secrets of military craftsmanship, as well as the techniques of attack, retreat, and hand-to-hand combat. Then they began to practice a parade march. I observed it diligently, catching every word. I concluded that the Banderites were waiting for

---

29 *Another derogatory term used for Poles*

someone, preparing for some sort of celebration. I was not wrong. In the afternoon, a new military branch arrived. There were ceremonious greetings between the commanders, a parade, and finally a joint supper by the fire. Of course, the ground around was heavily sprinkled with alcohol, which unraveled their tongues, resulting in increasingly loud conversation.

The new branch evidently came from the areas of action because the tales about the fallen inhabitants of the Polish village of Dąbrowa, who they had trapped in barns and lit aflame, hurt my ears. Those stories were not only about Poles who were murdered in an elaborate way, but also about Ukrainians who refused to kill their Polish neighbors. Full of indignation, a Banderite was talking about the liquidation of a nine-member Ukrainian family, and a Ukrainian peasant who struck a Bandera with an ax, wrestled him, and took his submachine gun, defending himself to the last bullet.

The camp was getting louder and louder. Harmonica tunes filled the air, and the shooters were dancing with girls arriving from a nearby village. A dozen or so couples danced a Trepak, a Hopak, a Cossack, and a sentimental tango. It was then when a familiar feminine face flashed at me in the crowd. Another person I know? I repeatedly stared at her. Yes, it was Wierą, my schoolboy infatuation! Impossible. Had fate so decided to mock me before I die? A flash in her eye made me realize at some point that she also recognized me. The remembrances, like lightning, flashed through my head—after all, it was only a year or two before.

* * *

When the Germans took over in the summer of 1941 and Reichskommissariat Ukraine was created, the local Ukrainian authorities started organizing schools, and Mother—who spoke perfect Ukrainian—managed to sign me to the technical institution. There, I found myself alone, except for that one half-Polish, half-Latvian girl, who hid her origins carefully from the Ukrainians. The first youthful spring feeling of love enveloped me like a flame. I thought about her during the day and at night. We went to school and returned together; we spent every free moment together. Soon, the times became more and more restless, and the school was closed down. The authorities sent the young people to work, and students from the village returned to their families. The resulting farewell with Wierą was deeply sorrowful. We both cried, promising ourselves that we would find each other again when it all calmed down. And we did! Yet, who would have thought the circumstances would have been so tragic for me?

* * *

The atmosphere at the camp was joyous, as people danced and sang late into the night. When darkness fell, the exhausted soldiers collapsed one by one into a drunken sleep. The flames dimmed, and only the choral snoring revealed the existence of the resting people. The sentry in front of the commander's tent had also apparently drunk well because his head dropped repeatedly, and only from time to time did he spy the dormant camp with his cloudy eyes. I also began to take a nap as the quiet sound of the forest calmed me down—until suddenly, my ears were alerted by the sound of sneaking footsteps.

After a moment of uncertainty, I felt that someone was slashing my bonds behind me. I glanced at the guard in front of the tent: luckily, his head was drooping. In a second the ties fell, and a girl's soft voice whispered to me.

"*Vtikayte* (Run away)." It was Wierą.

I stood still for another moment. The guard raised his head, looked around the campsite, and fell asleep again. This was my chance. I slowly moved into the shadow of a tree, step by step, and sneaked up to the adjacent river. A few dozen steps more, only a few dozen steps... An intense fear told me to rush while my reason warned cautiously. I treaded carefully, stopping every few steps, sharpening my hearing to detect possible movement. The sound of the river seemed to be the most beautiful music: there was freedom, there was life, there was salvation.

Holding my breath, I approached the shore. I was expecting another guard—but apparently, the Banderites decided that this side did not threaten them, and therefore, the sandy beach surrounded by reeds was free.

Tied to a wooden pole, a boat swayed gently on a wave. I carefully searched the boat—it was completely empty, without even an oar. I untied it from the pole and slowly pushed it to the river's current. Being chased from this side was no longer a threat. I looked behind me: the camp stayed asleep, and the faint glow of the bonfire only illuminated the low trunks of pine trees. I crossed myself, dipped into the cool riverbed, and hopped into the boat right before the main current swept me away. One last time, I adjusted my ears to confirm that I was not being followed.

It was a beautiful August night. The starry sky glowed over me as I glided down the river free as a fish, and every movement pulled me away from the terrible martyrdom of death. I felt like a newborn, as Horyń, my beloved mighty river, carried me like a mother carries a child to bed.

Suddenly, the current of the river accelerated. I raised my head and examined around carefully. In the faint light of the stars, I discerned a high, precipitous bank nearby on the right. I realized that, in a split second, I could find myself in the middle of a dangerous whirl created by the river, twisting and bending under the steep, jagged shores. A few energetic movements of my body, and I managed to land happily in a steady place—many inattentive daredevils had paid for their carelessness with their lives in such areas. Horyń is a beautiful but dangerous river.

I had already traveled a good chunk of the stream, maybe two or three kilometers, when a shot blasted in the camp, followed by a second or third—my escape had been noticed. Which way are they going to chase me? Despite that, I accelerated: it was my only option. They could look for me in every direction of the world, although the lack of boats would give them a trace.

The sharp current of the river carried me quickly, which I could tell by the speed of the shifting banks. I did my best to move as fast as possible, as I knew I could be pursued.

The sky in the east brightened, the silver glow on the waves announced the coming of a sunny day, and a light fog floated on the river, reminding me that there was another threat ahead—the bridge. A road bridge, closely guarded by the Germans, was a dozen or so kilometers away from the encampment, from where a floating man could be spotted and shot, defenseless as a duck.

I was tired now, but I accelerated, wanting to pass the bridge with the onset of fog. I was looking for it on each bend of the river, praying in spirit until I finally saw the bridge in the distance, rising high above the water, guarded by bunkers on both abutments. The fog was slowly falling when I found myself closer to it, and fortunately, there were no outposts on the shores. I continued to float downstream, carried only by the swishing current of the river, knowing that any careless move could betray me and lead to a series of machine gun shots from a distance that would ensure certain death.

A splash of water on the pillars of the bridge made me realize that I had left half of the dangers behind. I took deeper air into my lungs, and I continued to let myself be carried by the rapid current until I had lost the bridge behind the river bend. I drifted off several kilometers and went out onto the reed-covered shore. The sun had already risen and warmed my cold body, but my teeth were chattering, and only then I realized that I had not felt that sensation before: in the struggle for life, such minor details do not count.

I was sick and hungry—since the previous morning I had consumed nothing. My clothes were steaming on me, and I was frantically wondering what to do next, which way to go in order to avoid more unpleasant meetings. In this area the Banderites prowled less frequently; here there were Soviet and Polish partisans. I had enough encounters—I wanted to get home to my mother, who was likely weeping at the disappearance of her only son.

I was pondering where to go next. I figured I was approximately twenty kilometers from Równe and about four kilometers from the road that would lead me home via the forest. Deciding to make it there, I set off through the young, deciduous woodland, stopping every few moments and pricking up my ears. In the pine forest I saw blueberries, which I gathered, tearing the bushes with two hands and pushing them into my mouth. I can still feel their heavenly taste and smell to this day. For a minute, I had forgotten everything else—and by this, I also mean caution—when suddenly in front of me, as I rubbed my eyes, a Polish soldier appeared.

Yes, in full uniform, a Polish soldier with an eagle on his hat, and he spoke to me in Polish: "What are you doing here?"

I froze; the Banderites sometimes used tricks with Polish uniform camouflage, but when in a moment a few other soldiers sprang out, I regained my speech. The fear and tension of the previous days had found an outlet—I roared with tears.

"Don't cry," an older non-commissioned officer, with three beams on his shoulder pads, said as he patted me on the shoulder. "You are among your own. Tell me your name—and how did you get here?"

"Right, but let me eat. I have not eaten for a long time," I replied, wiping my tears. "I will tell you everything."

They led me deep into the old hornbeam forest by the river, where several shacks stood and a gurgling cauldron was hanging over a fire. A piece of bread with bacon and a sip of homemade moonshine built up my speech and confidence. The commander with the captain's emblem on his uniform listened to my story and asked a few detailed questions.

I could have been a Bandera spy, but when I told him the name of my third-grade headmaster in my pre-war school in Równe, he knew I was telling the truth. In the end, he asked if I remembered a teacher named Hlond.

"Naturally," I said, "He taught Polish."

And it was then that I recognized my teacher from elementary school. It was him! It took him a little longer to remember me.

He thought for a moment and spoke, "Listen, how old are you?"

"I will be seventeen in December," I confessed sincerely.

The captain looked with a critical eye at my frail figure and murmured: "You are too young and too weak for a partisan," he proclaimed. "I will send you back to your mother."

I did have a really miserable posture; my mother could only feed me on rations, and I had now had almost a week of strict fasting.

"Get a little sleep; after all these adventures, it will do you good," decided the captain. "There is a free hut over here," he pointed. "Lie down and sleep."

I buried myself in fragrant hay, was covered with a blanket, and fell asleep.

I woke up when someone nudged me on the shoulder.

"Get up, let's go," a man nudged me once more, and I rubbed my sleepy eyes. "You have gotten a sleeping melody; you have slept for over thirty hours," he added.

It was already the next afternoon, and I could tell a storm with heavy rain had recently passed over the ground, as the trees and grass glistened with moisture. I slept through it without even blinking an eye.

The division was ready to leave the encampment. The well-dressed platoon, partly in Polish Army uniforms, partly in English battledress, presented itself splendidly, and their weapons were a mixture of the armament of many armies. On one of the wagons, I spotted a Soviet Maxima covered with hay. Military discipline and order could be seen at every step. Seeing the Polish Army again lifted my spirits: after so many years after the September defeat, it was apparent that "Poland Is Not Yet Lost."[30]

As I realized by the position of the sun, we set off north. After walking—or marching, rather—for a long time, the roads became narrower and gravelly. The beautiful, high-growing pine forest seemed to have no end. The area became more and more waterlogged, and sometimes, when walking on the green carpet of moss, I felt the water munching under my bare feet (my shoes had been left in the Banderas' camp).

When night flooded the sky, we camped on a dry hill. Everyone, terribly tired, lay on the moss and fell asleep immediately. Even now the commander did not forget about me, and covered me with a blanket—nights in August can be chilly.

Before the sun had risen over the forest, we were on our way again, and we walked all day. The landscape began to change: the pine forest had given away to swamps overgrown with rushes, proclaiming that we were in Polesie.

For three days, I wandered with the Polish partisans in the wilderness and the swamps of Polesie until finally the former-schoolteacher-commander decided I could go home. I knew we were near the railway line because I heard the whistle of a steam locomotive several times. I said goodbye to the platoon and the commander, who instructed me to hide in the thicket, wait an hour, then go on the barely visible path through the swamps, which was supposed to lead to a small railway station staffed by the Germans.

---

30 *Here, Zbyszek is referring to Dąbrowski's Mazurka (the Polish national anthem)*

I did everything he asked me to do. As I emerged from the swamp, I saw the building surrounded by a high palisade and barbed wire fence, with a watchtower imposing over it. The Germans guarded the railway lines with an eagle's eye. On both sides of the track, the trees were scored out for a few hundred meters, and the Germans would fire at any man approaching without warning—once, I had seen how a peasant searching for a missing cow was killed. I wondered for a moment, and courageously, although with my soul on my shoulder, I went out into the open space and slowly headed towards the station.

The guard from the tower glared at me and then turned a machine gun, taking aim at the sight. A devilish shiver traveled down my spine once more. Will he shoot or not? He could see me on the palm of his hand, and with just a tiny movement of his finger... I would have drowned by the river bank.

I went on more boldly—if at first he did not shoot, maybe he wouldn't shoot at all.

When I came to the gate, a voice came from above: "*Woher?* (Where from)?"

"I am a Deutsche Post worker," I shouted.

I saw a soldier pick up the phone, talk to someone, then creak the large, cobbled gate and let me in.

In a moment, I was standing in front of an NCO who studied me carefully and asked in German: "Who are you? What are you doing here?"

I told my story from the last few days, excluding anything about the Polish partisans. The non-commissioned officer took out a map, examined it for a long moment, shook his head, and murmured, "It's a long way you have traveled through the forest, boy. What did you eat?"

"Berries and forest herbs, officer," I answered.

"But why did you go so far?"

"I wanted to move as far away from the Banderites as possible and went astray."

"You did not find Polish or Soviet partisans? It is full of them in this area; do you see how we live here?"

"No, I did not see any," I denied.

The petty officer thought for a moment, picked up the telephone, and connected with Równe. After a minute of waiting, a short conversation transpired, and he hung up the handset.

"You will take the first railcar to the city," he muttered.

A railcar armed with a heavy machine gun stopped at the station as several soldiers patrolled the railway track. I hopped on, and by the evening I was knocking on the front of my house in Równe. My mother opened the door. I fell into her arms, and she held me for a long time.

I felt her tears on my cheeks, and after a long moment, she asked, "You must be coming from the other world, Son?"

"Yes, Mother, I've come back from that world, and I've met many familiar people there."

— 11 —
The "Trial" Against Poles

A month before my forest adventure, in early July,[31] as we were going to sleep our neighbor knocked on the door and yelled: "Come out to see what's going on!"

We ran out into the yard, and it was as light as daytime. A huge wreath of fires surrounded the city—it was at the call of UPA chiefs that a general "trial" had begun against Poles. We did not sleep until morning; terror hung over our heads. Continuously from that summer, the glow of fires constantly flooded the night sky as the Ukrainian nationalists bloodily cleared Wołyń of Poles. It is not possible even now, after more than half a century, to think calmly about what was happening in this real-life hell. Poles from the villages fled to starving cities, and a paradoxical situation arose: for fear of Ukrainians, the Polish population protected themselves under the wings of a second enemy, the Germans.

* * *

It is difficult to say or describe the views I saw when we were traveling to fix the telegraph poles after my return from the "other world"—and we were traveling day by day. We saw many burnt villages and massacred corpses of adults and children that lay in the ruins of the burnt huts. Whoever survived the attacks protected themself in the forest, where they formed Polish partisan units, or fled to cities, where German or

---

31 *July 11, 1943, was considered the bloodiest day in the Wołyń Massacre of Poles by Ukrainians. On that day, the attacks commenced at 3:00 a.m. A reported 167 towns and villages were targeted.*

Hungarian garrisons were stationed. Polish self-defense centers[32] began to appear in several towns, which saved many people's lives. The Przebraże Defense and Huta Stepańska Defense were the largest and strongest of the defense centers. Przebraże survived until the arrival of the Red Army, although Huta Stepańska could not withstand the massive UPA attacks. Some people there were murdered, while others desperately defended themselves, managing to run to Równe. There, the Germans provided freight wagons and took the refugees away—where exactly it is not known, although likely to the General Government or to Germany.

One day, I was returning from work when I spotted a crowd of people: men, women, and children, barely managing to walk down the street. I stopped. Fatigue and despair were visible on their emaciated faces; some had to be supported under their arms, while others were carried.

I watched for a moment longer and then, hearing Polish speech, asked: "Where are you coming from?"

"From Northern Ukraine," replied a man passing by, whose voice sounded all the bitterness of despair and defeat. "Only half of us survived," he added.

I soon found out that they were the refugees from the broken self-defense center of Huta Stepańska, about sixty kilometers from Równe.

Mother, Father and I slept in our clothes with well-sharpened axes under the pillow so that in the event of a raid on the city, we were at least defending ourselves, at least not giving our lives away.

Soon, we received news about what was happening with our extended families in the province. Father's brother Gaj was killed by the UPA with an ax in front of the eyes of his Ukrainian wife and several of my cousins. She herself was killed a year later while escaping to western Poland, shot by a Soviet officer. Mother's sister Maria, who previously lived in Tiutkiewicze, died with her husband Stanisław and five children; they were murdered somewhere near Zdołbunów on that memorable July night.

The rest of the large family from before the war, both on my father and mother's side, dispersed in the turmoil of the conflict or were

---

32 *Around a hundred self-defense centers were created in response, in the Wołyń region. It is also estimated that two to three thousand Ukrainians were killed by retaliatory Polish acts in 1943.*

slaughtered, disappearing without a trace. Tens of thousands of Poles were murdered in Wołyń at that time.[33]

My Ukrainian friend Sławik Dejko was also missing then. Sławik worked on the railway. He did not notice the oncoming train in time and was killed under its wheels. As he was an Orthodox, I carried a cross before the funeral procession at his mother's request. A priest followed me, and then the casket was carried, followed by his distressed, heartbroken mother, sisters, and a crowd of friends. It was a typical picture of Wołyń. I, a Pole—a Catholic—carried a cross before the Orthodox funeral procession, in which friends of many denominations walked. Nationalism, a plague of the twentieth century, had not eaten as deeply into our hearts as the prophets of the new religion attempted to spread. However, not all Ukrainians succumbed to this terrible plague. I knew many Ukrainians who remained decent people until the end—many Poles saved themselves because Ukrainian friends warned them in time. Even so, the nationalists murdered any compatriots who refused to participate in their crimes.

From my childhood group of friends, only I remained. Jankielek and Masha, both of Jewish origin, had been lying in clay pits outside the city for two years, and Sławik rested forever in the Orthodox cemetery.

We thought about the coming autumn with fear and anxiety. The front was approaching; the Red Army was already standing on the Dnieper River. Ukrainian, Soviet, and Polish partisans dominated the province. The employed lived on miserable assignments while the unemployed were condemned to starvation. The Germans kept order in the city with utmost difficulty, only by frequent punishments of death. Attacks on Germans were common, for which they retaliated by shooting hundreds of innocent people.

We breathed a sigh of relief when our boss finally announced that the "field trips" were over. There was no point in going, as the partisans destroyed the telephone lines instantly after repair.

---

33 *Yale historian Timothy Snyder estimates that the UPA's actions caused between fifty and a hundred thousand deaths, including possibly thirty thousand Ukrainians who refused to participate in their acts. Tens of thousands of others were forced to flee.*

Just before Christmas, our truck took us to the railway station. There were empty wagons at the ramp. The gendarmerie surrounded us.

"*Einsteigen!* (Get in!)" roared a big gendarme.

And so a new phase of war adventure began—deportation to Germany. It is possible that we have moved from the drainpipe to the gutter. We'll see—I thought.

— 12 —
Eve

The early winter twilight had already fallen when the freight wagons were ready to leave.

"*Schnell! Schnell einsteigen!* (Quickly! Quickly get in!)" throaty German screams repeated.

We hurried out of the station's warehouses and climbed into the wagons. From the corner of my eye, I saw the figure of my mother, who stood with the crowd of other parents at the gate of the station, surrounded by barbed wire.

* * *

A large crowd of young people, who had been picked up straight from work on trucks, were brought to the warehouses all day. Chattering from the cold in the substantial unheated space, we prayed for it to be over soon because the night in this icehouse did not promise to be fun. News of labor deportation to Germany spread like wildfire around the city. The parents came together as the sentries allowed them to approach the gate and pass on some of our belongings. My mother gave me warm socks, her wool sweater, and a loaf of hard, bitter barley bread. That was all she could give me for the long journey into the unknown.

Before the wagons appeared, the gendarme with a translator ordered us to form a double row, then he carefully counted us twice and called the translator to speak a few sentences.

"I warn you," he informed us, "the wagons are being escorted. Every escape attempt will end in death. Oh, and there will be absolute silence in the wagons. No light, no loud conversations, no singing. You drive through terrain where partisans prowl—if they hear that there are people in the carts, they will shoot you like ducks."

They will shoot here, they will shoot there—it was no news for us. It was something we had gotten used to during the years of occupation. I don't think there was any city where shootings took place as willingly and often as there.

The wagon door closed with a clatter. Darkness reigned. Beyond this door had been a happy childhood, family, and finally the hell of the recent years of occupation, where the Germans, the resisting Polish Home Army, the Ukrainian Insurgent Army, the Soviet guerillas, and hell knows who else clashed in that city in those times—life was easier to lose than it was to sneeze.

And so we were leaving this behind! But what was ahead of us? We knew that we were not going to a health resort. We lay side by side on the hard boards of the wagon floor, as at last the train jerked and the wheels rolled.

A grave silence fell in the wagon. Alternately, we hung on the bars of the window to take a last look at the ground where we saw the world for the first time, and where our loved ones stayed, but unfortunately, the opaque darkness of the night covered our view.

"Look, there's the first star in the sky!" someone called out at the window.

"God, of course, it's Christmas Eve today."

Silence returned as the workers crowded by the window—everyone wanted to catch sight of the Bethlehem star.

Someone began to hum "Silent Night" in a thin voice. The whole wagon quickly picked up the song in full chorus.

Another one shouted, "Sing as the train moves, and go quiet as it slows down!"

Soon later, the train slowed to a halt in the middle of an open field, and the singing in the car died down. On the night horizon, the glow of the native land bade us farewell.

The train stood for a long time. We learned from overheard conversations of the guards that partisans had blown up the tracks ahead of us, and a hasty repair was underway. Finally, the train jerked abruptly and moved slowly. Where is it taking us? What will tomorrow bring? Thoughts such as these rambled in our heads.

The hush in the wagon lasted a good while; someone took a piece of bread and shared it with a colleague. The too distant glow of fire did not allow for recognition of any neighbor's face. We each broke off a piece of food, exchanged wishes, and swallowed our tears in the dark. One and the other mourned sorrowfully—but quietly and surreptitiously, to not let his colleague notice—wiping his eyes with his sleeve. Youth cannot bear sadness for long. Soon someone hummed the carol "In the crib he lies," and the whole wagon joined in eagerly to sing.

Through the rumble of the train wheels, we heard other carts singing the same song. Suddenly shots rang out, the music died down as if a knife had cut it, and we threw ourselves on the floor and huddled together, waiting for what would happen next. Luckily nothing resulted. The train rushed into the darkness—so they were only warning convoy shots. We breathed a sigh of relief.

The train stopped at a small but fortified station in the woods. A military transport train flashed east, and a second later another one passed by. Several wagons with wounded soldiers from the Eastern Front were attached to our train, and after a while, we took off again. To not sing on this holy night—when our hearts were yearning for our loved ones and were fearing the unknown ahead of us—was beyond our strength. Soon, someone hummed another carol, and we again took it with our whole voice, attempting to drown out the sorrow and anxiety of our hearts.

An older one always reminded us, "Sing as the train is going, silence when it slows down."

The singing wagon would die down, but not for long. The train was speeding in the dark of the winter night; it stopped, slowed down, accelerated again, and the chorus in the wagons would grow enormous. Then it would be silenced and rise in an instant again, to cheer the hearts and ears with the beauty of Polish carols. The escorts would induce terror with bullets in the air from time to time, but when they finally heard "Silent Night," they gave up—perhaps they were also in a festive mood.

A pale winter dawn was already peering into the window of the wagon as the train thudded onto a bridge over a large river.

Not long after crossing the waterway, someone peered out the window and cheered: "The sun has risen, the day is here!"

So we sang for the whole Christmas Eve. With the grinding of the brakes, the train stopped at another station. Soon, near the wagon, we heard a conversation in Polish.

The one from the window called out: "Terespol Station, and there are Polish railwaymen!"

We threw ourselves into the windows. Two Polish railwaymen were walking along the windows with long hammers in their hands. So we're in Poland! Conquered, enslaved, but in our homeland, Poland. Our hearts jumped into our throats.

Even though this was a comforting checkpoint, the journey had only just begun.

In Germany

I spent Christmas 1943 traveling. It was neither a voluntary nor luxury winter travel in a freight car. Just before Christmas I was picked up, with a dozen of my peers from work, and taken straight to a standing freight car at the station. Fortunately, someone notified my mother, and she brought me a sweater, a change of underwear, and a piece of bread. There was not even a wagon stove; we dreamed of the whole journey terribly. The train started at night, and Ukraine said goodbye to us with a glow of burning land.

RAILWAY LINES OF EUROPE, AND THE FRONTS AT CHRISTMAS 1943

By the end of summer 1943, the Germans were on the defensive. Through the remainder of the year, Soviet victories resulted in the recapturing of most of Ukraine, and the Allies launched the invasion of Italy, which capitulated soon after. By Christmas, Równe (Rivne) became close to the Eastern Front Lines. Knowing this, the Nazi authorities sent many young people, like Zbyszek, by trains for labor further into central Europe. This map illustrates the railway lines of Europe and where Zbyszek was taken.

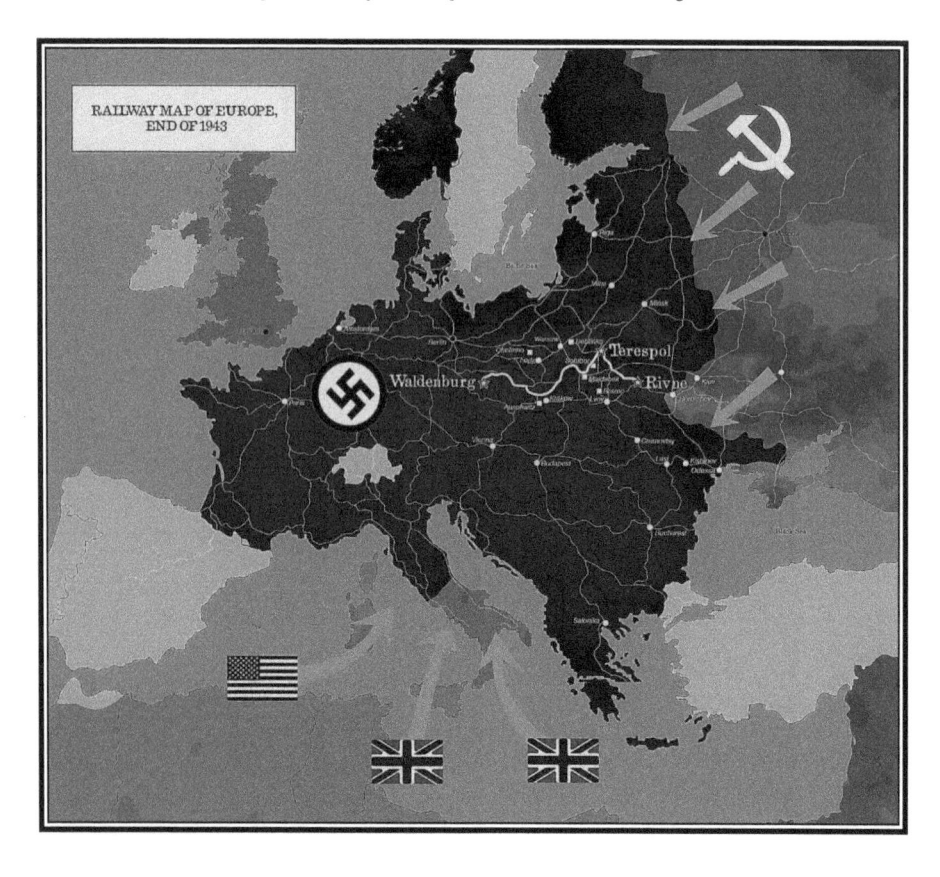

Back in Wołyń, our families were destroyed by the Ukrainian Insurgent Army and were left behind. The rest of the large family before the war, both on my father and mother's side, dispersed in the turmoil of war or were slaughtered, disappearing without a trace.[34]

The trip lasted almost a week.

At last, the train stopped and made a loud clamor, after which an order was heard: "*Alles aussteigen* (All get off)."

We spilled quickly out of the carts. Only three wagons remained from the entire transport; the rest were unhooked somewhere on the way. Our freight cars stood on the railway siding, and in the distance we could see a substantial train station with a sign of "Waldenburg."[35]

On the way, we had wondered where they were taking us—are we going to go from the drainpipe to the gutter, from the UPA hatchets to the Allied bombs? Fate turned out to be kind this time. On the horizon, we could spy a large city, surrounded by hills, and there was peace and quiet all around. Waldenburg and the surrounding Lower Silesian area were the most peaceful places in war-torn Europe.

Under the watchman's escort, we reached the barracks standing near the station. A barbed-wire fence surrounded the camp, but the gate was not closely guarded. The guards only told us that we must not leave without permission of the *Lagerführer*.[36] We shuffled up on empty two-story bunks, and soon it turned out that our location was a real international place—young people were gathered here from all over Europe. My neighbor on the bunk floor was Czech, and on one side Ukrainian, and the other side Croatian or Serbian.

Everyone was asking for tobacco or cigarettes. I didn't smoke, but my mother had given me a full slipper of light brown tobacco, which I soon distributed to neighbors. It was a mistake. I did make friends; they were smiling from all sides at me, and they patted my back, but I had lost my most valuable goods to exchange for in the camp—tobacco was more

---

34 *This was also the last time Zbyszek apparently saw his father, and although he spent many years after the war attempting to find records of where he went, he never found out what truly happened to him.*

35 *Now Wałbrzych*

36 *"Camp Leader" title of the SS, referring to the Totenkopfverbände (Concentration Camp Service)*

important than bread there. Soon we were served dinner in the evening; it was a soup that my colleagues called "gastric-rinsing fluid." Several cubes of turnip floated in the water, and no fat was visible.

Damn it! How to fall asleep here after such a "dinner"? Hunger twisted my gut.

My neighbor Zdenek gave some good advice. "Drink a lot of water, and you will fall asleep," he said with a smile. I soon found that everyone did it.

In the morning, the sound of a piece of rail banging on the gate set the whole camp on its feet. Breakfast was not rich either. A bit of bread (two hundred grams), a decagram of margarine, and a brown liquid considered coffee made the whole meal. That portion of bread was to last the entire day. Lunch was equally modest—a watery cabbage soup, six potatoes in natural uniforms (i.e. unpeeled and rotten potatoes were also counted), plus a large spoon of black flour mash. We won't be able to carry on for long, fed on such a menu, I thought.

After breakfast, under the watchman's escort, the majority of the workers went to the mines (under protruding shafts that we could see on the horizon), and a dozen or so of us went to unload carriages. Watchmen divided our work into two people for each wagon. They were carts loaded with twenty tons of cement blocks—ten tons for each of us to be removed from the wagon and placed on the truck. We worked like oxen, being told that it was to be emptied by evening, and whoever failed to do the work would stay longer—even until past midnight.

Despite the frost, our shirts were wet with sweat. The Germans had already taught me hard work in Ukraine, but here it was murder. At home, I knew that after returning from work, my mother would go to any extent to dig up from the ground something more to eat… but here? The only dinner waiting for me in the barrack was a soup with several cubes of unappetizing turnip.

It was dark when we finished work. I glanced at my colleagues, barely standing on their feet, a few leaning on poles. In the barrack, everyone swallowed their soup quickly and fell like a log on the bunk. And so the murderous labor began and lasted until spring.

"What the hell are these building materials for?" I asked Zdenek once. "What are they building here?"

"They say tunnels in the mountains and underground factories," he spoke quietly, looking sideways and then biting his tongue.

"You can't trust any people in this Tower of Babel," a Pole from Radom then warned me.

In March, some forced laborers working in mines were asked to remain there in the barracks—but others, including myself, were ordered to prepare for the road. Where are they taking us now?—we were thinking—please God not to the west, near the bombings. The news about what was happening in western Germany was heard more and more often.

This time the trip was short. A faded white inscription of "Jelenia Gora/Hirschberg" caught my eye on the train station building. The watchmen this time led us in a direction where, beyond the city, a tall factory chimney protruded up to the sky. It stank terribly. The stench instantly blocked my nose. Dreary gray residential barracks, fenced with barbed wire, stood near the factory. This incredibly buggy barrack was to be my new home, accompanied by the same international company.

The bugs hit us the first night. Bites all over my body left burning bubbles. I didn't sleep at all, although others from the factory were snoring, tired from another day of labor. In the morning, it turned out that meals did not differ from before; however, workers did receive one cigarette a day.

The factory—named *Schlesische Zellwolle* (Silesian Cotton)—was a beautiful, modern cotton facility. From one side of the workshop, wagons were constantly importing spruce wood, and on the other side, they exported beams of beautiful, white, shiny wrapped rayon. It was whispered quietly among the workers that ammunition was also produced here.

The factory was a technical wonder at the time, although the conditions of the workplace itself were horrendous. The basis of production was highly concentrated lye, which overflowed everywhere like fresh honey. In addition to the unpleasant, suffocating smell, every drop of lye on the skin resulted in a burning stain. Great concrete pools were filled with the substance, which flowed through complex machinery, undergoing chemical treatment. Work itself in the lye workshop was not hard, but arduous and dangerous, and for every wrong move you could pay with your life. My predecessor slipped at the edge of the pool, fell in, and... There was nothing left to pull out. Lye digests everything.

I worked in this department for a month. The strenuous work, inadequate food, and the chemical fumes were taking their toll. People working there were easy to recognize: a pale and yellow complexion, with an odor escaping from them that kept everyone else away. Even in the barracks we slept in a separate corner. Everyone said that three months of work would be enough in this facility to finish off the healthiest. However, I was lucky one day when the Lagerführer called for me.

The older gray-haired man looked at me closely and then asked: "You speak German?"

"Yes," I responded.

"What does that mean?" He put a table of chemical formulas under my nose.

"These are chemical formulas," I replied. "And this," I added, pointing to another card, "This is the Mendeleev table."

"And that?" He continued to ask me, showing me several further chemical formulas.

"It's water, it's salt, it's chlorine, it's sodium," I recited smoothly.

Chemistry had never been my favorite subject, but I knew the basics well. This short exam changed my life.

The Lagerführer wrote something on a piece of paper and stated: "You will apply tomorrow morning in the energy department."

I left the office feeling light, as if I had wings. Tomorrow I would be away from the damn smell! The factory stunk absolutely everywhere, but at my current workplace, the stench was so strong, it could stop you from breathing. I don't think I've ever prayed as fervently as I did that night, thanking my guardian angel for this change. I didn't know what awaited me, but could it be any worse?

In the morning, I reported to the head of the energy department, and he led me to the boiler room: "You will be a stoker's helper."

The stoker (named Helmut) was a middle-aged man, which was strange to me because Germans of his age, except for professionals, would be on the frontline. He shook my hand and introduced himself. I looked with curiosity around the big boiler room: I had associated it with dust, dirt, and shoveling coal, but it was clean as a laboratory here—only the noise of engines and the rumble of devices made me realize that this was a modern industrial plant. A miracle of technology.

My new boss showed me around the boiler room, explained the machinery, and introduced me to my task. It was child's play: Helmut was to walk on one side, along the enormous cauldrons situated in rows, and observe indicators of temperature, pressure, steam, water supply, and other measurements. My role was to do the exact same, walking instead on the opposite side. We would meet in the middle of the hall and repeat the procedure for all eight hours. Every hour, data on the indicators had to be written on special sheets in a notebook.

The only troublesome activity was blowing the boiler out. This activity consisted of turning the appropriate cranks, which led the steam to clean the inside of the boilers, for which two people were needed. To accomplish this task, I was accompanied by a young Hungarian Jew called Mosze from Feikesfehirwar (It took me three days to learn the pronunciation of this town—Hungarian is a hellishly tricky language to learn). I was always hungry, but the poor man could barely stand. I shared my bread with him. I even offered him a piece of bacon, for which I got cigarettes. Despite the prohibitions of his religion, he ate this "unfortunate" food with no resistance. I've seen worse things people have eaten.

The end of spring brought a new source of supply—digging gardens. The young and healthy German men were at war, so cultivating home gardens became a duty for women. They were not very good at it. A young man with fluent knowledge of the local language seemed a real treasure in the countryside desolate of young men. After work I dug gardens, so I never became hungry again, and I was abundant enough in supply to continue to help my Jewish friend from Hungary.

The ladies from the factory offices liked me very much. Hildegard, a thirty-year-old widow, pointed out to me several times that I was badly shaved. However, I did not have much to shave on my youthful chin—my first few hairs stuck out like lonely trees on a clearing. Even so, this seemed to disturb the happy widow. Why? The matter was cleared up very soon.

"Come to me this afternoon," Hildegard decided one day. "You will dig my garden."

And so I did, and then I was invited to the table for dinner. Afterward, Hilda set two cups of deliciously scented coffee on the table and sat down next to me.

"You are unshaven again," she observed.

She stroked her hand over my cheek, immediately embraced my neck, sat down on my knees, and started kissing my face. Under her silk dressing gown, I could feel her naked body. I jumped up as if I had been scalded, and pushed her away. She gaped at me, surprised and disappointed. I was a complete layman in these matters; I didn't know how to behave.

Hilda glanced at me mockingly and then asked: "You haven't had a woman in your life?"

"No," I admitted.

My previous contact with girls had been only a handshake or delicate kiss on the cheek. This first contact with the opposite sex had turned out to be a complete disaster.

Not long after this incident, I came into a clash with the Gestapo. One day, when I was cranking the valves with Mosza, I noticed that my boss Helmut was standing by one of the boilers, looking up at the water level indicator and scratching behind his ear.

"*Was ist los, Herr Heizer?* (What's going on, Sir Heizer?)" I asked, coming out from behind the cauldron.

Suddenly, an awful banging came into our ears, and a cloud of hot steam and smoke surrounded me. I thought a bomb had fallen somewhere nearby. I only managed to reach the electric dashboard and flip the switch before I lost consciousness.

I woke up in the factory infirmary. My face and hands stung mercilessly, but what was worse, next to the bed in a chair sat an individual in a black uniform—a Gestapo officer. He scrutinized me carefully; looking at my burned face and seeing that I had opened my eyes, he took out his notebook and began to interrogate me with questions.

I told everything how it was. There was no point in lying—there were no jokes with these people. The Gestapo expression itself aroused terror, prison, or death behind it.

"Did you turn off the power switch lever?" he asked, looking into my eyes.

"Yes. According to the instruction manual," I added hurriedly.

From the questions of the Gestapo officer, I guessed that the case smelled of sabotage. The investigation was ongoing for a few more days, which I spent in the Gestapo prison.

"*Bist du Pole?* (Are you Polish?)" the investigator inquired, shining a lamp into my eyes. "And how do you know German so well?"

I told them again and again that I was brought up among the Germans in Wołyń, hence my language knowledge. They seemed to suspect me of being a saboteur as they also X-rayed me thoroughly. That lever saved my life. Further operation of the machinery threatened an explosion all over the boiler room, so it was just an automatic response.

When I returned to my old place in the factory, everything was fine. I had another boss now. Helmut didn't come back, and I don't know what happened to him; I never saw him in my life again. Two scenarios could have occurred: he either died from burns or remained in the hands of the Gestapo. My new boss, named Bruno, was an invalid in his thirties. His hand was "forgotten" on the Eastern Front, as he often stated humorously—but it was humor through tears. Bruno was a decent, friendly man, whom I soon became friendly with, and I spoke to him on informal terms, which was strictly prohibited.

The war had bypassed these sides of Germany so far—the people lived here as if living the "life of Riley." Although, the first waves of refugees were beginning to flow from both east and west, and the fronts were approaching. On a beautiful spring day, heavy bomber squadrons flew high in the sky, pulling white braids behind. The sirens woke up the already forgotten feeling of anxiety in our hearts.

These sirens gradually became a more common occurrence.

On Palm Sunday, I had a day off from work. I lay down on the grass, on the hill's southern slope near the barracks, and fell asleep. I was awakened only by the thunder of cannons on the hill and the distant murmur of the bomb expedition engines. A split-second later, the first squadron appeared in the cloudless spring sky—I counted twenty-seven four-engine bombers—followed by the second, third, fourth, and eventually tenth squadron. When I added to a total of over two hundred bombers, a strange sound caught my attention: one of the aircraft fell out of formation and dived straight to the top of the hill. I jumped up and looked around for shelter.

A heavy bomber is not a light plane attacking from a mowing flight—and thus it had been shot down. The parachutes confirmed my thoughts. Seconds later, the heavy machine hit the top of the hill with a deafening bang. The parachutes with airmen were blowing somewhere beyond the horizon. I ran to the crash site, and German soldiers were already there. Stacks of sheet metal were falling within a half-kilometer radius, and the engines were still burning, covering the field of view with clouds of black smoke.

The sirens continued to blare daily into the summer. On July 20, 1944, I came as usual for work. The head of our department had sorrowful eyes.

"What happened?" I asked, thinking he was troubled by some ailment.

He gaped at me, tears streaming down his face. "The assassination attempt[37] on Hitler," he murmured. "They wanted to kill our Führer."

The response of my direct boss Bruno was extremely different. When he next saw me, he looked sideways and whispered in my ear: "Did you hear? They sought to assassinate that bastard, and they failed. What a shame!"

Newspapers and newsreels began to broadcast the results of the investigation. I saw later, in the *Polish Film Chronicle*, a general—who participated in the conspiracy—holding his falling trousers in his hands while testifying before a "popular court."

The Germans fell pale in fear, but the worst was still ahead of them.

---

[37] *The July 20, 1944 assassination plot on Hitler, also dubbed as Operation Valkyrie, was a coup attempted by many of the Führer's inner circle, led by Claus von Stauffenburg. A bomb was placed by Hitler's conference table in the Wolf's Lair, but it ultimately failed to kill him. Over the following weeks, the Gestapo arrested (about seven thousand) and killed (about five thousand) anyone who apparently had the remotest connection to the plot.*

— 14 —

Escape from Hell

"Wake up, Zbyszek! Get up! You have a guest!" An acquaintance shook me as if I were a ripe pear tree. "Stand up. You have a guest, wake up finally, see what a guest it is!"

I woke up and rubbed my eyes. In front of me, smiling slyly, stood Irmi, my German sweetheart. In a moment when I had pulled myself together, warm, tender arms wrapped around my neck.

"Irmi, what are you doing here?" I finally choked out of my throat.

"I came for you from Bavaria. I'm taking you to Rosenheim, to my parents' house; we'll wait for it to calm down," she chatted.

A gloomy reality was slowly reaching my sleepy head. The glass in the windows trembled at the artillery cannonade, and the room was light, like during the day, from the fires. I had already gotten used to these typical symptoms of war, and it was only Irmi's attention that made me realize how restless it was here. From the right bank of the Oder River, the Russians shelled the city at night, and the Germans pounded them with cannons during the day when the targets were visible on the opposite bank. The beautiful town on the great river, as well as its surroundings, slowly turned into a desert.

The snipers, ambushing on both sides of the river, were effectively extinguishing all the signs of life, resulting in the blood of many careless or too-curious colleagues soaking into the coastal sands. The day before, we buried a companion who carelessly tilted his head out of the ditch while repairing trenches damaged by artillery shells.

As frontal steel claws tightened from the east and west, a blizzard of fire and iron raged over the German Reich. The Allied air forces turned German cities and communication lines into ashes and rubble.

"How did you make it here?" I asked Irmi, looking at her cheeks slightly flushed from the frost.

"All of Germany is under bombs... For you, I would even make it to hell," she whispered.

Unfortunately, real hell was indeed ahead of us.

"Eat quickly and change," Irmi insisted, finally unpacking her backpack. "We don't have much time. We have an evacuation train in two hours," she added.

There was some food in the backpack that I shared with two friends, and deeper in the bag, there were beautiful shoes and a navy blue ski-suit that fit me perfectly.

"It used to belong to my fallen brother," Irmi whispered, with tears glistening in her eyes.

I changed quickly, gave my old clothes to my friends, packed my poor belongings in my backpack, and headed for the door. Then a sudden thought came to my mind—I don't have permission to leave my workplace. I stepped back from the doorway: an attempt of escape can end in you being put up against the firing wall.

Irmi was a little worried but finally decided: "In this terrible chaos, who will ask you for your identification? I will say that you work for my parents in Rosenheim."

It would be an easy lie to detect, though, as the *Ausweis*[38] I had found was from a factory in Gelsenkirchen, on another side of Germany.

At seventeen, decisions are quick—you do not think about what such recklessness threatens. Just an hour later, I was waiting with Irmi at the station for the long-awaited train to Dresden. We were lucky: the freight train soon arrived, although it was incredibly crowded with refugees. We squeezed into the wagon with great difficulty, and in a second, the locomotive started. Farewelled by the bloody glow of fire and the thunder of cannonade, we were going to meet an unknown future.

In another hour, the train stopped in the middle of nowhere, and a shy whistle of the locomotive warned passengers of an air raid. High above the ground, aerial flares appeared, whose awfully bright light seemed to allow even needles to be visible in the snow-covered field.

---

38 *ID card*

We jumped out of the wagon, and Irmi clutched my hand. We hid in a furrow, and with bated breath, accompanied by hundreds or maybe thousands of people, we waited for what would happen next.

The barely audible murmur of aircraft engines was rising somewhere from the east, and a hail of bombs spilled onto the standing train. The wagons were luckily empty; several bombs hit the train, and the rest went into the field. When the raid stopped, the dead and wounded were collected and placed at the track in the red light of the burning wagons. We both gaped at this view with horror. Irmi was trembling as if in a fever. Soon on the neighboring railroad, a second train arrived, and we squeezed into an open-sided wagon with a crowd of people and moved on.

"To Dresden, to Dresden," sighed Irmi. "Hopefully, it will be safer there."

It was terribly freezing in the open carts: people clung to each other like chickens in a coop. In the morning, the train arrived in Rottenburg, and only there we drank an icy cup of herbal tea. The train to Dresden departed at noon, dragged on, stopped, waited for hours, and again we hid in furrows several times. Above us, hundreds of bomb squadrons flew high in the sky, although these were bomb expeditions for which the train was too poor of a target.

In the evening, we got off at the Dresden train station, and Irmi suggested accommodation from her aunt, who had lived here for years and would be happy to receive us. I agreed to it without a second thought—all the more that spending the night in the cold, dark, crowded station, where the gendarmerie patrols circulated, did not seem wise.

We wandered and got lost several times in the big, dark city. We asked several strangers for the address, but nobody was familiar with it, as the town was full of strangers, refugees from all over Germany. When we finally came across a native who showed us the way, sirens squealed.

"It's a pre-alarm," Irmi reassured me. "Maybe they have a different purpose. Dresden has no industry. What would the bombers look for here?"

We stood for a moment, turning our ears. The sirens did not stop, and soon they howled in a broken tone. The distant roar of anti-aircraft artillery made us realize that Dresden was indeed visited by guests for an undesirable goal. We listened for a while, deluding ourselves into thinking they would choose a different target, but when the deep bass of hundreds of bomber engines reached our ears through the roar of artillery, we ran behind a white arrow to a shelter in the basement of a multi-story building, barely visible in the shadowed darkness of the wall. Then the first bombs fell somewhere nearby.

There were already several dozen people in the shelter: residents of the building, their children, and several military personnel. I crouched with Irmi in the corner of the basement and listened diligently to the residents' conversations: the general belief was that it was just some stray squadron getting rid of bombs, and as Dresden had not been bombed so far, the alarm must be canceled in a moment.

The deafening roar of anti-aircraft artillery and the monstrous thunder of exploding heavy bombs intensified. A deadly silence fell in the shelter, which was interrupted only sometimes by the crying of a child. Dozens of people held their breath as explosives were falling somewhere nearby. Irmi clutched my hand tightly, and I felt a terrible powerlessness and fear that I think a man only feels before the power of the elements.

"*Terrorangriff* (Terror attack)," someone next to us said.

So, we had hit the eye of the cyclone, a terrible bomb attack in which hundreds or even thousands of heavy Allied bombers took part, raids that wiped German cities from the face of the earth and which the Germans themselves called "*glatt rasieren*" ("a clean shave").[39]

Several minutes passed; the rumble above us did not stop even for a moment. The shelter was shaking and trembling, and eventually the light went out. A few candles were lit—even the crying of the child ceased—and above us continued what appeared to be a gruesome dance of giants, with no end in sight.

I felt drowsy, and I nudged Irmi. She was sleeping carelessly, leaning on my shoulder. Dreaming in this hell? So there is a limit to the human

---

39 *In four raids over February 13-15, 1945, 722 heavy bombers of the British RAF and 527 of the American AAF dropped over 3,900 tons of explosive devices on the cultural city of Dresden. It was later estimated that around twenty-five to thirty-five thousand people were killed, nearly all of whom were civilians and refugees. By this time, the Luftwaffe (the German air force) was unable to fight off any of these attacks, and it was considered a highly controversial move by the Allies, given the imminent ending of the war.*

psyche's immunity to fear, a mechanism that protects our consciousness from excess sensation. I didn't move; I let her sleep—maybe at least in this way I would save her a few moments from this nightmare.

Bombs were falling closer, at one point the shelter trembled, and plaster fell from the ceiling and walls.

The candles went out, and a man in a terrified voice cried out, "They hit us!"

And then tense nerves let go: the baby's cry and the desperate lament of women were heard from all sides. Coughing, we choked on virulent, limestone-plaster dust. Someone lit a candle, then a second and a third. Several men threw themselves at the door, but it did not yield. In a few turns of banging our arms, the iron door did not budge—so we were buried in the rubble of an apartment house bomb. The ceiling, however, withstood the impact.

The shelter became stuffy, as prayers, weeping, and the panicking of the women created an unbearable clamor. I felt my shirt wet with sweat, fear bristled my hair, and Irmi sobbed silently.

In the flickering light of candles, someone spotted and pointed to a rectangle painted black on the wall—so there was some last resort. This rectangle was a place where a wall should be pierced if the house was bombed and the door blocked, so behind the wall should have been the basement of the neighboring house. Forging tools, cutters, and hammers cluttered the floor of the shelter.

Our time was running thin, and our shortness of breath in the shelter increased. Two men took hold of the tools and started forging, and every few minutes, others replaced them.

Most noises were stifled, and all eyes were on the hands of the working men, seeing in them the only hope of survival. Sweat flooded my dust-covered eyes, my hands were bleeding, there was still gigantic drumming above my head, and I was forging like Satan, seeing nothing and hearing nothing. Someone snatched the tools out of my hand and ordered "rest" in German.

This race with death probably lasted for half an hour, as oxygen particles had been replaced with the dust from plastered walls. Our survival was decided in minutes. Finally, a chisel flew with a clatter to the other side—we had pierced the hole.

We enlarged it laboriously (the wall was thick—made of firm, hard brick), and finally, a breath of fresh air blew from the neighboring basement. Women, kneeling on the concrete floor of the shelter, prayed earnestly. The adjacent basement was empty. Several men crawled over to the other side while the panicked crowd cluttered into the hole. Someone tried to bring order, but only the loud "*Ruhe!*" ("Quiet!") controlled the panic. Even in such a tragic situation, German discipline proved its good side.

A queue quickly formed. We helped push women and children through the gaping hole from our side of the basement as the men on the other side pulled them through. Nobody paid any attention to what was happening above us—we were seemingly saved.

An older man as fat as a barrel approached the hole several times, and while we pushed him, they pulled. None of this worked: the hole was too small. After several minutes, the shelter was empty, and only the large man continually tried to get to the other side again. His desperate maneuvers and the kicking of his arms and legs were pitifully comical. Suddenly, in this terrible situation, we looked at each other and began to hysterically wallow in laughter. That's how in this nightmarish performance, our fate had given us a scene from a Chaplinist farce.

My conscience did not allow me to leave the fat man in this buried shelter, so I shouted through the hole: "Let's expand it!" and grabbed the chisel.

Someone took another, and we started forging again. It lasted quite a long time, and finally, the overweight man squeezed through.

"Thank you, sincerely thank you," he squeezed our hands and thanked us effusively in German. "I am Doctor Schmidt, and I will always be grateful to you for the rest of my life."

It was now possible to breathe freely in the neighboring basement. We looked for a way out in the dim candlelight. We traveled up the stairs to the ground floor, then to the hotel lobby full of patterned stucco walls, mirrors, and marble. It was as light here as daytime. I went to the swinging door and peered out into the street. Fire and a terrible heat hit my face—what I saw could not even be imagined by Dante when describing hell in his poem of *Divine Comedy*. The street had turned into a burning tunnel: the high houses on both sides of the road burned like torches. In the middle of the street, people ran in both directions, and many fell down, choking on the terrible heat and smoke of the conflagration.

I returned to the lobby. Irmi was waiting patiently in the crowd of panicking people. The hotel was also in flames; the fire had already made contact with the upper floors and was inevitably approaching us, so an escape was necessary. The fire would reach us in only a matter of time. People pushed towards the door and instantly returned, terrified of the fire, a terrible death that was clenching its jaws.

Sparks started falling from above, and then they became burning torches. I hesitated, thinking frantically of which way to run. I did not know the city, and the fire was coming from all sides. We finally bolted out of the hotel, choking on smoke, and headed towards where most people were running.

We were as if plunged into the crater of an active volcano. The terrible heat and smoke clogged our lungs, and our clothes began to smolder after a dozen or so steps, as somewhere high in the merciless night sky, the rumble of the engines of hundreds of bombers threw their terrible load on the unfortunate city. From the phosphor bombs, the road's pavement was burning with a white, blinding flame in many places.

Pulling Irmi by the hand, I tore through the burning tunnel, avoiding the sizzling spots on the road. Panting, we stumbled on a pavement of shrunken human bodies, whose moans and cries for help penetrated our ears, despite the roar of the fire and the blasts of the explosions. Nobody, however, could save anyone, nobody could help anyone; older people and children had no chance in this race with death.

Suddenly, a vast pool of water fenced the road: a bomb had hit a pipe. Without hesitation, I dragged Irmi to her knees and splashed us both with water because our clothing was already smoldering on us. This water was a gift from heaven in hell.

Dante's scenes were happening around us, as people burning like torches ran from the houses to the streets, dying in terrible torment on the pavement of the road, grabbing the legs and clothes of the escaping, while all humane responses froze.

We kept running until the flames formed a colossal vortex in front of us that suddenly shot high up, carrying burning objects and people. We backed away, petrified—all who were within the range of this vortex were sucked in by monstrous air pressure.

I wanted to say something to Irmi, but the roar of raging fire, the explosions of incendiaries and anti-aircraft artillery, and the bombers approaching us stunned me completely. I moved my mouth without hearing myself.

A sudden breeze of cool air refreshed us for a moment—apparently, the vortex sucked in a stream of fresh air from somewhere outside. It lasted for only a second, but it gave tremendous relief to our choked-with-smoke-and-debris lungs. We moved on, although more slowly. Rescue could only be reached through escaping. Our clothing boiled on us again, and our footwear burned through the soles, which only forced us to flee faster. Irmi stumbled once and then twice; I felt her weakening, and I saw a deadly fear in her eyes.

A young woman sat on a suitcase by the wall of a burning house, holding a small child in her arms. I ran to her, wanting to pull her away from the wall of tongues of fire. I struggled to get her to her feet, stared into her face, and felt a shiver run through my back despite the heat—those eyes were blinded by fire and insanity. She pushed me vigorously and started singing a lullaby, rocking the baby in her arms. At one point, she collapsed on the ground, letting go of the dead baby—my help was no longer needed.

I felt dizzy. I was panting heavily and now could only drag along, tugging a barely alive Irmi. I clenched my teeth. A few more steps, a few more... Maybe around the corner of the street I will see an island in this sea of the raging element, maybe some help will come, some help...

And the raid continued, as still, new and upcoming squadrons threw thousands of tons of bombs to the untouched districts of the city, turning them into one huge bonfire. Rescue for Dresden was out of the question—if someone hurried from outside the city with help, they would have got stuck somewhere in the distant suburbs, not daring to venture into this volcano crater of certain doom.

At one point, I felt my shoes cling to some fluid. The cobblestone street had ended, and the asphalt which covered this part of the road had turned into a smoky, sticky black goo. Further movement became impossible as our shoes clung to the asphalt, and the sidewalks under the windows of burning and collapsing houses were inaccessible.

Initially, I was surprised at where all the people fleeing or dead on the streets had come from, but in the end, my semi-conscious awareness told me that the city, in addition to containing permanent residents, was full of refugees from the east and west of the Reich, who had taken refuge in Dresden from the impending fronts. No one will ever determine the true number of victims on this horrible night. Tens, perhaps hundreds of thousands of people must have died in collapsed shelters, burned or suffocated in the smoke and fire of the inferno.

I became indecisive as to which path ahead of me to take, as both were bad, both threatened with destruction, as the heat of the air continued to burn our hands and faces mercilessly. Our clothes were charring on us—these seconds decided life or death.

I walked down the middle of the street, barely pulling my shoes out of the liquid asphalt at this point, trudging an almost defeated Irmi. I took her in my arms and got to the intersection of the streets with incredible difficulty. I looked to the right, and suddenly, a miracle emerged—the road was dark inside, so it was only a few hundred paces to live, which gave me determination. Staggering under Irmi's weight, I walked like a drunk in the middle of the street, with my heart in my throat. Just a few more steps, yet...

I tripped over a body lying across the ground and collapsed like a log. Irmi fell out of my hands, the world whirled in my eyes, something hellishly hot burned my side, and I lost consciousness.

I opened my eyes, and instead of the expected angels in heaven, I saw an angel in human form. A young woman dressed as a nurse of the Red Cross had bandaged my burned side and arms.

"Does it hurt? It will pass, we will give you an injection, the pain will pass," she smiled sadly at me.

"Irmi, where's Irmi?" I whispered.

"Say thank you to God that you survived yourself, boy," she shook her head. "You were extremely lucky. Two people from the fire brigade saw you fall a few dozen steps from the fire-free zone. You were still breathing, so they carried you out."

"And the girl?" I asked hopefully.

"*Tōt* (Dead)."

After a short pause, the nurse continued, "There was no need to take her out of the fire. She was already dead; we save the living."

So she died quietly in my arms, without complaint, and I didn't even notice. It was hard to believe it. I got up with a struggle; I wanted to look for her—maybe she is still alive—but the firefighters forcefully stopped me.

The second bombing raid after midnight completed the work of destruction. The great, beautiful city, the capital of Saxony, ceased to exist. Only settlements on the outskirts survived, where loose buildings inhibited the spread of fire.

It was only after two days, when the firefighters extinguished the flames and the heat cooled down, that the rescue teams could enter downtown. There was no one to save. They picked up dead bodies in the streets and laid wreaths on the rubble of collapsed and burnt houses.

Some strangers took care of me in a cottage in a distant suburb, and they fed and comforted me. On the second and third day after the bombing, I wandered the streets of the suburbs and focused on the wagons, full of bodies from the road that were being taken to mass graves. I believed that I would see a green, plaid skirt and a blond head in this mass of corpses. I wanted to see her, touch her, say goodbye—unfortunately in vain.

Carters completing the ungrateful work recognized me as I looked into the carts several times.

One of them, an older gray-haired man, finally asked: "Who are you looking for, boy? Family or maybe your girlfriend?"

And when I answered, "I'm looking for my Irmi, a tall, pretty blonde," he just nodded and sighed.

"We took thousands of blondes to our brothers' graves."

I continued my search persistently until the last day that the final carts with bodies arrived, and when this sad procession ended, I wandered to the city, or to what was left of the city. However, admission was still strictly forbidden; under no circumstances could one enter, and from time to time, explosions testified that the city's hecatomb was not over yet. It was unclear whether delayed-ignition bombs had exploded or if sappers had accidentally blown up faulty explosives.

After several days, the posts were finally taken down—you could enter the city. I wandered in a sea of ruins hoping that a miracle might happen and I would unexpectedly see the one I was looking for so eagerly. Hundreds or maybe thousands of people were looking for their loved ones about the streets covered with debris, topped with wreaths.

I returned deeply tired, my benefactors gave me something to eat, and they tactfully asked if I had any news or found anything. Then the hostess changed my dressings, after which I went to bed and fell into a restless sleep.

In my dreams, I saw Irmi, as I remembered her: a charming, smiling, pale blonde with whom I sat on the inviting Oder River on warm summer evenings. Holding hands, we looked at the rapid current of the river and talked about what people in love talk about—the future. The war was inevitably approaching us, and Irmi told us how we would go to Rosenheim in Bavaria, how we would get married, how we would live in a house from which the snow-capped peaks of the Alps could be seen in the distance.

"But I am Polish, and you are German," I once interrupted her daydreaming. "Between us, there is a massive void. You know that if someone found out and reported us, we would both regret it bitterly."

"But I love you, Gustl (my second name was Augustine, hence this diminutive), and I am not afraid of any rules. My father said that all of this nationalism is idiotic—no one can forbid me to love you."

I knew that, but still, I only arranged to meet her in the evenings when hostile eyes could not see us.

* * *

This whole story began on an evening in the summer of 1944. I worked as a laborer at the Hirschberg chemical plant when one day my boss named Bruno, a handless German, told me: "Tomorrow morning the whole assembly, in the yard of the factory, will go somewhere to dig trenches at seven in the morning. Do not be late."

I left work cheerful as a bird—so tomorrow I would be riding into the unknown. I was fed up with this smelly factory. Nightly alarms and then working on the boilers, poor food, and no entertainment whatsoever—after each shift I had had enough and only dreamed of eating more and getting enough sleep, which was rarely possible. Set on a hill several hundred meters away from our barracks, the battalion of heavy anti-aircraft artillery defense often opened fire as soon as bomber engines thundered in the sky, and there were more and more of them every day. Apparently, some bombing route led above our heads because often Superfortress squadrons flew to the south or southeast. I couldn't hide my joy that I would leave this unpleasant everyday life and go somewhere that might be different. It couldn't be worse than here.

The train stopped at the station in a small town on the River Oder. We got off efficiently, dozens of young ragamuffins, instinctively peeking at the sky and alerting our ears. There was peace and quiet—a real idyll after the gloomy past. An elderly German soldier, who picked us up from the train, walked us through the streets of a quiet, charming town. Located on the high west bank of the Oder, it had an iron lace road bridge that connected the city to the other, lower bank.

We were accommodated in a few houses of the town, and when we got dinner from the military kitchen, I thought that we had at least reached the vestibule of paradise. The work was also light and pleasant. I was assigned along with three other boys to a group of German girls. We cut branches from bushes in the coastal forest, which "our" girls entwined for fascine in trenches.

Beautiful and serene was the summer, while somewhere in the east and west, the fronts thundered—the Reich was crackling under the impact of giant bombing raids, yet here on the Oder, there was silence, peace, as if there was no war in the world. Having laid a supply of branches, I lay on a sunny spot in the forest and took a nap, sweetly lulled by the noise of the river and the buzzing of insects. This calm did not last long, however; there was an attack from the least expected side—on the part of the girls.

"Have you had enough sleep, Gustl?" sweet redhead, blonde or brunette deity asked me. "What time is it?"

Irritated, I looked at my left wrist, and then the right hand; I did not even dare to dream about having a watch, so I finally stuck a stick into the ground and carefully examined the sun, the shadow of it. Then I stated solemnly: "Half-past three, nice lady."

Astonished, the group of girls asked me where this skill came from.

I seriously answered: "No watches are needed in Ukraine. Everyone walks with a stick and always knows what time it is."

"And when the day is overcast?" they asked slyly.

"In our place, there is always sunshine," I declared.

"And at night?"

"That's what the roosters are for. There are several in every home."

The girls laughed out loud. The international company grew more and more alive.

My work colleagues (who were Poles, Czechs, and Serbs), along with more and more German women, came to my bonfire, which I started lighting somewhere on the riverside. Someone told jokes, and here I saw how silly and fragile all of the bans and barriers of Nazism and nationalism truly were.

A particularly frequent guest by my fire was Irmi, a slim, shapely blonde who spent every spare moment in my company. She told me about her life in distant Bavaria, about working in the chemical laboratory of a factory in Leverkusen, about her brother who fell on the Eastern Front, and about her parents, who lived in a small town at the foot of the Alps.

Once, sitting by the fire next to me, she took my hand, gazed into my eyes, and announced briefly: "Gustl, I love you. You must be my husband."

I looked at her in amazement. Does she really mean it? Raised on *The Trilogy* (a novel series by Henryk Sienkiewicz), where the man long sought the girl's favor, I felt like these words had hit me with a stick to the head—I couldn't recover for a long time.

I was attracted to Irmi; she was pretty, shapely, graceful like a deer and a light blonde—I liked this type of beauty, but a few days passed before I came to my senses. We began to meet not only at work, but also in the beer hall and in the park, one of such meetings I still remember today.

It was a dark, starless, temperate evening. I was sitting in the park on a bench with Irmi, embracing her tenderly, when a few lads with *Hitlerjugend*[40] uniforms, armed with rifles, shone flashlights in our

---

40 *The Nazi youth organization*

eyes. I instantly became numb, and Irmi squeezed my hand—we could pay dearly for such a meeting. Escaping was out of the question. I put everything on one card and boldly looked the boys in the face. Fortunately, I did not have a diamond with the letter P on my sweatshirt.[41] In spite, I never wore the symbol—I felt like a dog who had to wear a badge around his neck, and it usually didn't seem to be a problem. This time it also served me well. Once again, the young Nazis looked at us closely, and without seeing fear in us, they even began to joke.

One patted my shoulder and said: "*Na Deutschland Zukunft* (The future of Germany)."

They laughed loudly and disappeared into the darkness. We were silent for a long moment.

I felt my fear slowly evaporate, and finally, Irmi murmured: "Idiots."

Summer was coming to an end, and we felt that the day of separation was not far away. Some of our girls left in mid-September, while the rest, including Irmi, left at the beginning of October. Departing, she gave me her parents' address and promised that she would come for me. I felt a strange emptiness in my heart for several days, but the increasingly hard work, digging trenches and building fortifications, left me little time for longing. In the evening, half-dead from fatigue, I crumbled on my bunk and fell asleep immediately.

Initially, letters from Irmi came regularly, but then as the war situation deteriorated in Germany, there were increasing breaks in between, although every letter was still cordial and affectionate.

Around Christmas, the frosts gripped, so forging the frozen ground was becoming a heavier and more exhausting task. We crossed the river bridge and built fortifications on the other bank of the Oder, where the Germans planned to maintain the bridgehead for future offensive activities. In mid-January, snowstorms came, and work in the open fields became torture.

The road from the east began to pull carts of refugees. At first, somewhere from afar, then from Poznań, and closer and closer. The coaches rode in the raging snowstorms along a four-lane highway full of people and belongings. Whenever wagons broke, the refugees threw

---

41 *The "P" badge was a Nazi symbol used to detonate forced Polish laborers*

them, including their belongings, down into the ditch. Finally, when German tanks began to drive along the road, they unceremoniously made their way into the crowd of scared civilians.

The traffic on the road became more and more chaotic and hectic, and at noon one day, when the distant rumble of cannons in the east began to intensify, the route became hell. The stronger people would push to the bridge, trampling and shoving the others to the side. We threw our tools and ran to a boat hidden in the coastal brushwood. The river was already partly frozen, but I had gotten familiar with this section during these six months, and the crossing was short. We traveled to the high bank and glanced behind: in the distance, we could spot Soviet tanks trampling unfortunate refugees, and in the afternoon, the right bank was already in the hands of the Russians. The first cannon shells began to fall on the town, and the fires spilled a wide, bloody glow in the gray winter sky.

THE FLOODS REACH GERMANY, EARLY 1945

Through 1944, the Soviet eastern offensive continued to rip into German-occupied territory, and the Finnish signed an armistice with Russia. On the sixth of June (D-Day), the Americans, Canadians, and the British Allies launched the invasion of Normandy, and two weeks later, Stalin launched Operation Bagration to great success. By the end of the year, the fronts had reached the borders of Germany. The Nazis surmounted one last offensive in the Ardennes, known as the Battle of the Bulge, to no avail. By early February, a spearhead of the front stood on the Oder, only forty miles from Berlin.

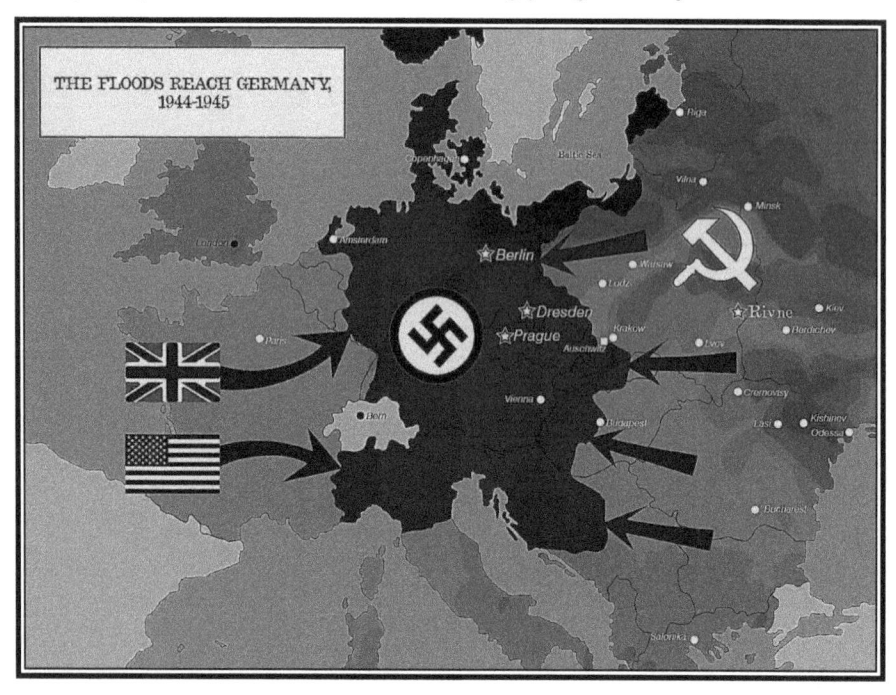

Note: Western Allied symbols and arrows do not necessarily show the exact location of each country's troops or direct goals. Also, be aware that it was not only the Americans and British fighting the Germans in the western theater.

The town was in the direct range of Soviet artillery, so our quarters were moved to a suburban village, and this time I found the worst possible occupation, repairing trenches damaged by artillery shells.

The fighting on the Oder line intensified, and artillery from the right bank destroyed bunkers and trenches made in such a vain effort. After combat, we workers were called down under sniper fire to repair the damage—the everyday game with death continued until the arrival of Irmi...

* * *

For another few days, I wandered around the destroyed city. I had not been to Dresden before, but after what was left, I knew that it had been a magnificent place. One time, I arrived at the banks of the River Elbe. The remains of the royal palaces and the famous Zwinger lay in pieces, but even the debris testified to the size and beauty of these buildings. Hundreds of years of work by artists and builders had gone to waste in one single night.

Every morning, a new hope told me to go to this sea of ruins. I searched, waited for a miracle, but it did not happen. My great love had been lost in a conflagration of the great, merciless, total war.

My wounds healed quickly, and I was increasingly thinking about what to do next. Going back to Hirschberg didn't make sense. Was I to push towards the front that was approaching the heart of Germany? Staying in Dresden was also impossible: my benefactors were polite and gentle, but they reminded me often that I was a burden to them.

The days were flowing by, and I still couldn't decide which way to go. Finally, the idea came to me to travel to Prague. I even had close relatives there, and the railways were still functional, but traveling by train without any documents worried me. Absolute war law, or rather lawlessness, allowed a death penalty for even the slightest offense. Even with such risks, there was a chance to make it—how could I use it?

— 15 —
Victory Day

A joyful spring day found me in the Czech village of Sýkořice, about forty kilometers west of Prague. This wonderful day almost ended in a tragedy, however.

In 1945, on the night of February 13-14, I managed to make it through the Allies' relentless bombings of Dresden. I saved my skin, but it was severely burned and scarred, which allowed me to have a few weeks of rest in the suburbs—but what to do next? Going back to the factory where I worked as a forced laborer made no sense, as the front stood on the Oder River, and the city was under siege by the Soviet Army. I couldn't live with the Germans who were sheltering me, either. Any controlling authorities could pick me up and force me to work, removing rubble from the city and burying the killed. There was no other way than to run—you had to escape before the Nazi government recovered from the shock of the great raid. I decided to go to the "Protectorate" (during the war, that is what they called the Czech Republic), as I had cousins in Prague and near Beroun.

At this moment, I have to move back a while in time and space. In 1914, the tsarist authorities deported all foreigners from the near-frontal territories of Eastern Prussia to Siberia. My mother's sister, Tekla, found herself there with her husband, a Pole. The husband soon died, and then the young widow, who had a child, married a Czech who came to Siberia as a prisoner of war of the Austro-Hungarian Army. After the First World War, they and their children returned to Czechoslovakia. The elders stayed in the countryside, and their two daughters got married and lived in Prague.

I remembered the names of those people in Prague and their addresses there, so I decided to travel to them. Trains between Dresden and Prague ran; however, I didn't have any documents, which could have ended badly. Instead, I counted on my bandaged head, hands, and charred face. Everyone was still under shock from the terrible bombings that had wiped the city off the face of the earth.

On the train, German gendarmerie patrols kept passing by, but apparently, my bandages were a valid pass as nobody stopped me. Prague, a beautiful, big city on the Vltava River, was vibrant with normal life. The Allies bombed armament factories in many Czech towns, but not even a single bomb had fallen in Prague.

Without difficulty, I came across the address of my relatives. My cousins lived in a large Art Nouveau apartment house in the Smichov district, near the Vltava. They received me warmly and hospitably, although there was a problem: I could not live with them for long—one of my cousins was a policeman. On top of that, there was a requirement to register strangers who came from outside of the city, and I didn't have any identity documents. After a few days, under the excuse of "escorting a detainee," my cousin Antoni took me by train to the small town of Zbečno in the mountains, and from there it was only two kilometers on foot, across the pass, and we were at my aunt and uncle's place in Sikorzyce.

The area was similar to the Polish Bieszczady Mountains. My cousins' house stood near a steeply slanted hill by a ravine through which a stream flowed. The village was small and scattered over the steep slopes. It was an idyllic, angelic view during the war. Silence and tranquility prevailed, and the roosters crowed good night and good morning. Here you could forget about the fighting, and only sometimes, on clear days, you could notice the roaring engines of bomb expeditions that flew over Germany, high in the sky.

I registered with the local authorities as a refugee from Dresden. To the clerk's question of where I came from, I stated that I was born in Ukraine. I had finally received a registration certificate, along with food stamps and a work referral in the woodlands. Those were beautiful days. Together with several girls and boys, under forester supervision, we planted trees in the forest and counted the bomber squadrons flying in the sky in our free time. Europe was on fire, the fronts rumbled, millions of people were dying, yet here I was: surrounded by singing birds in the spring forest, planting trees, counting airborne planes, and admiring beautiful mountain views.

In the evenings, together with my uncle, I put my ear to the radio. You were only allowed to listen to the official broadcast, which unfortunately told very little truth—for listening to the radio signal of London on shorter waves, you could still pay with your head.

We knew that the war was coming to an end. The Allies broke the Siegfried line and were pushing deep into the Reich. The Soviet army had reached Berlin.

Like all happiness, this idyll did not last long.

When I had gotten back from work one evening, my Uncle turned on the radio and directed, "Listen!"

"This is Prague radio, this is Prague radio!" a voice sounded in the speaker. "An uprising has broken out. The Germans are trying to destroy our capital; hurry to help!"

This was repeated every now and again in several languages: Czech, Russian, and English. The quiet village was suddenly boiling. Everyone was hurrying to the square in front of the local school. Some men spoke briefly of what was said on the radio.

The recruitment process was concise—nobody was ordered to undress or had their teeth examined.

"Women and children to the right, men to the left," a man ordered.

Of the group of men, the elderly were asked to leave. After that, there were only twenty people left, myself included. Suddenly and unexpectedly, I had become a soldier. When you get among the crows, you have to crow like them, I thought, at the very end of the war. A Pole as a Ukrainian, I had become a Czech insurgent. Knowing the Czechs' dislike of Poles in Zaolzie, I didn't want to reveal my true nationality.

In the school hall, we were given weapons: brand-new Mauser rifles, not yet shot, with only ten bullets in the pocket. It was almost a useless gun. The rifles had no ejection springs (a part that automatically ejects an empty core, in place of which a new one jumps); therefore it was necessary after each shot to turn the rifle upside down, throw away the thimble, insert a new cartridge, shoot and repeat. This gun had the medieval efficiency of a musket, but it was still a weapon.

A train was waiting for us at the station in Zbečno. On the way, the commander taught us how to use the Mausers. The train stopped at every station, where new warriors boarded. We drove like this all night. Dawn was already brightening the sky when the train halted at a small station near Prague. In the distance, you could spy the towers of the city.

Westwards towards the downtown, you could hear the shooting of hand weapons and machine guns, as well as more impactful explosions from time to time. Fighting continued in the city, and houses were smoking. Getting closer to the center of the action, we crept along the streets. The volume of explosions and shootings increased, and reflexively we pulled our heads into our arms when bullets appeared in the air close by. We entered a large empty apartment house near the Charles Bridge, over the Vltava River. The Germans attempted to keep the main roads, railways, and leading bridges through Prague in their hands, as Wehrmacht troops from the east retreated to the south.

The insurgents had conquered the downtown and were attempting to block communication routes. Our task was to paralyze German movements on the bridge. Several times soldiers approached it, but they retreated under a barrage of bullets.

The situation became direr. Ten bullets are only ten shots—by the evening, I had only two cartridges left in my pocket. In the dark, the shooting stopped, the area around became eerily quiet, and we anxiously waited for the morning. What will it bring? There was news that Berlin had fallen and that the Americans and Russians had already met on the Elbe, but here on the Vltava, it was anything but cheerful—hell could break loose at any moment.

At dawn, a long freight train full of troops and equipment rolled over the Vyšehrad Railway Bridge, three kilometers from the Charles Bridge. Someone spotted, through binoculars, German uniforms. Our faces sulked; we were expecting the worst.

Unexpectedly, a furious shootout broke out from the central station. Windows trembled from the explosions of hand grenades.

"What the hell is going on there? Who's beating who?" we asked, stunned.

Soon we were ordered: "Everyone to the downtown!"

We were moving like geese in a row by the walls, passing the bodies of German soldiers. The news soon came: the Russian division in service of Hitler, under the command of Andrey Vlasov,[42] had made it to the central station by train and unexpectedly turned on the Germans. This turn of events was incomprehensible. The unanticipated help reversed the fate of the uprising and perhaps saved the city. Surprised by the sudden attack and encaptured Germany, the remaining soldiers hurriedly began to leave Prague.

Joy was unanimous. There was no end to the cheers and shouts—until someone present brought a message: the radio stated that the Soviet tanks were only several kilometers from Prague. The news hit our new allies like lightning; in a flash, they unloaded the equipment from the wagons, and a moment later, they were gone.[43] The square in front of the station became empty.

"What shall we do?" our commander wondered. He then glanced around and at last waved his hand, giving the command: "Well, the war is over. Let's go home."

There were several locomotives and trailing wagons at the station. At the order of our commander, the railwaymen arranged the carriages, and the train set off to Beroun. As we loaded the train, our lips whistled the tunes of victory.

In the evening, already in Sýkořice, we met again with our Russian friends from Prague under the command of Andrey Vlasov. They found a full tank of spirits at Zbawcza station and drank it all night. At dawn, the whole unit went west towards Pilsen, not far from the German border.

After several social and noisy days, it once again became quiet in the village. The war was finished, and people split up to continue their duties. The group of soldiers and I were accommodated at the school.

---

42 *Andrey Vlasov (b. Sept. 1901, d. Aug. 1946) was a Red Army general, who was captured at the siege of Leningrad. He defected to Nazi Germany, and became the leader of the Russian Liberation Army, until the end of the war, when he ordered his men to turn on the Germans during the Prague uprising of May 1945...*

43 *...Andrey Vlasov knew that if they were to come in contact with the Russians, they would be captured and imprisoned for their collaboration with the Nazis. His squadron attempted to escape to the Western Front, where they would expect better treatment from the British and American Allies, but on the way they were still captured by unforgiving Soviet forces.*

In the yard, on a high mast, a white-red-and-blue-wedged flag of free Czechoslovakia flapped in the air. In front of the school gate, with a rifle on his shoulder, stood our sentry, Honsa. Someone brought several cases of good beer from Pilsen and as we were drinking, we commented on the events of the previous days.

It was almost noon. The day was quiet and clear, and time passed merrily as we were chatting and gulping beer, when abruptly, one of my colleagues looked out the window, cursed an ugly word, and shouted, "*Nemce* (Germans)."

We rushed to the windows. Along a winding mountain road that led from Prague was a convoy of trucks, full of soldiers, armed to the teeth. There wasn't a moment to lose. We forgot about our weapons and rushed through the fence like rabbits into a field. Fortunately, the rye was high. Hidden there, we gawked at what was happening in the village.

The convoy of vehicles slipped around the bend of the roadway and stood in front of the school. One soldier jumped off from the first truck, stepped towards our guard, took the rifle from his shoulder, threw it onto the car, and then the whole convoy moved on. A short time after reaching the spiral road, they disappeared from our view.

Without looking into each other's eyes, we began to descend to the front of the school. Our sentry, Honsa, stood as pale as a corpse and did not answer any questions. Only a juicy slap on the cheek brought him back to consciousness. We returned to the beer, but strangely, we suddenly lost taste, and we sat, feeling bitter.

A boy came with a message that the Germans had abandoned a truck on the spiral road. This unloaded our gloomy mood. We ran with weapons in hand to the indicated place. Left on the side, there was a broken truck full of military goods. As a "souvenir," I took several sets of soldiers' underwear, which served me well through the poor post-war years.

Today, I'm a bit ashamed to admit that on Victory Day, which was on May 9, 1945, we had disgracefully run away. On the other hand, what chance did we have? A dozen or so boys armed with single-shot rifles against a frontal battalion armed with machine guns. They would shoot us like ducks and let the village smoke. As you can see from this, you can have different memories of Victory Day.

Over the evening, Soviet tanks rolled into the village.

PART III

The Post-War Situation

— 16 —
The Long Return

Victory Day in Sýkořice had passed. Residents returned to their duties. Nothing here is left for me, I thought—and said goodbye to my aunt and Uncle Zaspal. I made my way to the railway station in Zbeczek and hopped on the first train that arrived.

I got off at the large train station where the German inscription "Pilsen" was already blurred with paint—someone had underlined the Czech name "Pilsno" on the right. On the streets, humming jeeps and military trucks filled the roads with substantial white stars on the doors and hoods. Groups of adolescents, joyous and enlivened, skipped along the pavements. Here, Victory Day was only now celebrated, and the euphoria of freedom hung in the air. Young couples were hugging and kissing. There were American soldiers in the crowd, cheering and saluting. They gave out cigarettes to the right and left, which I did not like (I did not smoke), but to be honest, it was difficult to refuse: the white and black soldiers' enthusiasm and laughing mouths were very captivating. They were glad that they had survived the front, that the nightmare of the cold and hungry war years had passed.

These were beautiful days—of spring, freedom, and youth. Magnolias bloomed in the square, and their sight and smell, and the atmosphere of those times have long been remembered.

Several days passed. I slept like many others on the bench in the station waiting room, and there was time to think about what to do next. French, Italians, Dutch, and other residents of Western Europe were slowly leaving the hospitable city. Like me, other Russians, Ukrainians, and Poles did not know what to do with each other, where to go—to the east or to the west? There was news that the Americans would soon retreat. The matter of our return was becoming ever more urgent.

At the train station, we created several Polish discussion clubs. Some said to go back, others said to stay, and the third group suggested we withdraw with the Americans, who were already packing their bags for departure. According to the post-war declarations, the entire territory of Czechoslovakia was to be handed over to the Soviets, so time was pressing. The Americans and English were deploying the Polish Home Army, and some of the Poles were stating that for the soldiers who would complete service in those military units, the door into the far West would be open. Going back to the motherland, which had been destroyed by war, famine, lawlessness, and worst of all, the Soviet governing—which I had seen from the worst side—was the argument to stay in Czechoslovakia.

Stay, or go back? I turned all night on the hard station bench. Longing for my homeland and my mother became more painful and troublesome. After a sleepless night, in the morning, I made up my mind—I'm going back! What will be will be. Yes, I shall go back, but where to? To Wołyń? Where so many Poles were tortured and killed at the hands of Ukrainian nationalists?

I was perplexed and tormented, but the thought of not returning did not leave me in peace, and finally, I stated firmly to my company from the station waiting room: "I'm going back, everyone!"

"I will go with you," said Benek Bednarski from Bielsk Podlaski.

A silence fell and lasted a long moment. Some looked at us as traitors, others as heroes.

One of the opponents came up to me, put a pistol in my pocket, and whispered: "It might be useful to you. There are twenty-five bullets in the spare magazine."

A second man put twenty American dollars in my pocket.

I'm going back, but how? There were several wagons at the station, yet they were without steam locomotives. Benek learned from a Czech railwayman that one of the trains was voyaging to the east. We said goodbye to the company from the station and rushed to the wagons. Standing on one of the sidetracks was an old-type passenger car with a dozen open coal wagons. We both jumped into the first compartment in the passenger coach, threw backpacks on the luggage racks, and glanced at each other. The same thought suddenly occurred to both of us: what shall we do? What do we eat? How long will this journey take?

We had a loaf of bread and several cubes of sugar together. Here fate came to our aid. Near us, by the loading ramps, was a series of long American trucks unloaded with all sorts of goods. I went exploring, and the property was guarded only by an African-American soldier who slept peacefully, snoring like a horse in the cab of the first truck, leaning on the door. I hopped onto one of them. It was loaded to the brim with wooden boxes with "corned beef" inscriptions in English. I already knew what it meant, so I hijacked one of the boxes and sneaked to our wagon. Benek also brought one case of cans, which, to our surprise, turned out to be sweet condensed peaches. We wanted to replenish our supply once more, but unfortunately, the other Americans arrived, and the convoy went on its way.

The wagon jerked again and again. New carts were attached; this time, they were open platforms. Our carriages filled up with people, and when space ran out, they slowly began to fill up the coal wagons and finally the open platforms.

We were waiting impatiently for departure. During this time, someone brought news that the Soviets were occupying the city. This was confirmed shortly afterward by the rumble of tank tracks on the cobblestone of the city's main street. Soon, the first "watchmen" (Soviet soldiers who stole watches from anyone they encountered) appeared. We didn't have watches, so we missed out on the pleasure of an encounter with them.

The train stood still all evening and night and finally departed early in the morning. Our route was unknown. All we knew was that we were traveling through the Czech territory. Finally, when more and more damages and traces of fighting could be seen, we knew we were going through Germany. The train finally stopped at a siding in… Dresden.

The steam engine was disconnected, which meant that we would have a long break before traveling further. Passengers disembarked and set off in search of food. I went too. The beautiful old city, the capital of Saxony, was still in ruins. I'd survived the most terrible moments of my life here, and I'd lost my beloved girlfriend. Now again, I was getting lost in a sea of ruins that was full of impoverished people.

I understandably didn't get any bread. I came back inhumanly exhausted, opened up a tin of peaches, ate half of its contents, wrapped myself up in a blanket, lay down on my bench, and fell asleep.

I woke up the following morning. The train supposedly rushed all night, yet when it finally stopped, I rubbed my eyes in amazement: the board with the name of the station—Pirna—was only a dozen or so kilometers east of Dresden.

"To hell with that," I cursed like a shoemaker.

At this pace, the trip to my homeland would take a month. I wasn't wrong—it lasted over five weeks.

The locomotive was detached, so there was a long stop again. All company of the train spilled onto the tracks. It was a very international group—Poles, Russians, Ukrainians, Latvians, and Lithuanians, and many Germans returning to Silesia, Pomerania, and East Prussia.

The evening had come. There was not a single steam locomotive at the station, so we anticipated a long break in our travels. At dusk, dozens of fires lit up around the train as everyone attempted to bake something to eat. In a few days, most had consumed all of their supplies, and an unsatisfying, albeit likely familiar feeling crept into everyone's stomach. Only Benek and I felt secure that there was enough for us for a long time—we looked at our boxes like treasure.

People began to gather around the bonfires, each a different nationality, so I joined the Polish group. Most of the participants of this feast under the stars were my peers or men only slightly older than me. As a result of all the stories I overheard, my head began to ache. Each of the narrators was of the highest class Casanova—their conquests were in the tens and hundreds. I felt like an ashamed orphan. I had returned from this hell of war, almost eighteen years old, as innocent as a lamb, which I naturally did not admit. All of my love adventures came down to delicate caresses, at most kisses. Raised on Sienkiewicz, I saw love only as a great and wonderful feeling you only experience once in your life. I considered ordinary physical love as something for an unworthy man. Now, under the influence of these stories, I felt a sudden hunger for lust, this simple physical encounter of male and female. An opportunity to meet this other side of love came soon.

The next day, a young German woman came to me with a request. Her older sister had a cold, a high fever, and further journey on the platform under the open sky threatened her life. After a brief consultation with my traveling companion, we agreed to accommodate them. We decided that we would now rest on the shelves, and they would sleep on the benches. The girls moved in immediately. The repeated words of "there are no women in our hut" came to an end.

The older one was indeed very sick, and we could not help her much; we only fed her with aspirin, which I had obtained an ample supply of. After a few days, she recovered, and we even accepted them at the table, as we still had the collection of cans while they had nothing and were hungry. It became happier in our hut on wheels, but the next stop, unfortunately, promised to be long. Through the main track were trains running east, loaded with troops, military equipment, artillery, and tanks.

"What the hell?" we were puzzled. "Are the Russians running away or what?"

In transport, word spread about a third world war, this time between the Soviet Union and Western Allies—but why would the trains rush to the east? We hadn't seen any of the air force…

The next day around noon, a locomotive was put in place, and transport started. Several hours of traveling, with short breaks, and then another long stop halted our journey. This time we reached Meissen, still only a couple dozen kilometers or so northwest from Dresden. Near the tracks, there was a tall factory chimney and buildings. Soon, someone broke into the factory and brought joyful news—there is flour! Whole sacks of flour. I ran as fast as I could. There were tall, evenly arranged stacks of bags with white, coarse powder in the factory warehouse. I took a little bit of this powder in my fingers; sniffing it, a thought suddenly dawned in my mind—Meissen, Meissen? This is a porcelain factory, and the white powder is kaolin, clay for its production.

"Don't take it! It's clay!" I yelled, but no one listened to me.

They were tearing the sacks and powder and distributing it into whatever they could—saucepans, sacks, or bags.

Soon, bonfires burned along the train. Noodles were cooked, pies were baked. I also tried these specialties. It was like chewing gum, tasteless and odorless. I spat it all out, although others ate it as if it had great flavor. On the following day, everyone was twisted with stomach aches.

Our travel mates, younger Krystyna and older Irmgard, continued to be nourished on our "bread" (more precisely, the canned goods), and it turned out that they were attractive and charming girls. As usual between young people, the conversation went down on an eternal topic—love. I was ashamed to admit I still didn't know the taste of physical love. Krystyna's eyes widened.

"You still haven't had a girlfriend?" she asked, surprised.

I blushed like a virgin, which I, in fact, was.

"Well, I see that I have to be your teacher," she added with a mocking smile. "I promise you that."

Our journey dragged on forever. The train went in all possible directions through the terribly destroyed Reich. It was difficult to spot an undamaged house. People were wandering among the ruins and ashes. Stations were overloaded with burnt-down wagons and steam engines. Roads were full of damaged, empty horse carts, cars, and tanks. There were signs of fierce fighting and fresh graves at every step. Germany had paid a terrible price for its dreams of power.

The central railways were still occupied by military transports rushing east. Our train was either put aside somewhere or directed to a free sideline at every stop.

At the end of May, we arrived in Magdeburg. The stop in the destroyed and starved city lasted twenty-four hours. Famine harassed the passengers on our ghost train. They searched for last year's mounds in the hope of finding forgotten potatoes and searched the basements of decimated homes. It didn't help much. At every stop, the corpses of children and elderly people who could not stand the hunger and hardships of the long journey under the open sky were laid next to the tracks.

At this point, I reduced food rations for both of us and the girls. Our canned food supply would be enough for a few weeks, although sometimes we were approached by people dying from hunger, who were difficult to refuse. The plague of Soviet soldiers, who walked along the train and innocently asked about the time, visited often. Whoever looked at his watch and responded said goodbye to it forever. One of the Red

Army soldiers, when asked by me about how many wristwatches he had, rolled up his sleeve, and then the other. On his hands, from the wrists to the armpits, dozens of them were pinned. Wow, I thought, this one will have enough "time" for the rest of his life.

Nightly visits of uniformed bandits were worse than those of watchmen. They entered the wagons, plundered everything, and took young women with them for a known purpose. We did not miss such a visit either. At dawn, during a stop at the siding of a small station near Berlin, someone banged on the wagon door.

It opened, and promptly a man peered into the compartment and roared: "Women!"

The girls were sleeping on the seats. Benek was high on the luggage shelf, and I was on the floor.

"*Zhenshchiny vykhodyat!* (Women get out!)" The order was given.

I saw in front of me the mouths of two soldiers, their odors like that of a distillery.

"*Zhenshchiny vykhodyat!*" The one who stood at the door screamed for the second time.

"*Net, oni nikuda ne denutsya* (No, they are not going anywhere)," I said firmly, raising my head.

"*Eto nashi zheny; nikto nikuda ne idet* (These are our wives; no one goes anywhere)." My Russian came in handy here.

Both Red Army soldiers opened their mouths in amazement.

"*A vy kto?* (Who are you?)" The second one asked.

"*My Polyaki* (We are Poles)," I replied.

There was a moment of silence. On the top shelf Benek moved, I heard the click of a pistol, and I, too, imperceptibly under the blanket, took the handle of the Mauser pistol and pushed the fuse away with my thumb. A shooting was potentially hanging in the air. However, the word "wives" seemed to work on them. We had the advantage over them in that they had their PPSh-41 submachine gun strapped on their chests, while we had hidden pistols, already primed to fire—one step ahead of them. But if there are more Russians nearby? Fortunately, the conflict ended peacefully.

"*Polyaki, Polyaki, oni nashi soyuzniki* (Poles, Poles, they are our allies)," said the closer one.

"*Nu, trakhni ikh* (Well, fuck them)," he swore and waved in a dismissive gesture.

"*Zdes' dlya nas nichego net* (Nothing here for us)," he said, and they went along the wagons.

There was a deep silence, and finally, one of the girls whispered in German: "*Was ist denn los?* (What happened?)"

I looked at her with a smile and murmured: "*Dein Schicksal wäre miserabel, wenn du ihre Pfoten beendest* (Your destiny would be miserable if you ended up in their paws)." We promoted you to our wives, and that saved you from rape."

"And this?" Krystyna asked, pointing at the gun in my hand, which I uncovered.

"Ah, that?" I put the gun under my blanket. "Just in case we need it," I added.

After this moment of the highest tension, our conversation became more lively. "But you are the loser, Zbyszek," Benek's bass voice from the top shelf sounded. "You wanted to shoot the Russians for the German girls?"

"Well, you see, this is how it turned out, as I was brought up in such a way that I can't stand it when someone vulnerable is being mistreated—and what would you do in the event of a shootout?" I asked.

"I'd shoot a full magazine and run," he replied.

"So you see, we're both the same," I stated.

"Our" girls gazed at us with admiration. In their eyes, two young boys grew to the rank of heroes, while for us, it was only an adventure during the times of travels. And this dragged on unforgivingly; another few kilometers drive, and we had to stop again. In addition to hunger and unwanted guests, one more plague arrived: uninvited hair lice. We were constantly scratching. It was hard to sleep at night. Someone suggested that we shake our shirts and pants over a bonfire. It didn't help much; I only burned the sleeve of one of my two shirts. The girls attempted to wash our underwear every day, but soaking them in cold water without any soap had no effect.

The following day, we were again stuck on the railway siding of a small town southeast of Berlin. The railwaymen once again unhooked the steam engine, so we had to keep waiting. I walked with Krystyna to the town in the hope of getting a loaf of bread. It was empty and uninhabited. The apartments stood as if residents left them yesterday—sometimes pots were still on the stove. We went to one such abandoned apartment, located in a charming villa with a spacious garden.

Krystyna suddenly took my hand and dragged me onto the couch in the room. She undressed quickly and began to rip my clothes off. She hugged me with her body, and the world swirled before my eyes. Her cuddles, like iron hoops, gripped me and pleasured me as if a high voltage spark had flashed through my body. This first love rush, like a May storm, short and violent, stunned me.

When I returned to my normal self, I got up on shaky legs and whispered: "Come on, because the train will run away."

I walked beside her, daring not to look her in the eye, full of shame and suppressed fear. All my ideas about women from romantic literature fell like a house of cards—her passion and lust were like a lightning spark, seeking an outlet to earth.

I avoided her mocking smile in the compartment until the end of our journey, which was gradually approaching its conclusion. Around noon, another steam engine was replaced. We set off, and after an hour, the locomotive slowly entered the high wooden bridge over a wide river. It continued to move little by little, and on the other bank of the river, there was a border sign with white and red stripes, with a soldier wielding a rifle standing next to it, wearing a Polish uniform.

Someone then shouted: "He is a Polish soldier, this is Poland!"

What was strange was that the soldier did not have a crown on the eagle on his uniform, although that didn't bother us. After so many years of uncertainty—we were finally in Poland! There were sobs from several sides, my eyes were also wet, and a few tears dripped onto my chin.

A half-hour later and the train rolled onto the platform of a large train station. Someone had spotted a white and red flag on the roof of the town hall, an inscription on the boards with the name of the Sorau station—so is it Poland, or still Germany? When the steam engine was detached, I decided to check.

"Watch the suitcases," I told Benek. "I'll go see how it is here. Maybe I will get bread."

The town hall was not far from the station. I reached it in a few minutes and instantly was surrounded by some amicable young ladies glancing at me curiously.

"Are we in Germany or Poland?" I asked, embarrassed.

"It's Poland! Poland!" They called out in chorus.

"The border is on the Oder," added a plump blonde.

I asked for bread. "Bread, naturally, maybe mister, you are hungry; we have a delicious pea soup," they spoke one by one. In a moment, I was sitting over a plate of steaming pea soup with fresh, homemade bread in hand.

"God! What a delight!" After so many weeks of canned beef and sweet peaches.

The blonde was peeking at me curiously. She added another plate of pea soup and then invited me to her home for coffee.

"My name is Jadzia," she introduced herself. "I have a beautiful apartment. Maybe you will stay here, mister; so many flats are empty," she chattered sweetly, peering into my eyes.

"I'd love to stay, but I need to go home to Równe in Wołyń—my mother is waiting for me there. I will come to see you later," I said.

"In Równe? In Wołyń? It's beyond the Bug," she peered at me closely. "Don't go there—it's not Poland anymore—the Soviets took it away," she added with sorrow.

THE NEW POLISH AND EASTERN EUROPEAN BORDERS

At the Potsdam Conference of July-August 1945, the allied leaders of Britain (represented by Prime Minister Churchill), the USA (represented by President Truman), and the USSR (represented and led by Josef Stalin), met to settle the final borders of Europe. The map below showcases the new boundaries of Poland and the territory it annexed from, as well as ceded to, neighboring nations.

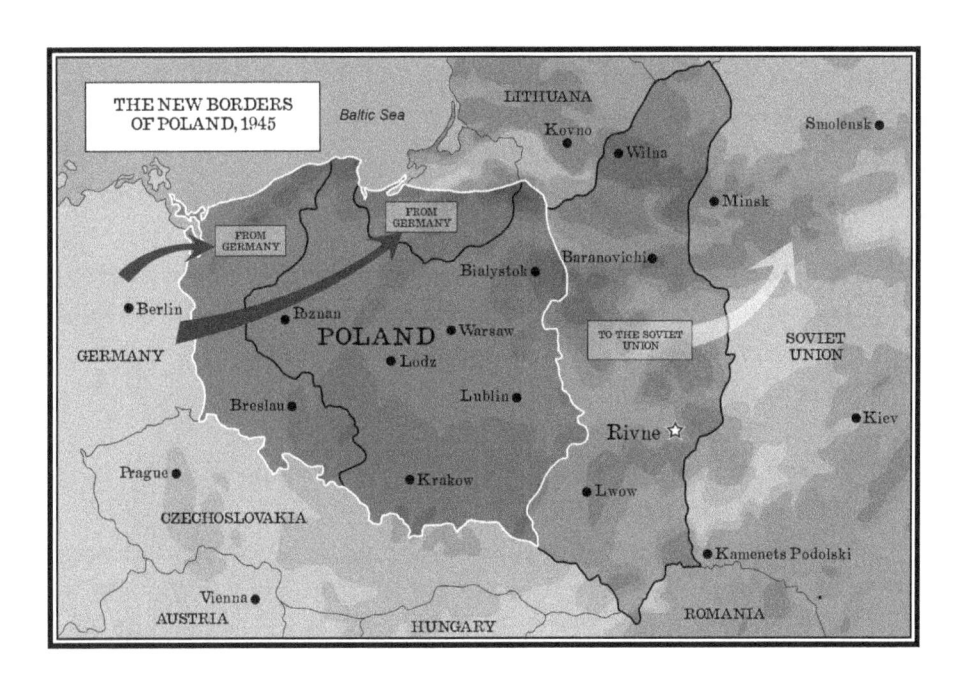

This message worked on me like a blow to the head. Równe, Wołyń, no longer ours? So I don't have a home anymore, no more motherland? I thought bitterly.

"Don't worry," she looked at me sympathetically. "Over there are only strangers. You have no reason to go back there. There is so much space here; half the city is empty." She urgently attempted to persuade me, "Please stay here, mister."

Jadzia poured me a cup of coffee, and some sweets also appeared. The atmosphere became more and more pleasant. The girl was getting closer and closer, and she put her arm around my neck and pulled me onto the bed. Luckily, my guardian angel saved me before sin because someone abruptly knocked on the door. Jadzia released from my neck, running to answer it, and I cooled down instantly. A whole cheerful company of young girls and men appeared through the door, and I recalled that my transport was at the station. I promised the amiable hostess that I would come back to her, said goodbye to the pleasant company, and rushed to the station.

An unpleasant surprise was waiting for me here. My train had left!

"It went half an hour ago," a railwayman in a Polish uniform—again without the crown—informed me.

"Where to?"

"Perhaps to Rawicz."

"And what about the steam engine that is standing here?"

"It also goes to Rawicz."

And indeed, the steam engine was going to Rawicz, but Russians operated it: for my request to get a ride with them, they told me to "get lost" in harsher words. I left their sight, came back, and quietly, from behind, climbed into a coal carriage and hid behind the heap. The locomotive soon started, and after three hours, it stopped at the station. I arrived at the perfect time. Benek—with my suitcase—and the girls all stood on the platform.

"You're lucky," he smiled with his whole mouth. "We're just saying goodbye. I'm going to Katowice, and the girls are waiting for the train to Koszalin."

Soon all of the transport company broke up. I was alone, and the evening was falling. Then I remembered the address that Jadzia, my new acquaintance, had given me. "Visit my family. My parents and younger sister will welcome you with open arms," she had assured me. And indeed, they actually received me with open arms. A sweet young lady opened the door for me, Jadzia's sister Marylka. The parents—a very kind, elderly couple—greeted me like an old friend and invited me to the table for dinner. The divine smell of fried eggs and bacon filled the air. I talked about their daughter and myself until late at night, and at one point, my head dropped onto the table. I was delicately woken up, and after a soothing bath in an actual tub, in clean pajamas, I lay down under fresh, fragrant, cool, linen bedding.

"What a delight!" I think the gods of Olympia do not experience such pleasure.

I rested for three days after the hardships of my travels in that hospitable Polish household. I enjoyed the atmosphere of that family, and Marylka's parents probably wouldn't have had anything against me becoming their son-in-law. This experience had turned the wild youngster from after the war to once again a well-behaved young fellow.

Marylka often smiled amicably at me. On the second day, I went with her for a walk through the streets of the city. I felt uncomfortable with myself—in a tattered suit next to a pretty girl wearing a colorful spring dress—but I had no other choice.

In the city, many Russian and Polish troops occupied the streets. As we passed next to a group of Polish soldiers, who were smoking joints and hiding alcohol in between newspapers at the corner of the road, a familiar borderland accent of their conversation reached my ears. I apologized to Marylka and approached them, asking politely where they came from. God! They were my compatriots from Wołyń; one from Zdołbunów, the other from Łuck, the third from Kostopol—so they were my former neighbors.

"I'm going there to find my mother. I am from Równe," I confessed openly.

The soldiers looked at me and smiled pityingly, then one of them told me: "You have nothing to go to there—it's not Poland anymore. Our families are leaving from there. The UPA is still crazy, and the Russians are having problems with them."

So that confirmed what I'd been told so far: the country's borders had been moved, so my homeland was no more. I didn't sleep all night. I rolled from side to side until I finally made a decision. In the morning, I told my lovely hosts that I was leaving that day. I had to find my mother. As an only child—it's my holy duty. Marylka was upset, but I comforted her, affirming I would write and come back. Over the evening, I said goodbye to the hosts.

Marylka escorted me to the station. I had decided to go to Warsaw. This time, I didn't wait long for the train, maybe an hour. Hissing with steam, in rolled the locomotive, followed by a long series of passenger carriages. So many people loaded the cars that you could not even stick in a needle. I walked around the train once, then again—there was no free place… except for on top of the wagons.

I climbed one roof and strapped myself to a ventilator with my belt. Soon the train set off. The night was beautiful; the full moon flooded a silver gleam on the passing landscape. It was a cold June night, so I wrapped my blanket tightly around myself. Not that it helped. I froze so substantially that when the train finally rolled into the central station in Warsaw at dawn, I was so numb from the cold that the luggage men took me for a mute who couldn't speak a word.

I spied diligently around the small waiting room of the station. The traffic of the crowd was heavy: people hurried with huge bundles in all directions.

In front of the station stood carts with horses, and their owners shouted, "To Praga! To Praga! To Praga!"

Since I was there, I decided to spend my time seeing Warsaw, the capital of Poland, which I had never visited before. I left the station and turned left onto a wide street named Jerozolimskie Avenue. Looking ahead, my breath was taken away. Ruins, ruins, ruins! Only here and there a surviving apartment building stood. In front of the Marszałkowska intersection, on the right, the Polonia hotel had survived, and on the opposite, a single house protruded. Otherwise, it was a sea of ruins. I was used to this view in Germany, and it seemed that I was expecting it not to make a significant impression on me. Nonetheless, here, this view hurt me like a terrible wound.

Though in front of me, deep down the broad avenue, there were some survivors on the right—the buildings of the National Museum, which miraculously still stood, as well as others further down by the fallen ironwork of the Poniatowski Bridge. I turned left into the thoroughfare of Nowy Świat. From the perspective of the street, only the remnants of burned houses still stood. In front of the devastated Holy Cross church, the statue of Christ carrying the cross lay face down on the ground. On Krakowskie Przedmieście, the only surviving wall of the Royal Castle also shone with emptiness, surrounded by scorched ruins. Zygmunt, fallen with his column, stared into the sky with lifeless eyes.

The fiercest fury of destruction was visible in the Old Town, where there were almost no ruins, as the buildings were severely demolished with explosions enough times that it turned them into piles of clay.

I looked at it all with wide, open eyes. God! What had happened here, I could only imagine.[44] I simply stood and stared, gaping. After a long moment, I noticed a young girl trudging around, appearing disorientated.

I awoke from my trance, approached her, and asked: "What are you looking for, madame?"

She glared at me without a word, and in her eyes I could detect insanity. I'd seen a lot, but this terrible cemetery—the Old Town—and this girl shocked me deeply. I was reminded of the image of the woman with a dead child in her arms in the flames of Dresden. How much evil can one madman do to his own neighboring nations in the pursuit of world domination?

I retraced my steps to the station and strolled deeper into the Old Town. Peeking into the backyards of the burned houses, a dead silence prevailed everywhere. The yards had turned into cemeteries. Rarely on these lifeless streets, a man passed along. It was lively again only on

---

44 *By 1945, 85% of Warsaw's buildings were completely demolished. The majority of this destruction occurred during the Warsaw Uprising of August-October 1944, which was planned to coincide with the Soviet army advance. Even as the Polish resistance army attempted to communicate to the Russians (on the other side of the Vistula River) that the uprising had begun, Stalin ordered them to be ignored. This resulted in brutal German massacres of civilians and soldiers alike, numbering around one hundred and fifty to two hundred thousand people. After an armistice was signed, the Germans expelled another seven hundred thousand people from the city to camps, and continued to flatten every building they could. The Soviets didn't enter the city until the following January.*

Jerozolimskie Avenue. Towards the Central Station, you could occasionally spot a car, as well as hear and see the rattling of the iron-rimmed wheels of loaded carts riding along the cobblestones.

Tired, I arrived at the Central Station. I ate at the station cafeteria, picked up my suitcase, and hurried to a horse-drawn cart going to Praga. The wagon, loaded with people and bundles, rolled and rolled along the avenue towards the fallen Poniatowski Bridge, then it traveled over the pontoon to the right bank of the Vistula. Finally, the cart stopped before Wileński Station. I jumped off. Other passengers were scrambling slowly with suitcases and bundles.

"Pay now," the driver ordered.

"How much do I pay?" I asked.

I had a few small bills in my hand—the rest of a hundred zlotys that my hospitable host in Rawicz gave me for the road—and the twenty US dollars from Pilsen.

"That much," the carter snapped, ripping the green American banknote out of my hand and disappearing into the crowd.

"Oh boy, that thief has robbed you mercilessly," remarked an old man, looking at me with compassion.

At the station, I asked how to travel to Sokołów Podlaski, where I knew some of my relatives lived.

"Tomorrow before noon, there is a train to Białystok, where you can get off at Małkinia station and change your destination to Siedlce," a railwayman informed me kindly.

So I spent one more night on the bench, in the miserable barrack waiting room, under the great signboard of Wileński Station.

I glanced around. Traffic here was heavy. There were crowds of people nearby in the Różycki Bazaar. On the opposite side of Radzymińska Street, there were magnificent buildings—the former residence of the Polish National Railway head office—that housed the Polish government and president. This was indicated by the flag of the president of Poland with a white commander pattern that fluttered on the mast above the roof of the building. So I'm in good company, I thought, feeling touched.

I spent the night on a hard bench with a suitcase under my head. In the morning, the station platforms flooded up with people, and around midday, a long freight train consisting of cattle wagons was set up, and the crowd fell in, as well as I. So this is the last stage, I thought gladly, when all of a sudden, some screams on the platform woke me up from reflection. Two Soviet soldiers were marching along the platform with pistols drawn.

"*Krest'yane von! Teper' eto voyennaya mashina!* (Peasants out! It is now a military vehicle!)" One of them yelled in full throat, brandishing his gun.

Slowly, with resistance, we emptied the wagons and crawled out onto the platform. The Soviets walked along the train, still screaming, "*Voyennaya mashina!* (Military vehicle!)"

Soon, a Polish railway man appeared with a hat in hand. He collected donations to pacify our threatening "ally"'s ransom. They quickly estimated the value, filled their pockets with money, put away their pistols, and without looking back, left.

The crowd rushed to the wagons again. On the other side of the parallel street, the flag of the Polish president proudly waved. Now I know who really rules here, I thought. Those who stayed in the west were right.

After a few hours of travel, I got off in front of a miserable barrack, by the sign of "Małkinia." I asked the railway man for a train to Siedlce.

"Maybe tomorrow, around noon," he replied curtly.

So again, a night on the bench potentially awaited me. There were many dodgy characters around the station, as well as drunken Soviet soldiers. Searching for an alternative, I noticed several wooden lodges standing across from the station. I took the advice of one of the railwaymen and went looking for accommodation there. An elderly, gray woman pointed to a wooden bunk with a mattress of straw. I paid for the night and wrapped myself in a blanket, falling asleep heavily.

In the middle of the night, I woke up to someone lying next to me, with their arms wrapped around my neck. What the hell? I thought. Could it be my hostess? Was she in need of companionship? Carefully, I began to grope the intruder gently. I identified that it was a girl wearing only a skimpy t-shirt. The early summer dawn had entered the room through the window, and in its dim light, I spied a Soviet greatcoat, belt, and a soldier's hat. Ah, so that's the girl, I thought, and all my involuntary excitement faded as if I had been splashed with a bucket of cold water.

Such accidental love contacts had to be avoided, like a devil avoiding holy water.

Gently, I slowly pulled the blanket over me. In a moment, the woman woke up, dressed, and after a stream of flowery Russian curses, she left, slamming the door.

The railroad man confirmed yesterday's message at the station: the train to Siedlce would be here around noon.

"You have a lot of time," he added.

What to do with this time? I thought—I will visit Treblinka. During the train ride, I had heard a lot about this German extermination camp. The railway man showed me the way.

"Not far," he told me. "It's only six kilometers. You go along the track, then when you reach behind Treblinka station, turn right into the forest."

It was a beautiful, warm day as I walked along the tracks. Nightingales sang in the riverside bushes of the River Bug, and further along the path, I reached Treblinka station. Like many others on the east of Warsaw, it was a small station built during the Tsarist times. A kilometer further, the track turned into the forest, and a narrow, paved road appeared nearby. Both the track and road ended in a great clearing, surrounded by a pine forest. The frail grass was covered with fish-scale-like white petals, glistening in the sun. I picked up one of them and squeezed my fingers slightly. The petal broke down and fell to dust.

"They are burnt human bones!" I said out loud in horror.

How many people were murdered here?

Soon, my ears reached a loud conversation. I came closer to the voices. Several men were sitting on the edge of a pit, handing each other a bottle in turn, taking great sips. When they noticed my approaching footsteps, they stopped drinking and peered at me with wide eyes. The first of them rose and stepped towards me.

"What are you staring at? What are you looking for?" He questioned in a raised voice. "Get out of here or...!" He pulled a revolver out of his pocket and pointed the barrel at me.

What the hell were they doing? Something strange is going on here, I thought. Still, I knew it wasn't worth the confrontation. I turned and walked away, not looking back. A gust of wind brought the familiar stench of decaying bodies.

Further down the track, I met a woman with a basket of berries. This one seemed to be less hostile and more talkative.

"Oh, mister," she started, "What happened here is beyond human comprehension! In one year, hundreds of trains with Jews entered this forest. Then the guards must have shot at them because gunfire could be heard all the way in Małkinia. Then they were buried in huge, excavated pits. When the Germans got beaten in their skin by the Russians, they remembered that someone would discover these pits one day. They ordered these graves to be dug up and have the corpses burned on piles of wood. The stench was so horrid in the whole area that it was difficult to withstand."

"And who is digging them out now?" I asked.

"They are cemetery hyenas—they seek treasures," she replied. "Not all the mass graves were unearthed and burned by the Germans in time. The Jews who were forced to burn the bodies revolted, and they killed some of the guards and fled. Oh, mister! What was going on here then! In all the surrounding villages, the Germans and their helpers turned everything upside down, looking for the fugitives. Some, however, managed to escape."

"Was there supposedly a concentration camp for Poles?" I asked.

"Oh yes," the woman said. "You will turn back, mister, before the clearing in the forest, you will turn right, following another field road. A kilometer further, you will see a huge pit in the ground; it's a gravel pit. Thousands of Poles lost their lives there. My neighbors were hiding Jews. The Germans discovered their hideout, but luckily my neighbor managed to escape. His wife and their two young children, however, were dragged to Treblinka. None of them returned. The penalty for helping Jews was death," she sighed heavily.

I glimpsed at the sun; it was still a long time until noon, and I turned back as guided, taking the road to Polish Treblinka. Several meters deep and two hundred meters wide, the pits stretched for half a kilometer. The Germans had ordered their prisoners to dig gravel for road construction. How much sweat, how much blood, how much torment of innocent people was created from this terrible pit? Nearby the hole stood a tall wooden cross with a wooden board. Ten thousand Poles, dead from hunger and the hardships of backbreaking labor, who will never return to their own homes.[45]

It was time to return. My train is probably on its way, I thought. I strolled, pondering. The forest, field, and Bug River meadows had taken on a look of strange gray, as in old, colorless films. I peeked up at the cloudless sky, and the sun was always shining. Evidently, the angel of death is covering the sunlight of the day with his wings, I mused.

I waited another hour for the impending train's arrival, and then the freight wagons rolled up at last... The final stage of the long return to my mother.

---

45 *Although Zbyszek visited the Treblinka I labor camp constructed around that gravel pit, Treblinka II, the dedicated extermination center, was located nearby. Between July 1942 and September 1943, an estimated 925,000 Jews were killed in that camp, and a selection of them there were ordered to burn many of the bodies on "open-air ovens" at that site of the pit. As the lady said to Zbyszek, a Jewish resistance group was formed in 1943. In early August, hundreds of prisoners attempted to storm the gate, and many of them were mowed down by machine guns. A total of three hundred managed to escape, but two-thirds of them were found by the German SS and other auxiliary forces shortly afterward.*

ZBYSZEK'S JOURNEY BACK TO HIS MOTHERLAND

Through the immediate month and a half after the war ended, Zbyszek traveled through some of the most war-torn regions of Europe. Every station mentioned in this chapter is located on the illustration below, although the path itself is not an exact replica, as the route itself represents highways in Europe. Note that the map itself shows the borders of central Europe today for reference, except the division of Czechoslovakia.

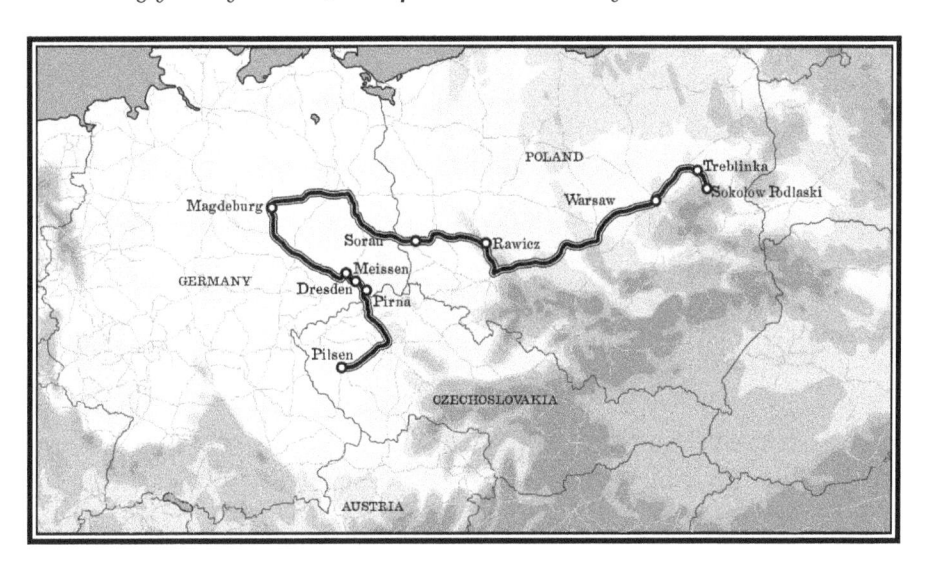

After an hour of travel, the train stopped at the platform of a charred railway station, with a "Sokołów Podlaski" board on the post. I jumped off. Dozens of people soon split up, and I was left alone on the platform with my suitcase in hand. I peered around carefully. In front of me were the ruins of the burned station, a dozen or so residential houses, and a partially destroyed town on the hill in the distance, about a kilometer away. I looked into the opposite side—on the left, a few hundred meters from the railroad, there were ruins of a burned factory and a nearby estate. From the same distance to the right, an old park was visible, within which the walls of a palace or manor were still standing. Which way should I go, where to look for my mother's family?—I wondered for a minute.

"What are you thinking?" a senior railwayman in a worn uniform asked me.

"Does any family by the name Wojewódzcy live in this town?" I questioned.

The man considered for a moment, and he finally replied: "I know two families with that name. One lives in town, the other somewhere near the hospital—it used to be a palace, now it's a hospital."

I departed towards the hospital.

Upon reaching the former castle, in the old gardens, several wooden houses stood for the staff. I asked the first person I met about my relatives.

"Is there anyone with the last name Wojewódzcy around?"

"Let me check for you, mister. Wait right here."

And shortly after, the nurse returned. And there was a lady beside her. It was Mother.

Ursul

It was the end of 1945. I had returned to Poland after the war and lived in a town in Podlasie. My mother and I inhabited a small room, and my work was unsatisfying and boring—there was no future in it. That was until one day when I caught sight of a poster with a large inscription: "Go to Recovered Territories." I was always drawn to the sea, and now an opportunity had come!

"I am going to look for a better future tomorrow; I see no future here," I declared to my mother.

I chose Szczecin as the destination.

Two days later, I took a night train with a loaf of bread, a piece of lard, and a gas mask all in my bag (that's how the authorities advised you to travel in those times), and I went to the so-called recovered land. Partially destroyed by bombing, depopulated, and completely robbed, Szczecin was an unsettled city. Groups of looters and all sorts of thugs were taking what the Soviet occupiers had left behind.

I moved into a small room on the first floor of a huge, empty apartment house near the port district. I gathered some three-legged stools, an equally lame table, and a bed, and then went searching for a job. I found one in the accounting department of the first Polish newspaper, the *Szczecin Courier*. Accounting and bills had never been my strength, though, so I was often contemplating changing jobs. I spent my evenings with a candle in a large, empty apartment, reading books that had been left on the shelves. I would hear echoes of shootings from time to time, and hand grenade outbursts disturbed my blissful peace.

I was drawn to the sea. In my spare time, I walked to the port and would peer north towards the banks of Świnoujście, from where the seagoing ships arrived and sailed down the River Świna. Rumors spread that this was a city like "El Dorado"—a land of prosperity. Unfortunately, it was closed for ordinary mortals: permission to live there was only available to former soldiers.

I was wandering around the waterfront, pondering to myself how I could make it to this El Dorado when a Soviet speed boat moored to the wharf. A lightbulb went off in my head.

"*Tovarishch?* (Comrade?)" I looked at the sailor standing on the board of the Russian speeder. "*Mne nuzhno dobratsya do Swinemunde* (I need to get to Świnoujście)."

He looked at me closely and murmured: "*Dva litra vodki—odin seychas, a drugoy litr pozzhe* (Two liters of vodka—one now, and the other liter later)."

We had a deal. I brought a liter of vodka, and the second I promised to bring in the evening when I boarded.

I packed my miserable belongings, bought another liter of moonshine, and went to the port in the evening. The Russian, named Matros, was waiting for me. He took the alcohol and told me to follow him quietly, tip-toeing along. He opened an iron hatch.

"*Vlezay* (Get in)," he murmured and shut the panel.

It was cramped here, like a hollow tree, and it stank of grease and oil. Sitting like a mouse under a broom, heavy crew shoes boomed along the deck, and somewhere above the engines roared, spewing exhaust into my hideout.

The speedboat started off. The rumble of engines and the smell of exhaust gas stunned me to such an extent that I didn't notice when the sailor opened the hatch.

"*Vylezay* (Come out)," he shouted, tugging my arm.

I scrambled out of my hiding spot, gasping for air like a fish, and followed him. The boat stood at the scarcely lit dock, surrounded by the ruins of houses.

It was dark, gloomy, and silent as I glanced around and wandered along the waterfront. A blinding light suddenly struck my face when a Soviet patrol noticed me.

"*Ruki vverkh!*" A familiar shout came, and I obediently raised my hands.

The patrolling sailors, shadowed by their torches, searched my pockets and ordered me to march ahead. I felt the barrels of machine guns on my back. We didn't walk far; the patrol handed me over to the nearby security office. Here, a guard, poking me in the back with a rifle, led me to the head officer.

"Name, organization, where are you from, and where are you going?!" the officer roared at me.

At that time, Świnoujście was known as an asylum route for Polish underground organizations and people leaving the country. The security officers interrogated me for three days until finally I convinced them that I had recently returned from Germany and had nothing to do with politics.

Seventy-two hours later, the key gnashed in the cell lock, and an officer escorted me to the door and growled: "Clear off straight to the ferry and to the other side!"

Yeah right, I'm here now—I thought and went to explore the city.

Before the war, Świnoujście had been a military and trade port, with a Prussian fortress and cozy high-rise houses that formed the downtown area. There also had been a beautiful residential district, a spa building, and a large spring by the sea. After surviving a large English bombing expedition in March of 1945, much of the town presented a deplorable view: many structures were demolished, and windows were smashed out.

When I reached the port, by the branches of the River Świna and the Piastowski Channel, I learned that over a dozen ships had sunk—likely as a result of a bombing raid. Among them were two armored cruisers; the crew of these ships, not wanting them to get into the possession of enemies, had sunk them with their own hands. Only a steam ferry, which connected both banks of the Świna, and a small steam antediluvian ship with one very high chimney, had survived from the entire port fleet. I returned to the central square, and above the town hall, the white and red flag of Poland was flying.

In the lobby on the ground floor of the town hall, I asked an amicable young man: "Where can I apply for residency?"

"Do you have a permit?" he questioned. "If you don't have it, you won't be able to register. Take a room somewhere among some Germans, stay quiet and look for a job. I am from Kraków, my name is Kazimierz

Hasny," he introduced himself. "I live in Matejki 29a, if you do not find anything, come to see me, and maybe I can help you," he smiled.

I quickly found a room in an apartment belonging to an older German couple. Work was not as easy to find here, though. I spent my days wandering around the city looking for opportunities, and in the evenings, I chatted with my hosts. They were a lovely, childless couple who enjoyed having a young, calm, familiar-with-their-language tenant.

Sometimes, my host's sister would come and visit. She lived with three adolescent children on the opposite side of the corridor. She also accommodated two men who seemed suspicious—they spoke in Polish but with a strange Russian or Ukrainian accent.

On New Year's Eve, at a late hour, my hostess's sister came in. The women whispered among themselves, and finally, the neighbor turned to me: "My tenants and some other man want my daughter to go and clean an apartment with them. What do you think about this?"

What could I think about it? I knew these two were suspicious by sight, and the third was a complete stranger. Also, the hour for cleaning was rather unsuitable, on a late evening...

The neighbor whispered "goodnight" softly and left.

Maybe a quarter of an hour had passed since that conversation. A sudden, loud, violent knocking on the door put us on our feet. The hostess opened it, and a girl ran into the room with insanity in her eyes. It was Ursul—our neighbor's daughter.

She threw herself on my knees and yelled: "*Um Gottes willon, retten sie mich!* (For God's sake, please save me!)"

There was no time for questions: I raised her from my lap, led her to my room, and hid her in the wardrobe full of clothes. I locked the door to the room.

Three drunken, armed lads burst into the apartment.

"Where is the bitch?!" screamed the one with a gun in his hand. "I will kill her! She cut me!" And indeed, blood was flowing from his hand.

"Where is she?!" the other attacker hit the hostess in her face and kicked her husband.

Long knives glistened in their hands as they demolished the apartment. I stood at the door of my room with the key in my hand.

"Maybe she is there?!" one of them roared.

I opened the door, walked enthusiastically to the closet, moving to the side my coat behind which Ursul stood, and showed them the interior. They took a quick glance and left in an urgent search. There were shouts on the opposite side of the corridor, then upstairs, and throughout the apartment houses, indicating that the investigation was ongoing.

In the end, everything went quiet. I let the petrified girl out of the closet. She shook like jelly and began to explain. Cleaning had just been an excuse—they offered her vodka, and when she refused, two grabbed her hands, and the third began to pour vodka on her lips. During the struggle, one of them staggered and banged his hand into the table full of glasses, and the girl escaped in the confusion.

The sudden thud of steps on the stairs made me realize that this was not history yet. Time was running thin. I opened the nearby dresser door quickly, and with help, squeezed the girl in, who was now curled up like a caterpillar. The door popped open with a bang, and the gang burst into the apartment once more.

"She must be here!" one screamed.

The hunt began again.

They brutally searched all the corners, but it did not occur to them that the girl could be hidden in the closet. Finally! With relief, I heard a click of the door. Ursul was close to suffocation. I pulled her out—she seemed half-dead—and with difficulty, put her on her feet. She trembled like a leaf. Her aunt handed her a glass of cold water, and she came back to herself after a while.

What's next? We have to run from here, but where to? It's the middle of the night, and there is a curfew! I dressed quickly, Ursul pulled on her mother's old sweater, and quietly tip-toeing, pricking up our ears, we went out into the yard, through the garden, to the neighboring street. Only here did we breathe a sigh of relief, and she clutched my hand. I remembered the address of my acquaintance from the town hall: Kazimierz Hasny, Matejki 29a. We walked carefully, slowly, with our ears pricked up like a dog. We hid several times in ruins when voices or footsteps were heard from a distance, portraying a military patrol or other people you should avoid meeting with at night. I could feel that my shirt, despite the frost, was drenched in sweat—I had enough excitement for one night.

Will my new friend be home? How will he welcome us? I was asking myself these questions. After probably two hours of Amerindian sneaking, with reassurance, I spotted the lighted windows of his apartment. At the apartment door, we heard music, and in a moment, a cheerful young man, from whom the smell of alcohol came, opened the door for us.

"Ah, it's you, Zbyszek! With a girl! Here you are!" He led us into a room where several couples danced to the music from a gramophone.

They welcomed us warmly. The atmosphere was frozen, for a second, by the fact that I had come with a German girl. I told the events of the night, they became relaxed, and we danced until morning. Ursul, after a while, got used to the company and had a great time.

In the morning, the companions split up, and Kazio invited us for breakfast. Only then did I first peer at Ursul—a stunningly graceful, perfectly built girl. When the fears and stresses of the night passed, her charm and beauty glowed. She quickly took over the duties of helping with breakfast, and did so with elegance and a smile. Kazio stared at her like a magpie staring at gold, and sighed.

"Where did you find such a beautiful girl?" he finally asked. "You are lucky."

"A total accident, my dear," I confessed. "Yesterday, I didn't know her."

At one point, Ursul took off her watch from her hand, came over to me, and put it on my hand. I shied away from accepting the gift—what I did to save her was a simple response in solidarity for a person at risk of death. I wasn't expecting anything in return.

The watch hadn't been warming up on my hand for long when Kazio turned to me with a request: "I'm going to Karsibór. Lend me this watch. I have to be punctual."

I gave it to him willingly. After an hour, Kazio left us alone in the apartment.

I decided to look around. In the daylight, I could see that it was a beautiful four-story villa that stood in the spa park near the city's stadium. The houses stood only on one side of the street, and on the other side, a small, devastated castle was located on a wooded hill.

Each segment of the house had a separate entrance, each decorated with large finials on stone columns. After several steps towards the villa, you would approach the bottom platform foyer of the front door to that apartment. The inside consisted of two rooms, with a kitchen and a bathroom on the ground level, and a similar layout on the second floor. There was another small room with a kitchen and bathroom supposedly for a *Dienstmadchen* (maid) in the empty attic.

The quality of the furniture testified that the original owner of the apartment had to be a rich man. There was contemporarily-shaped furniture made of black mahogany, a piano, and three comfortable, bright, leather armchairs in the office. The bedroom was probably the top dream for a young, wealthy couple: standing next to each other, there were two comfortable, wide beds with cupboards, a four-door wardrobe, a three-wing mirror, and a dressing table, all made of golden birch on black ebony bases. The furniture could satisfy the taste of the most demanding lady of the house.

You could go straight to the terrace through the ground floor hallway, which was surrounded by a garden with a wire mesh fence. Behind it, an old pine forest grew, stretching all the way to the other side of the border, by the German health resort of Ahlbeck. The border ran about one and a half kilometers from the home, more or less through the middle of the coastal forest.

But what's next? The girl, fearing revenge from the thugs, did not want to go home. We spent this first day entirely in conversations and jokes about our incredible adventure.

When evening came, I fell asleep like a stone. However, I woke up in the middle of the night, feeling someone cuddling my neck. A meek whisper of "I'm afraid to sleep alone in a stranger's apartment" let me know who lay next to me.

I fought two powerful forces for a long time: the passion of a young man and the dignity of a gentleman who was inclined to be respectful.

We lay in the embrace until the morning. I had won the internal battle, probably the most difficult one of my life. Days and nights flew by like a wonderful dream. I only went out to shop and, as if on wings, I would return to "my" home, to my dream, the sweetest of all dreams.

Kazio did not return. I did not miss him at all, wishing in my spirit that he would not return at all—and apparently, he fulfilled this wish.

After four days, a postcard came, and in it, a few words were written: "Zbyszek, don't be angry; for the watch, you can take the apartment."

And this is how accidentally, in one night, thanks to some unknown luck, I was granted a girlfriend and an apartment. A great gift of fate, but again, what's next? We were having a wonderful time, and when her mother came with a visit, it was evident, of course, that Ursul couldn't return home. We decided that her best option was to run away through the border to the west, through the Soviet occupation zone.

From that moment on, an angel of sadness covered us with his wings. Our kisses, as equally passionate as our first night, tasted of the bitterness of looming separation. I understood that postponing this moment for too long did not make sense.

One evening I decided it was time for her to go.

"In the morning, I will lead you across the border," I whispered, and a painful contraction seized my throat. Ursul cried quietly, longingly, and painfully.

I woke her up as soon as dawn shone in the window. We dressed quickly, swallowed something without looking at each other, and left the house. The border was nearby, only a kilometer and a half through the woods. We strolled slowly while holding hands. German signs made me realize that we were already in Ahlbeck—so she is among her people now—and it was time for me to go back to my own. I kissed her tenderly, squeezed her hands tightly, and without a word, turned around. The rising sun emerged from behind the forest. My place is in my homeland, I thought—and took a deep breath.

The Asylum Route

In spring, life at the port began to flourish once again. Merchant vessels sailing under foreign flags traveled towards Szczecin on the river. In the city, a private trade began functioning, and there were several port taverns open, where guests would cheer and chant in the evenings while chords of instruments filled the air. There were several Polish and Soviet military ships in the port, so plenty of clients inhabited the pubs. Every step, you were met with Russian and Polish seamen. Another part of the port served as a Soviet military base, and the most beautiful part of the city, the seaside resort, was occupied by the Soviet Army and had been converted into apartments for the fleet of officers. Several minesweeper ships and transport barges at the deck and a modest one-story building (the quarters of the port authority) marked the presence of the Polish military.

I now decided to look for a job again. I had no trouble this time around, as straight away, I was able to become a senior waiter at the ferry-pier restaurant known as Portowa. Initially, the work of a waiter seemed to be a straightforward task: take the order, provide the ordered food and drink, then collect the payment. It appeared as simple as it could be. Unfortunately, this job is actually a higher study of the psychology of the guest. This had to be learned, especially regarding the specific type of client who visited Portowa.

Most of the guests were officers and sailors stationed in the Świnoujście Russian fleet. Serving them was a real "Russian roulette": will they pay, or will they not pay? You never knew how the guest would behave in the end. The Russians drank harshly. They were victory soldiers, the winners who had won the battle a few months ago, and so it was apparently different for them when it came to paying the bill. Some did honorably hand a larger tip than the actual bill, but a fair few also offered a pistol to my face. Often, the guests gave me a bunch of flowery Russian curses as a "thank you" when I left the table.

With time, I worked out a particular way of enforcing the dues. When guests were badmouthing me, I dropped to their tone of voice and sent them a bunch of equally rude curses, along the lines of "*Tak chto vy takiye otlichnyye soyuzniki, k chertu vas* (So you are such great allies, to hell with you)." They would look with astonishment for a moment—because referring to the Polish-Soviet alliance was already a political matter—and ask: "*Otkuda ty tak khorosho znayesh' russkiy yazyk?* (How come you know Russian so well?)" Then they'd pay without any resistance.

Similarly, it happened that many Russian sailors often drank and ate the whole evening, and when it came to paying the bill, they would turn their pockets and show carelessly: "*Smotrite, oni ukrali u menya den'gi* (See, they stole money from me)."

What was I supposed to do, call the police?

The Scandinavians, Swedish, Danish, and Norwegian, who often stood in the port waiting for a free way via the Piastowski canal to Szczecin, were a strange category of guests. They drank without moderation and most often had to be carried out by their colleagues, who would come to get them when the time of departure of the ship was approaching. Never short of money, they could often afford such drinking. Foreign currencies were so expensive that, for the equivalent of several hour-long parties full of drinking in Portowa, such a customer in his home country could drink only a single pint of beer.

The Poles were generally the best clients. They sat, drank, ate, paid, and went. Among them, the occasional annoying guest would not like to take the wallet out of his pocket. If he would not pay, there was one word that would work like an electric shock: "militia." With time, I got to know the reason.

The attraction of the Portowa house was its music band, especially one high harmonist, whose face was covered in scars from childhood smallpox. He was an artist, a musician of the highest class. The accordion in his hands turned him into a magician who hypnotized the guests. His fingers imperceptibly danced at the instrument's keyboard with such skill and speed, and his repertoire was so rich that the visitors came only to listen to his playing. Unfortunately, many of the guests offered him a glass of vodka—and this often ended with his own "rest" under a table.

One time, one of the guests, a corpulent older gentleman, asked me where I was from, then he murmured his name, said he came from a village near Sokołow Podlaski and asked for a private conversation without witnesses. You do not refuse the guest, so when the place was deserted in the evening, the visitor surveyed the room carefully and asked me to come to the table. He quizzed me, half-whispering, on where I lived and was pleased with my answer.

"That's right. It's close to the border," he answered. "Would you not give me a small favor? My cousin, a former Home Army soldier, was given a death sentence. He escaped from the prison in Siedlce and wants to cross the border to West Berlin. In this country, a sooner death awaits him."

I knew that through Swinoujscie an underground smuggling channel for doomed people led to the West. It was also the shortest way to Berlin, but his proposition surprised me. It smelled of provocation. Just in case, I asked him who he knew in Sokołów and who directed him to me. Everything was correct; he knew my relatives and several people from the town. However, I decided to think it over and made an appointment with him the following evening.

That night I did not sleep until dawn. I already knew the way across the border, and I knew the schedule of the change of guards and their positions, details which I had gleaned from drunken soldiers' conversations. However, I had to take into account the possibility that this information was inaccurate. The risk was high in the case of an accident—death was likely, or many years in prison. That was the standard punishment for illegal border crossing at that time.

The gentleman also brought me some news: in Sokołów, I was awaited by my old mother, who had been taking care of her less able sister. What to do? This question tormented me once again, raging all over my mind.

In the evening, the older man came to the pub once again. I definitively voiced: "No. I cannot risk it. I have a family to take care of."

And then tears filled his eyes. "Dear mister, it's actually my son," he confessed and pursed his lips.

It broke my resistance. "Alright," I uttered. "Tomorrow, at about 10 p.m., you'll report to my address. Besides, I see that you know my address perfectly well." (I wrote letters to my mother and hence the guest probably knew my address).

"Maybe today?" he asked hopefully.

"No," I answered. "The weather must be suitable for this 'adventure,'" I explained. "Besides, tomorrow is also uncertain."

"Why?" he insisted.

"You will find out in your own time," I replied.

All of the conversations that I had witnessed at Portowa led me to some useful information and conclusions that had to be taken into account. Since patrols passed along the border between the coast and the highway constantly throughout, the most convenient time for passage was during a dark night, when the sounds of the sea and the forest drowned out the steps of feet. The old, tall pine forest facilitated easy observation, but the gusty, frosty wintry weather forced the patrol to look for cover in the ever-growing clumps of young trees, and so in such places, you had to be vigilant, with your ears perked up. Luckily, the patrolling soldiers could not hold still without chattering or rolling a cigarette for two hours. The smallest embers of these cigarettes betrayed the place of hiding for the guards.

Again, it was a precarious task: I knew from conversations I'd overheard that the border guards, in the event of the slightest assault (such as crossing the border) first sent a series of automatic bullets in that direction and only then called, "Stop, who is there? Put your hands up!"

One more important message that I learned was that the guards changed positions every even hour. Fortunately, patrol dogs were not used in these times, and the moderate, snowless, coastal winter helped our adventure.

The older man and his son, about twenty-five years of age, appeared punctually the following evening. They apologized to me, then carefully checked all the angles of the apartment. I understood their caution. We did not know each other, and this was a high-stakes game we were playing.

"Please, take off your coats. Let's have a cup of tea," I suggested.

The younger one looked at me suspiciously. "Why aren't we going?" he asked, clearly anxious.

"Easy, young man, the time will come," I replied. "Let's talk inside."

"Let's talk now!" the younger raised his voice and instinctively put his hand in his pocket.

"Whatever you keep in your pocket, you will immediately throw in the forest."

"Why?!" He roared. "No weapons?"

"Yes, no weapons, young man. The privilege in the event of an accident costs us two years or longer or life. The crossing of the border with arms in hand is prohibited under a very strict paragraph of the law."

At the urging of the elder, the young man calmed down, and after tea, we even sat down to a game of poker. One round, a second, third, and my guest became disconcerted. The clock struck twelve, and he was nervous again.

"Why aren't we going? What the hell are we waiting for?"

This time I lost my temper; I stared into his eyes and asked: "You, the old partisan, do not know that the most convenient time for such actions is the hour before dawn when the most patrols are likely to be dreaming?" Then I added, "In the morning, the wind on the sea is the strongest, and we are not going for a stroll, are we? Hell!"

After two in the morning, the son and I left the house. We said goodbye to the old man and turned towards the stadium. The night was perfect for such an expedition. It was dark, though our eyes had adjusted, as a cold wind howled and hummed in the branches of the trees. The crashing of the sea would sometimes become thunderous.

"Stay two steps behind me! Drop your gun!" I whispered to my companion.

We were silent as ghosts. Every dozen steps, I would stand under a tree, set my ears, and try to pierce the darkness. My eyesight had become as good as a cat's.

We reached the border bridge and immersed ourselves in the forest on the German side of the border. Here, such precautions were no longer needed: the German patrols were not as ruthless as on our side. On the forest road far away, I noticed loud conversation and the glistening of cigarettes. It was just dark enough to lurk around and wait it out. Soon the voices died down, and we moved cautiously forward. The dusk had begun to brighten when we arrived at the edge of the forest. In the distance, a light flashed.

"It's the Ahlbeck railway station," I murmured. "Now go straight to the light, but watch out for any Russians. Luckily you will be able to hear them from a distance. From Ahlbeck, there is a train straight to Berlin. Keep well."

We shook hands and melted away like ghosts in the darkness.

The return path passed without hindrance. Good ears, eyes, and a little bit of luck—I thought to myself and walked one again upon the stadium.

I accelerated my pace when suddenly I heard a familiar command: "Stop! *Ruki vverkh!*" which knocked out my newly gained self-confidence.

Out of the darkness, three Russians jumped out with weapons in their hands.

"*Kto ty i chto zdes' delayesh'?!* (Who are you and what are you doing here?!)"

"I am a sportsman," I lied. "*Ya zhivu ryadom* (I live nearby)."

It was a Soviet patrol who was fishing out disobedient marines stationed in nearby barracks.

They believed me to be a sportsman only when I pulled out the key and opened my apartment door. Pacified, each of them gulped a cup of moonshine, and we parted as allies.

Two weeks later, my friend from Nieciecza appeared again with another asylum-seeker. The aftermath of the war in Poland wasn't one of peace; those who were resistant to the Soviet influence were threatened with death or a long time in prison and were saving themselves by escaping west. And so, the hope that change could take place began to expire in the nation.

I took several trips to Ahlbeck. During the last route, only the flash of a cigarette warned me before I would have been caught, and I decided to temporarily suspend the service. I felt I had fulfilled my patriotic duty towards my countrymen.

In April, my mother and aunt came to visit me, and I could not endanger them. I decided to change my job, as I had enough of those nocturnal returns home after a constant view of the drunken soldiers whom I had to wrangle for payment. It was necessary to look for another, more effortless occupation.

That guest from Nieciecza was still at the bar, attempting to persuade me to continue those trips. I finally decided to officially part ways with my endeavors only when a well-intoxicated, frequent visitor of Portowa, a clerk from the nearby Public Security Office, asked me, with drunken honesty: "Do you recognize me?" He then proclaimed with a mocking smile, "We met one time."

And indeed, I recognized him; a long time before, he was the officer who, upon my unsolicited arrival, gave me an "honorary greeting" while keeping me in captivity for multiple days.

"I will ask you something," he strained through his teeth. "Do you have many cousins who regularly visit you?"

I froze, and blood rushed to my head. So they must have known something about me—it was the last signal.

The officer drank until late in the evening. I didn't take any money from him and escorted him to the door. Outside the door, he stopped, wagged a finger in front of my nose, then grabbed my hand, shook it, and disappeared into the darkness. So there were still decent people at this time.

I sat in the nearest chair for a long time without moving. The manager of the bar came to me at last.

He peered at me carefully and asked: "What's wrong with you? Are you sick? Or did you see a ghost? You look like a dead man."

"Give me a glass of water," I trembled.

I drank one glass, then another, before I got back to my senses. Attempting to evade a conversation with the gentleman from Nieciecza, who was patiently sitting in the corner waiting for me, I whispered to my boss: "I will come back tomorrow afternoon and settle my bills." Then I left through the back door.

Everything was in order at home.

"Nobody asked about me? Nobody was here?" I asked my mother frantically.

"Nobody was here. No one asked," my mother replied. "Are you sick? You look troubled and pale." She gazed at me with worry.

"No, nothing. I'm tired. I'm going to sleep."

I did not sleep all night. I considered all possible scenarios, but apparently, the man did not know much, or I would have been found out a long time ago. It is not out of the question that the neighbor next door may have said something, as he also seemed suspicious. By the way, that officer was a decent man, I decided, who was also endangering himself to some extent. And at the end of the day, it was time to change my profession.

Life in the city and the harbor slowly returned to normal. More and more ships sailed to Szczecin and back. There were several fishing boats in the port, so I decided to try my luck at sea. Strolling by the wharf, I asked one fisherman repairing a net whether they had a full crew.

"We lack one. He was hospitalized for something serious—no one knows when he will come out," responded the fisherman, eyeing me carefully. "Do you want to try? If so, come around five in the morning with the documents." He then approached me and introduced himself: "I am Wilhelm Tonkiel of Chałupy. I am a skipper on this boat. I am from the region of Kashubia, and I only like hard labor. Think about it because the sea is not a caring mother but an evil stepmother." He gave me his rough hand, full of blisters, and added, "Today, fix the documents."

Well, it doesn't look like this fellow carries food and drink for his crew, I thought to myself. However, I still liked the skipper: he was an honest, open, rugged man of the sea.

At five o'clock in the morning, before it grew bright, I was there. The border control officer, a friend, looked through my papers and asked why I had left Portowa. Soon, the engine hummed, and the boat departed from the harbor.

The first issue that our skipper dealt with after the departure from the quay was the matter of my acquaintance with the WOPista.[46]

"Where do you know him from? How long?"

"He drank with us in the bar," I answered.

The usually quiet Kashubian carried out a meticulous investigation of my acquaintance.

---

46 *Wojska Ochrony Pogranicza (WOP): Polish border guard agency throughout the Cold War*

I assumed the reasons for his curiosity; in spite of the high penalties and sharp supervision around the boats standing in the port, it was also a second, naval route for asylum-seekers to travel abroad. Repression in the country intensified, and the authorities were destroying the underground opposition, so the traffic on the border grew. Perhaps this skipper, like me, was soaked in this business of smuggling, and he was nosing if I was a plug for the office of security. It took a few weeks before I gained his full confidence.

Promptly, the deck swayed underfoot as the engine increased power. We sailed out of the harbor, passed the breakwaters, the high lighthouse, and the old Prussian coastal fortress, which I previously didn't know existed because the Soviets occupied it. Then we sailed to the waters of the Bay of Pomerania. It was another world here. A high wave swayed the small boat, and the deck danced underfoot. A sharp wind cut across our faces like a nettle. In the outer port, just behind the breakwater, two large transport vessels sat deep—up to the top deck—in the water.

"Whose job was it?" I asked the skipper, nodding at the wrecks.

"I think the Americans," he muttered, "in March 1945. You see those torn apart ship decks? There is more wreckage under the water," he told me. "It's much deeper, you cannot see, and so you need to be careful with the net."

Shortly after, the shore and the city became a thin line on the horizon. The boat was rocking so badly that we had to carefully maneuver our feet to keep from falling overboard, and at last, the helmsman set the ship against the wind, and he made the command: "Set up the nets!"

By the end of the day, we had collected an entire net of silver-looking fish.

"Is it always so many?" I asked the skipper.

He took his pipe from his mouth and said: "Not always so much, but often. For a few years, few people were fishing here. The Germans did not have fuel for engines nor people to work at sea." He smiled, "So more is left for us."

Our skipper was a decent man: he was honest, cheerful, and witty. He liked to joke and drink. However, on the sea, every mistake was punished without mercy. Once, the rope had been carelessly tied at the bollard, and it came loose, throwing one of the men into the water. We miraculously managed to save his life, but we couldn't save him from the Old Man, who cursed him callously and threw him out of work.

Our fishing trips were often fruitful, and there was always a demand. Usually, our loading room was full by the early afternoon, and the deck was covered with fish boxes. Many carts and carriages waited on the dock. We sent fish boxes from the boat straight into the hands of the recipients. The transaction was amazingly straightforward; the recipient paid the crew on the spot, and our hearts grew when our pockets swelled instantly with cash.

The Old Man looked at me carefully, and when he saw my satisfaction, he replied quietly: "Today was a greasy day. There are days when you do not earn a broken penny."

Following the fisherman's custom, I invited the entire crew to Portowa to blend in. From the time of my employment in the bar, my former colleagues looked at me as if I was Croesesus when they noticed the royal tips I rewarded our waiter with. Drunken, I made it home without issue and was greeted by my mother, whose eyes almost fell out of their sockets when I emptied my pockets. I was so tired that I had fallen asleep in my clothes before my mother even calculated my earnings.

It was now summer. I got used to the labor. The Old Man put me at the helm more and more often, which was evidence for trust and recognition. Once while drinking, he mentioned a possibility of a pay raise and that I would probably manage to obtain a fisherman pension and eventually own a cozy place on the Baltic shore—if it weren't for my internal calling to explore the wide world.

We usually fished in the coastal zone, three nautical miles from the shore, and every time I would dream of distant lands, seas, and oceans. I was drawn to this far wandering, which I had read so much of in the books of Konrad Korzeniowski. It seemed to me that on the horizon, in a place where the sky merges with the sea, I was starting another fantasy that was more interesting, happier, and nicer than our gray everyday reality. Sometimes, in good weather, it appeared to be visible, looming in the distance. This was really the island of Rügen or Bornholm, which for us was enemy land, forbidden; for even just a voiced desire to visit it, you could be put in prison.

Exploring, seeing the world—only one road led there in this time: education. In Świnoujście, even a high school was established, with evening classes for youth like me, who were lagging behind in schooling due to the war. But how to enjoy learning while working at sea? How to reach for a book or notebook when after an intense day, I would fall asleep at the dinner plate?

I decided I needed to find another job. I found it without difficulty in a state-established enterprise for fisheries known as Barka. There, as a young man with a bachelor's matriculation and already knowledgeable of the sea, I was offered a job in the technical department easily. I had never missed the desk, but what was the other way out?

The problem was how to speak with the Old Man about it. I liked him and respected him, and he liked me too. For a whole year, he never said a bad word when addressing me. During my work, the crew changed probably three times. Despite the high earnings of those days, many of them escaped from the battle against the waters after three days of hardship.

On a stormy day when we were standing in the port, I invited the Old Man to Portowa for a drink. He was surprised by this sudden invitation but did not refuse. I ordered half a liter of vodka and an appetizer. We ate, drank the cup, and then, seeing his questioning look, I strained to find my words.

"Listen, I have to leave," I spoke. The words barely passed through my throat, which felt like it was fenced by barbed wire.

"Girl?" He asked.

"No, education," I answered. "I want to study, and I want to go on a large ship to see the world."

Silence fell. We drank silently.

After a glass, finally the Old Man spoke: "It's a pity, we worked well, and you saw how difficult it is to collect a decent crew, but if you want to learn, then go."

We shook hands and parted without a word. Something squeezed in my throat. I knew I wouldn't meet many others like him in my life.

Now I was forced to like working at the office. I stayed there for three years, and I can only remember the ships sailing down the Świna Canal.

These years passed like years spent in a boring, incompatible, and emotionally numb marriage. However, I did not waste any time. I enrolled in the nearby high school, and with persistence, made up for the lost education from the war. What else to do? My dream college, the Maritime University in Szczecin, was still being put together. I waited. Finally, the letter came: "Please report to the university secretariat."

The next morning at five o'clock, I rushed to the port on the pier, from where ships sailed daily between Świnoujście and Szczecin. An old German ship, a convenient connection with Szczecin, had a high chimney, with her name "Piast" bolded on the side.

I ran to the port as if with wings, and a surprise awaited me: the Piast had disappeared! Only a chunk of the ship's once-grand chimney protruded from the waters. At night, the old boat had begun to gain water; possibly its rusted rivets had given in, and when the crew came out in the morning, all they could see was the chimney sticking out of the water. There was a worried crowd of passengers on the quay. People shook their heads. "How could this happen?" they pondered, forgetting that inspectors had long ago qualified the ship only for a museum.

When I made it there the next day, there were many candidates for the "sea wolves," but I believed that fate, which had seemingly favored me for many years, would not disappoint me this time.

When the announcer dropped over half of the candidates, among them me, it was a devastating disappointment. What was it? I did not feel any special ailments, and yet there was something there, and I couldn't stop thinking about what it was. This was explained only by an official notice that I received one week later. A slight traumatic defect of the left eye was the doctor's diagnosis. And so from Dresden, a blow to my head had left its mark.

All my youthful dreams of distant seas, oceans, and lands burst like a bubble. It took me a long time to recover and regain my spirit. Fortunately, the testimony of the technical school in Równe, thanks to my mother, had survived, so I could learn in that direction. Close nearby, the local authorities had already organized an advanced vocational education in Szczecin, which I graduated from with ease. I said goodbye quickly to my desk, and I began my new career.

Towards the end of the 1940s, the reconstruction of the port and the devastated residential districts of the city started, so it was not difficult to get a job in my profession.

The mystery of my eye injury also came to light. After an examination at the health clinic in Szczecin, the doctors said my injury was caused by a tiny (the size of a nail's head) shard that had pierced shallow under my skin, in the left side of my skull. A surgeon removed the fragment, and after two weeks of staying in the clinic, I returned home.

During a summer holiday, I went to visit Sokołów Podlaski, the town where my destiny had thrown me after the war. I had many friends there, and passing a familiar street, I decided to visit one of my old sweethearts. She had left to study in Warsaw. My future mother-in-law gave me her daughter's address in the capital. Soon afterward, I received a letter from her address. I replied. And so this is how our romantic love correspondence began; half a year later, we married in Warsaw.

In the summer, my young wife joined me in Świnoujście, but to my surprise, she wrinkled her nose at the place. She only saw our future in Warsaw. After two weeks of stay, she left, expecting me to join her in the capital.

I found a small home for my mother, gave the keys to my apartment to the City Hall, crossed to the other side of the Świna River, and jumped on the train. I had crossed out six years of my life and assets.

Beginning a new life, I started off, not looking back.

PART IV

Life in the Eastern Bloc

THE EASTERN AND WESTERN BLOCS OF EUROPE AFTER WWII

The Cold War spelled a new era in world affairs, and Europe was split into two main spheres of influence: the Communist-controlled countries of the East and the United Nations-allied countries of the Western side. As a result of this divide, an "Iron Curtain" descended upon the continent. This map illustrates Europe's postwar borders, as well as the division between the East and West.

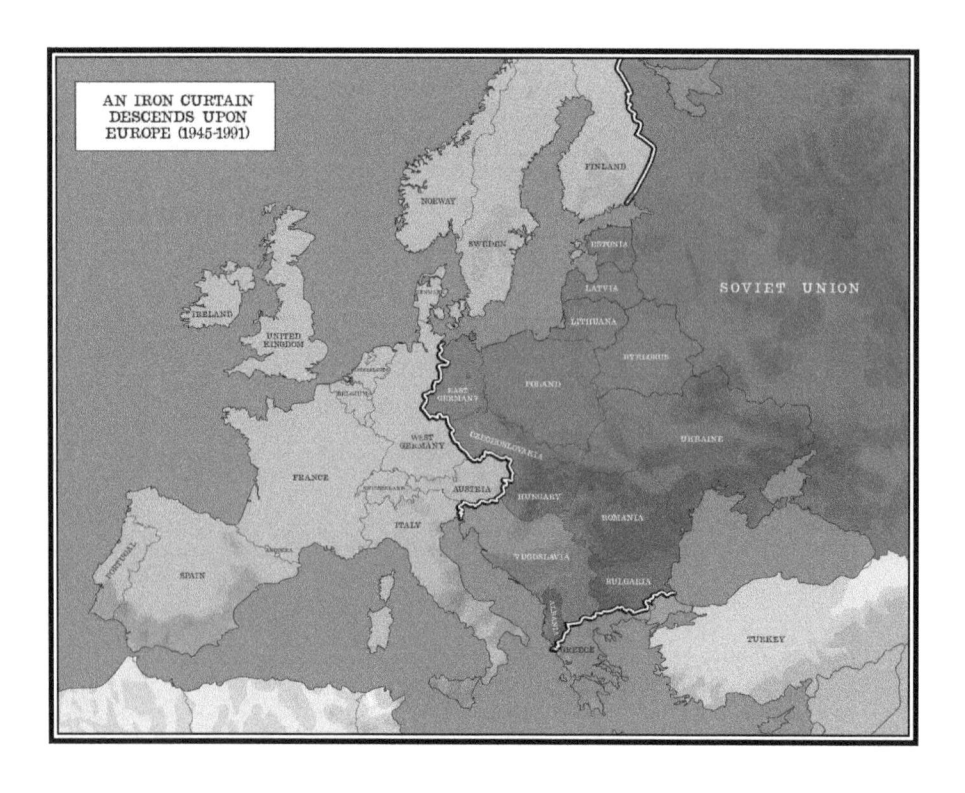

The Post-War Concentration Camp

The years following my departure from Świnoujście would often see me arriving home on Saturday evening and leaving on Monday morning while my wife took care of our child. Accessing the construction sites was only by public means of transport, and those in the 1950s were in desperate condition. Often, these vehicles were converted trucks, adapted to carry passengers. I would wait for transport for hours in the rain, in the heat, and the cold.

It was hard labor and a small income, but someone had to rebuild this Polish land. Whoever knows these times knows how difficult it was to buy even a piece of sausage in the store. Vodka, however, was never short. In the majority of the towns surrounding the region of Warsaw, finding a hotel was a dream of the beheaded, so I often stayed overnight in railway and bus stations. The seasoning of the war served me well.

A decade passed. You can get used to everything, including the gypsy lifestyle.

There were moments of joy and satisfaction. With all my prejudice to the authorities of that time, I could slowly begin to see that something was building up in this country, something was coming, and that my efforts and those like me—millions of us—were not in vain, not being wasted by unjust governance.

During my constant travels, I met many fascinating people. I experienced several accidents and witnessed interesting events. I can only remember a few of the incidents from those years, although some of them I remember as if they happened yesterday.

I stood on the platform of the railway station in Sochaczew, waiting for a train to Warsaw. When the train arrived with a terrifying squeal of its brakes, many people were standing on the platform. A twelve-, maybe thirteen-year-old boy jumped out of the wagon, bounced off the lamppost, and flew towards the wheels. I jumped after him: I grabbed his collar with one swift movement of my hand and used my other to grip his pants. Then, I jerked backward, pulling him from under the wheels in the last, hundredth of a fraction of a second. I vividly remember the wheels of the wagon in front of my eyes.

Both the boy and I were in one piece. The boy only peeked at me fearfully. Instinctively, I whacked his ear, sent a bunch of curses, and got into the wagon. The train started.

My travel companion, the director of a construction company in Sochaczew, gaped at me for a long time with stupefied eyes, and finally he choked out: "Mister, how did you manage to do that? You saved his life!"

"Yes," I cursed. "I didn't even ask him for his last name."

Was this just a simple case of instinct? Would I have managed to save the boy if it weren't for my near-death experiences of my former years? It's a question that I asked myself for a long time, only finally answered with the coincidental instances of the following decades.

A similar event happened to me later in the following year. My company received two "Stary-25" trucks, which greatly simplified our construction work. As I was heading back from a construction site in one of them, an unpleasant surprise awaited me on the road near Stanisławów. The vehicle stopped. My driver scratched his head for a long time and finally stated: "We ran out of fuel, but we'll come up with something."

He opened the engine hood (the engine in this truck model was in the driver's cabin), pulled a liter of gasoline from under his seat, removed the engine filter, and connected the bottle directly to the engine pipe.

"You look after this bottle. We can drive!" he announced triumphantly.

Indeed, we went, but before we traveled even a hundred meters, the engine sneezed, flames burst forward, and the whole cabin was on fire.

I closed my eyes, but I still held the liter bottle of burning gasoline in my right hand. Throwing the bottle down threatened to explode the flame further in the cramped cabin—it would result in certain death. Like lightning, my mother's story passed through my head, explaining what to do in such a case.

* * *

During the First World War, oil lamps for lighting were widely used. It was difficult to obtain kerosene, so it would often come from various sources; most of the supply came from soldiers; however, no one could guarantee it was legitimate kerosene. Often, with the operation of an underground market, the "kerosene" was actually gasoline.

And so one evening, when my mother was topping up the lights, the bottle suddenly lit aflame. Mother, conscious with a burning bottle in her hand, did the only thing she could do to save herself; she ran to the door, opened it, and tossed the bottle into the yard.

* * *

So, the only option I had was to throw out the bottle of gasoline! But how? I kept the bottle in my right hand, and the door was on the right side. I clogged the bottle with my thumb, and with my left hand, grinding my teeth with pain, blindly reached for the door handle. Finally, I opened the door, threw out the burning bottle, and jumped out of the wagon.

I had seen how in 1945, the Soviet soldiers jumping out of burning tanks put out the fires on their clothes. This experience came in handy. I began to wallow in the roadside ditch. From the back of the car, my workers jumped down and, using their jackets, put out the fire from my clothes. I stood on my feet, straightened up, and howled in pain. Both of my hands were burned black, and blood was dripping from them. I clenched my teeth, but despite this, the yells still came from my larynx.

Nearby, there were several peasant houses. We approached one, then the second, and the third. I asked and offered every sum of money to take me to the hospital in Minsk. However, it turned out to be impossible. The first one was busy because his horse was birthing a foal, the other had a broken car, and the third a sick wife. Everybody refused. Post-war numbness, or simple laziness? I stopped asking, cursed angrily, and set off on the road. I walked like a prisoner, my arms raised, blood running down my sleeves. Two of the men held me under my arms.

At dawn, we reached the emergency service in Minsk. At the sight of my burns, the nurse on duty paled and said she could not bear my wounds because she would faint. All she could do was advise me to go towards the hospital, which lay just outside of the town.

I made it there. Here, a young doctor who showed no interest ordered his staff to dress my wounds and give me three days of work release. I stood on the sidewalk for an hour, waiting at the bus stop. An overcrowded bus naturally did not stop at the station. Finally, a merciful soul by the freeway indicated that I could be given a ride. On the way, I lost consciousness.

I woke up in the hospital bed just on the outskirts of Węgrow. A transfusion of blood and some morphine had brought me back to life.

The senior doctor who was treating me shook his head: "How could they let you out of the hospital in Minsk? You could have died on the way from loss of blood," he said in a moment of sincere honesty.

And so I managed to escape the undertaker's shovel, once at the scene of an accident, and secondly from the carelessness of some medics.

The tragic incidents would happen not only on the construction sites. I clearly remember one incident while renovating houses in Pułtusk. The German-Russian front had stood there in August 1944, on the Narew River. The city, occupied by the Germans, was mercilessly bombed and shot at by the Russians. The entire coastal part of the city was destroyed. The only things that stood up were the burned walls of apartment houses.

One day, an employee named Edek disappeared from the construction development. A coworker found him and reported that he was drinking in a bar at the corner of the street. At our workplace, fantastic rumors circulated: Edek had won the lottery, he had gotten an inheritance from America, he had found a treasure. I figured what had happened when I went to the place where Edek had worked. I found an abandoned, pre-war, empty tin tea box. So what could have been in it?

After a few days, my worker came back, and the matter cleared up. He was sad, pale, depressed, and burdened with a sincere request to take him back.

"What happened to you, Edek?" I asked.

"This!" Edek replied, turning and pulling up his shirt.

There were several strips of bruises on his back left over from a severe beating.

"And what is that for?" I inquired further, showing him the tin tea box.

"That's it," he confirmed. "While hammering the grooves in the wall, I found, walled-up inside, a box of twenty-seven twenty dollar American gold coins. I had to celebrate." He added, "I managed to sell and drink two coins, the rest of them were taken away by the UB,[47] and in memory, they left the bruises on my back. They also interrogated me about where I had more of these coins, but I already took all of them."

Actually, this loss was quite significant. At the dizzying prices of gold, you could buy a detached house with a plot of land for these coins. I learned from one of the inhabitants of Pułtusk that the home at the construction site, rebuilt before the war, was owned by a wealthy Jewish merchant, who likely walled the treasures.

During the reconstruction of old houses devastated during the war, we often stumbled upon hidden banknotes and documents. Perhaps even gold and jewelry was buried inside, but it was not always easily detected.

Another event from those years remains. It was a cold, frosty morning as the bus stopped in Węgorzewo. The door opened, and up the stairs, a beautiful, maybe eighteen-year-old blonde with a long braid hopped in and sat down next to me. We exchanged a few sentences (I learned her name was Stasia), we promised to stay in touch, and because I repeatedly stared at her, I missed my stop in Liw. Getting off a few kilometers away, I had to walk back on foot in the crackling frost.

This seemingly unimportant event had a very surprising epilogue, which took place many years later.

It was now the end of the 1950s. After ten years of work, I had accumulated almost zero funds. Only dubious satisfaction remained as I traveled through the kindergartens, schools, health centers, or residential houses that I had assisted in rebuilding. Satisfaction is poor pay; however, it is not offered in any store.

---

47 *The secret police of the Polish People's Republic, then known as the UB*

Soon I decided to leave my state-employed career. I had decided to join the layer of independent workers, who were dismissed by the majority of people and barely tolerated by the authorities.

This new stage of my life began very successfully. By winter, when my first job was signed off, I hurried to the payment office. The cashier laid such a stack of banknotes in front of me that the eyes of the administration officials almost fell out of their sockets. This reward was the equivalent of three years of wages in my previous managerial position, working for the state.

I had a rule—I paid a lot more to employees than they would have earned in a state-owned company, but in return, I required honest work, which was the hardest thing to enforce, as I learned later on. Generally, employees did not respect the job, and the saying often went around, "*Czy się stoi czy się leży dwa tysiące się należy* (Staying up, or lying down, two thousand still due…)" and so even when the pay was more lucrative, it did not mobilize people to work. The principle "one works and two admire" was commonplace. This was perpetuated by overprotection from the government and usually low pay.

The so-called "tumiwisizm[48]" had become a universal phenomenon in the Polish People's Republic—which was organically derived from socialist realism—that demanded that the management of the construction companies have incredible gymnastic ability to satisfy the payroll requirements of inefficient employees and expectations to complete the required work. Luckily, the private employers had a more manageable task when taking on board laborers, as they were not backed up by the political party, management, or trade unions.

So I had indeed caught the wind in my sails. And after this first successful and timely job, the next orders began to fill in rapidly. There was just one more obstacle; self-employed relations with the Tax Office were very particular. It was often a game of cat and mouse. The office arranged traps in which the unwary delinquent fell easily, and there was no longer mercy. Such an insignificant "insult" could reach the size of an annual income, which is why you had to keep an eye on every step.

---

48 *An expression for a lack of drive to work, as coined by the Polish poet Julian Tuwim*

Financially, I was incomparably better off than before, but I needed to work hard and efficiently. Even so, I proved to myself that even in a post-war socialist regime, it was possible to live fruitfully. I could comfortably afford far trips abroad, I visited the whole of Eastern and Western Europe, and I bought a car, a beautiful apartment, and furniture. My daughter graduated after her final exams and left to study in Warsaw.

Although materially I was considered a wealthy man in those times, my private life—my marriage—began to deteriorate. I don't like to bring back the memories of these days, where the cause of the decay of my marriage lay.

At my mother's funeral, I stood alone over the coffin, with only the choir of the evangelists from Węgrów, who sang on the open grave, making it easier for me to experience the difficult moment. Further difficulties came soon after. One is not likely to call divorce a pleasure. I accepted all of my wife's terms: I left the apartment, furniture, everything. I got into my car, taking only one suitcase, and without looking back, drove away.

At the first intersection, I wondered where to turn, where to go. The first thought that came to mind was to drive around central Europe and take a bite into the memories of my younger years. From experience, I knew that nothing was as calming and enriching as traveling.

Behind the steering wheel, concentrating on the roads ahead, I was detached from the memories of unpleasant, gloomy events. After a few hours of driving, the tiredness of the senses excludes all thoughts.

For the first time in my life, I was without compulsion, without company, without worries and duties. I felt liberated as if I was a free Cossack in the Siberian steppe. My mother was no longer alive, my former wife quickly found a job, and my daughter was in university—so the page of this chapter had closed. What will the future bring? We'll see.

I decided to continue my traveling therapy. I traveled through Kraków, and then I reached my relatives in Wrocław. They welcomed me with open arms, but something inside of me pushed me to keep moving as if I could run away from my thoughts and lose them somewhere along the way.

The next step was Prague, where I also had relatives, which proved how good it was to have a large, spread-out family. I visited for three days. My cousins sat behind the wheel, and therefore the duty of tasting famous Czech beer and vodka fell on me. As a result, I was constantly tipsy, to their delight.

Slowly, my good humor returned. My cousins looked for even more places worth going to visit. And they have something to boast about; the Czech area was the corner of Europe which had probably least suffered from the wars that plagued the continent. We decided to visit Konopiště, the hunting castle of Archduke Franz Ferdinand, the late successor of the Austrian throne, which was decorated with thousands of hunting trophies. Thousands of animals from all over the world fell from his bullets before he and his wife were assassinated in Sarajevo in June of 1914.

It was time to return to say goodbye to my cousins. The farewell was extremely cordial. The female neighbors who knew me from previous visits opened their windows: "*Na zdar Zbyszek!* (Cheers Zbyszek!)" For a long time, their farewells rang in my ears.

I decided to head north, towards East Germany. I crossed the border without any problems and arrived in Dresden in the evening. I spent the night in nearby Radeberg, and the next day I returned to the city where I experienced the most terrible night of my life and where I lost my first real love.

The downtown of the magnificent capital of Saxony was already partially rebuilt, but the city was still curing its wounds. I slowly wandered to the banks of the Elbe. The freshly rebuilt, former royal castle prized itself with a new garment. The water shimmered and reflected the bright, blue sky as clouds like floating sheep passed by. I continued to stroll towards the central streets of the beautiful city, which were also flooded with sunshine.

I closed my eyes, and the past, the nightmarish night I had survived here, was brought to my senses: the clatter of bomber engines, the sea of fire, the thunder and whistling of bombs, the mad mother cradling a dead baby, the grip of Irmi's hand, all of which stood in my mind as if it were happening there and then. Perhaps her spirit is wandering somewhere in the alleys, I thought.

I opened my eyes. The Elbe flowed continuously, the birds sang in the bushes, and children innocently played on the riverside promenade.

Tremendously tired, after a long day of wandering around the city, I decided to go to bed immediately after dinner. I was hungry as a starved wolf, so I walked into the nearby restaurant, and to my surprise, all of the tables were occupied.

"What is it, a convention or a funeral?" I asked the waitress.

Before each of the guests stood a large pint of beer, yet there was complete silence. The guests, only men, sat quietly and stiffly, as if at a funeral feast.

The waitress glanced around the room. "No, they are our *stammgaste* (regulars)," she replied with a smile.

"But I am furiously hungry, and I do not see one free place here."

"Ah, there will be a place soon!" she grinned again and soon brought a chair.

The guests made a place for me at the nearest table, and I sat down to dinner with the silent company. These young Germans looked at me curiously, and in the end, one of them spoke to me: "From what country, mister?"

"From Poland," I replied. "I am visiting Germany."

They looked at me with surprise.

"Are you allowed to do that?" asked a neighboring lad from the table.

"It's possible," I told them. "Now I am going to Berlin, and later maybe to Paris."

The interlocutor shook his head; the German Democratic Republic was called the largest concentration camp in the world in those days.

"It's not so easy for us to have a passport," the other added on.

All of my plans for the evening went out the window. An entourage of captivating young people surrounded me, and the conversation ended around midnight. I had to watch out for every word—there could be a spy among these people. This conversation gave me lots of food for thought; the young Germans seemed to know almost nothing about Poland and Poles.

I have encountered similar conversations many times in both the German Democratic Republic and the Federal Republic. Our western neighbors, even some thirty years after the war, knew little about us.

Instead of getting up early in the morning, I woke up after midday. I did not engage in any conversations. After breakfast, I jumped in my car and drove straight north towards Berlin. I made it just in time for dusk. By Marchlewskist Street, I found a small hotel and spent the night.

In the morning, I discovered that the Berlin Wall,[49] which divided Berlin in the east and south part of the city, was located not far from the hotel. Cut in two by a three-meter-high concrete wall, they were two different worlds. From the eastern side, there was a belt of no man's land, barbed wire fences, guard towers, and minefields (although theoretically, at the request of the government of the Federal Republic and for fifty million marks, the mines were reportedly removed). The warning boards and eyes of vigilant sentries from the towers created the atmosphere of a concentration camp, and none of the locals approached too close to the wall. Several hundred young Germans and one young Polish girl paid with their lives here, as their curiosity led them to attempt to discover what was on the other side.

On the other side, life was carried on as normal. There was no surveillance, and no one was shooting anyone. For the curious who wanted to see a piece of the "exotic," there were even wooden platforms built right next to the masonry to peek into the paradise of the laborers and peasants of the East. I had visited West Berlin twice, so I had the opportunity to see both sides of the picture.

---

49 *The Berlin Wall (August 1961 - November 1989) was created in response to the mass emigration of Easterners to West Berlin, which, by 1961, totalled 3.5 million German citizens, 20% of the East German population. Eastern officials had feared a "brain drain," as so many younger and well-educated people of the GDR were leaving the country, depriving it of the working population and hundreds of thousands of professionals. The wall extended 155 km (about ninety-six miles) around West Berlin.*

EAST-WEST GERMANY AND THE BERLIN WALL

For about forty-five years, the new borders of Germany were split with the western occupation zones initially for the Americans, British, and French, and the east for the Soviet Union. Berlin was divided the same way. Soon afterward, the nation was officially split into the Western German Federal Republic and the Eastern German Democratic Republic. In 1961, the Berlin Wall was constructed, and it was only taken down some twenty-nine years later, with the collapse of the Soviet Union and the Eastern Bloc. This map showcases these borders of Germany.

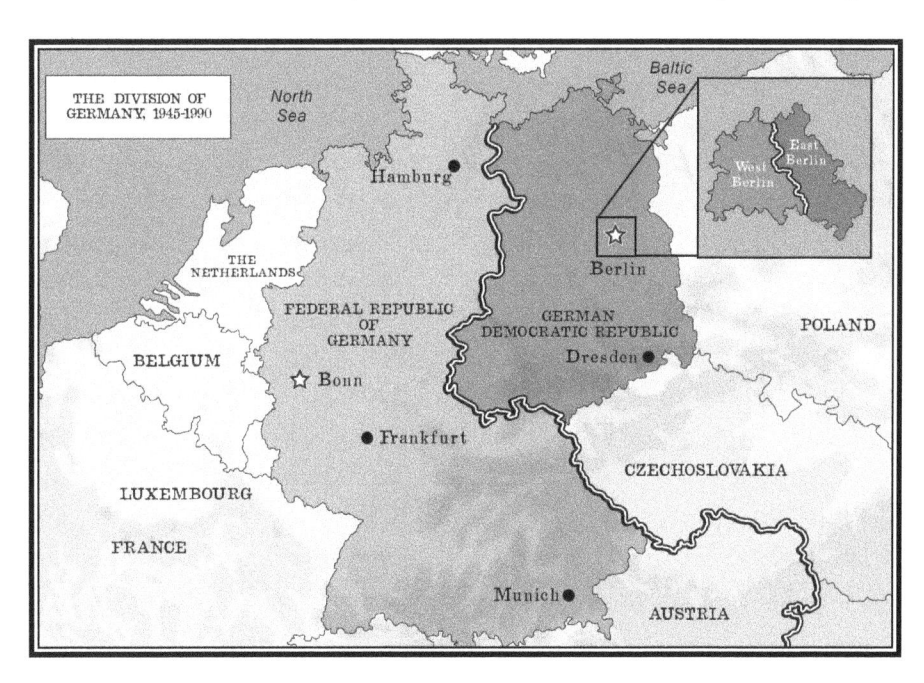

This time, I had a passport, but I did not have an entry visa, so access was closed—and this led me to come up with an equally genius and stupid idea. I decided to implement it straight away. No wall in the world cannot be overcome, I thought.

During my last stay in West Berlin, Ralf, an acquaintance, showed me this hole. The government of the GDR, like all Communist authorities, was in desperate need of foreign currencies, which were in the pockets of the residents of West Berlin, and therefore they created a clever setup.

The Berlin subway would not stop at the stations over which East Germany was running; they would just slow down and run through. Dangerous, armed *grenzschutz*[50] guarded the platforms. The wagon doors would not open. This applied to all metro stations belonging to the East, with the exception of the Alexanderplatz station. Here the train stopped, and you could take a high staircase to the top, to Alexander Square, where there was a big shop named Pewex just next to the exit. The only way to purchase items from that store was with Western marks or American dollars. The policemen stood on the stairs by the entrance and surveilled the travelers—every young man was stopped and scrutinized. This was to prevent the young people from escaping to the West.

The whole joke was that a resident of West Berlin could purchase from the shop, leave western hard currencies and go back the same way. The goods in this Eastern Pewex were much cheaper than in the shops of West Berlin. So I decided to test this loophole.

I left my car at the hotel parking lot, took out my essentials, and went to Alexanderplatz. At the entrance to the subway I made purchases, then confidently hopped down the stairs to the subway platforms under the diligent officers' eyes. When I got into the wagon, I breathed a sigh of relief. Phew—I had succeeded; I had crossed the border of two worlds with luck.

In the afternoon, I came to my dear friend Ralf, who, during the summer, lived on his vacation property in the northern district of Berlin, Frohnau.

"You can stay here with me for as long as you want," he stated when I told him my finances were already running out.

---

50 *Border guards*

Then he picked up the phone and called Zygfryd, whom I also knew. From the next day, I was able to start work in a book bindery. At seven o'clock in the morning, I stood in my new workplace.

I lived on the northern side in the Frohnau district, and the workplace was in the Kreuzberg district, which meant I had to travel almost across the whole city. Fortunately, the transport was efficient and punctual, just as the Germans always had been. A ticket covering two hours of all types of public transport cost two marks. The division of the city was confirmed only by the blind metro stops, where the train did not stop at all.

Work in the bookbindery was light. Two breaks for breakfast and lunch gave sufficient time for a meal and relaxing chats—and these were extremely interesting. There were four of us: "Redhead" Zigi (the boss), senior Alex (a Berlin socialist), a seventeen-year-old apprentice named Hansele, and I.

After a few days, I became one of the staff's brothers, and Zigi especially appreciated me. With time, it became a routine that on Friday, after being paid, my boss would invite me to the Italian restaurant on the other side of the street. He had six children and was in constant quarrels with his wife. After a few pints, he would weep all his sorrows onto my sleeve.

We would spend almost all Friday evenings together. Conversations went in various directions, and a few large beers would point us to political topics. Zigi confessed once that he was a part of the Hitlerjugend and the head of his group in school.

In a moment of regret, he would cry and tell me: "Our Führer was such a wise man, and this is what he did to us."

"He was not wise, only ignorant and stupid," I would reply. "At school, he was clearly weak in the areas of history and geography."

When I saw Zigi's surprised expression, I added: "If he knew history well and was aware of Napoleon's attempt to conquer Russia, and if in geography he knew the distance between Konigsberg and Moscow, he would surely roll his mustache before giving the order *Vorwarts* (Forward)."

"The Allies also helped him a lot," Zigi murmured. "Here in Berlin, the English and Americans gave us quite a whipping."

"You see, Zygfryd," I said, "only fools are cocky with the rest of the world."

"*Ja, hast du recht* (Yes, you're right)," he replied. "And we believed in him like God," he sighed.

On another occasion, Zigi asked me: "Where were you, and what did you do?"

"I was a long way from here, in Ukraine. I worked and saw what the Germans did there. I will tell you one day if you feel like listening."

Three months passed, and I was getting ready to return. Zygfryd advised me to apply for asylum or to put him and Ralf as witnesses in the law enforcement office and state that I was German and would remain permanently settled in West Berlin. These options did not suit me—I already had my homeland. Even though I knew I wouldn't stay, I kept delaying my return day after day.

A coincidence decided that I did not put off the exodus; one time, a beautiful, elegant lady stood with a little girl on the metro platform next to me. Suddenly, the little girl spoke in Polish, "*Mamusiu, czy pociąg zaraz nadjedzie?* (Mama, will the train come soon)?"

A heavy sentiment, like a dark and deep night, fell on my heart. Tears stood in my eyes. I decided to go back the following morning, despite the unhidden disappointment from a lovely neighboring widow.

In the morning, I thanked Zygfryd for his work, said goodbye to the others, and began to prepare for departure. I decided to take the same route through Alexanderplatz. The only problem was with money; I had earned a large sum. In the event of being caught, the devil will take my money, I thought.

Ralf agreed to transport my marks through the risky loophole. For him, as a citizen of West Berlin, there was no threat of search and confiscation when shopping in the Eastern Pewex. We agreed to go separately and meet in the bar at the top store.

As agreed, we did just that. Ralf went up the stairs from the subway, and I followed a little later. On this day, there were few people on the stairs. The grenzschutz surveilled everyone, and perhaps this time, my luck did leave me because the patrolling officer gazed at me with scrutiny and asked for a passport.

He examined it and questioned: "You were in West Berlin without a visa?"

I was prepared for this inquiry.

Staring into his eyes, I proclaimed, "Only fifteen minutes, sir."

"How so, fifteen minutes?" he growled. "How is that possible?"

"That's typical. I went to Alexanderplatz and walked down the stairs to the subway. I realized I had gotten lost, and I'm just coming back," I was lying brazenly to his face.

"I have not seen you here, mister," he responded, frowning. "*Kommen sie mit!* (Come with me!)"

Few people would run from West Berlin to East, and it was usually vice versa, so in the assumptions of the grenzschutz, I was either insane or worse—a spy. There were no jokes with the Eastern officers; you could live a sad existence in prison for years.

For a minute, I stood in front of the officer at the border-control post.

His brow furrowed, he eyed me carefully, and then he yelled to his guards: "Search the suitcase and check the documents!"

The grenzschutz told me to undress, and then he began to carefully rummage through my clothes' seams and stitches. I sat on a hard bench, bare as a Turkish saint, and despite the fears for my destiny, I laughed to myself in the spirit of their fruitless efforts.

In my pockets, I had only a comb, handkerchiefs, a pocket knife, my wallet with several hundred Polish zlotys and Eastern marks, and in my suitcase, there was only a change of underwear and toiletries. The officer finally made a note of the stamp, which was given to me in the passport when crossing the Czech–East German border three months previously.

"What were you doing in the German Democratic Republic the last three months?" he asked with gleeful wit. "What did you live off?"

"I visited your beautiful country, and I had seasonal jobs," I replied.

"Where? Who for?"

"I do not remember. I have been to so many different places."

Dial-up calls were made. I have hammered a nail into their head, I thought, and then suddenly I was overcome with a slight uneasiness.

The investigation was prolonged. Upstairs in the bar, Ralf is waiting, knowing him, most likely chugging beer, I thought. Certainly with my money. It doesn't matter, as long as no one robs him.

It was the evening. For the tenth time, the officer asked me how I had managed the miracle of getting downstairs without being noticed by the guards. And for the tenth time, I replied that they must have poor eyesight because I do not look like a dwarf. The devil took hold of him; he horribly criticized the other grenzschutz that they guarded the border poorly, and then again he dived deeper into studying my passport.

"You've traveled a lot around the world," he remarked. "So many stamps here, from almost the entirety of Europe."

"I only haven't made it to Greece," I added modestly.

Then a genius thought struck my head. In the passport, there was a stamp that said "This passport is valid in all countries of the world" or something along those lines. I could use it in my favor.

"Please read this stamp," I pointed with my finger. "I can ride around the world."

The officer stared intently at the stamp but did not understand much because it was only stamped in Polish, French, and possibly English. It was a standard stamp that was found in every passport.

"Call Hans—he might understand Polish," he ordered his subordinate.

Another guard appeared in a moment. This one was likely educated at a Polish school because he read the stamp without a hitch.

The officer in charge looked at me with respect, returned the passport, and spoke the final words: "I am sorry, it's all because of the inattention of my people," and he escorted me to the door.

How many times have I managed to escape free from the dragon's teeth? I thought to myself, hurrying up the stairs. The shops at Alexanderplatz were already closed, and my friend was fidgeting patiently at the table.

He spotted me and, with dreary eyes, murmured: "Where have you been so long? Was I supposed to stay here overnight?!"

He gave me the money and with the words: "I have drunk twenty marks worth," he gave me his hand to say goodbye. To hell with twenty marks, for so many hours of waiting, I thought to myself.

I made it to the familiar hotel, next to which I left my car. After an emotionally taxing day, I fell asleep like a stone. In the morning, I picked up my already washed car and asked around how to make it to the "Berliner Ring" (the bypass around Berlin).

From the beltway of Berlin, I turned onto the highway leading towards Frankfurt an der Oder, near the border-crossing in Świecko. I drove unhurriedly, cruising along the concrete "ladder" autobahn built during Hitler's time, but the closer I reached to the border, the more persistently dark thoughts circled my head, like angry wasps. What's next? I was alone again, without a home, rich only in new life experiences. I had to start over again.

The same wide river, bridge, border, and homeland, which I could not reject, was before me, yet it seemed to be a vast unknown. It was just like thirty years before.

The day was sunny and pleasant, and soon my heavy, sad pondering left my mind. I hummed the lyrics of my favorite song, the story of Medea, in a low voice—"*Jak Jazon naszych czasów ruszamy z Grecji w świat, by zdobyć złote runo... tram tara ramtam tam* (Like Jason of our time, we set off from Greece for the world, to get the golden fleece... tram tara ramtam tam)." Indeed, there was not much to worry about: I had a large sum of money in my bank account, a contract for the renovation of a large holiday resort in Masuria in my pocket, an almost brand-new car—which cost a fortune in those times—and my lucky star that never failed me before.

Masuria

Masuria greeted me with a golden autumn. The old holiday resort, named Rudziska Pasymskie, had several holiday homes and forester's lodges, surrounded by overgrown forest hills. It was located a few kilometers from the historic town of Pasym on the beautiful Lake Kalwa, which aroused my admiration. There aren't many such quiet and picturesque places in Poland, I thought the next day when I went to see the construction site.

A large, beautiful resort stood on the hillside in the old pine forest. Silence was ringing in my ears. During the times of the Third Reich, the residence was a Hitlerjugend sports center, as indicated by the traces of the ski jumps. Later, the conquering Russians devastated the center completely. Now, it was in the hands of the *Związek Socjalistycznej Młodzieży* (Socialist Youth Union) and was in desperate need of further renovations. It required injections of fat sums of money.

I occupied a small room in the main building of the resort, was given a small iron stove for warmth, then decided to explore the local area. And this place was really beautiful. The golden Polish-Masurian autumn painted the forest hills with all shades of color. Golden, bright red maple leaves, a delicate lace of yellow birch contrasting harmoniously with white stems, dark green pines and spruces, the blue of the autumn sky, and the dark emerald of the lake, was a truly breathtaking sight. Only a genius painter could record this fading beauty of autumn on canvas.

For two days, I wandered around, learning about the charms of Masurian nature. Twice I went astray and spent hours looking for a way back. However, I did not regret that hardship, as I discovered so many fascinating, interesting places. Hidden in the depths of the forest, there was an abandoned forester's lodge and concrete bunkers—which covered some grim war secrets because nobody had ever opened the thick armored doors—but above all, the beautiful, emerald lake with rugged banks attracted my interest. Here it was possible on a sunny day to sit for hours and gaze at the shimmering emerald waves.

    I dedicated the next few days to meeting the people. Apart from the night watchman and his dog, who generally slept all night, I met a forester, who was as large as a barrel, and his very thin, quiet wife. They were all of the people in Rudziska Pasymskie, except for the seasonal residents there.

    I spent the long warm sunny autumn evenings sitting in the yard and peering at the beautiful sparkling October sky, spying the stars and constellations that I knew. The Pleiades, the Usar Major, the Little Bear, and the millions of worlds that have been shifting slowly before our eyes.

    Inhabitants of cities never seem to know the power and beauty of the outer cosmos; as for this, you need the weather, a moonless night, silence, and no lights nearby. Only at times, the quiet sound of the forest, the long hoot of an owl, the clangor of cranes flying somewhere under the stars, of a distant whistle of the locomotive disturbed the harmony of the autumn Masurian night. How trivial, how little a man sees himself, with all his troubles, problems, and feelings. A few hours spent in such a starry, silent night is a natural bath for a harassed human heart. This is what I had just experienced.

    After a week of staying in this wilderness, I felt renewed in my soul and body. All black thoughts floated away somewhere beyond the horizon of time and space. I began to peer around the distant area. During the night, only the light of the small town of Pasym flashed in the distance, seven or eight kilometers away. With a narrow, winding, asphalt road, there were two farms along the way to the town. That was the only sign of civilization in this forest wilderness.

    I went to the town. A church in the Romanesque style, a city hall, the market square, and the remains of the old guarding walls testified to a medieval origin, of former glory and riches. The shops were poorly stocked; apart from everyday necessities, few items adorned the shelves. The shelves in the butcher shop were empty. Taking the advice of one of the residents, I wandered to the fishing base, and here to my surprise, I was offered a box of fresh, live eels straight from the lake. I bought a few kilos of this fish and took them to the address given to me, to the house by the lake of a Mrs. Gabryelowa, and by the evening, I had a delicious stack of smoked eels.

Along with three young workers, I spent the entire winter disassembling old, devastated sanitary and heating installations, hammering holes in the walls, and undergoing similar auxiliary jobs in the resort. I spent long frosty nights in my room, by the glowing fire of the stove, in the company of the old Masurian caretaker and his dog.

Sometimes, there was a distant howl of wolves in the cold nights, causing the dog to bristle and tremble all over, and "Grandpa"—what I used to call the old man—would begin his Siberian stories.

During the First World War, Grandpa Ernest spent some freezing winters in Siberia as a German prisoner under Russian enslavement. After the war, he returned, but with frosted fingers, so he was no longer suitable for the profession of carpentry. He worked as a caretaker the entire twenty years between the wars and somehow survived through January 1945, when he continued to caretake foreign property under the new reign.

He was an exquisite storyteller. He spoke so vividly in the beautiful Masurian dialect, which he had learned among his people in the town, that with some imagination, it was detailed enough to close one's eyes and see the unbelievable Siberian spaces, impenetrable forests, powerful, raging, foamy rivers, and hear the rumbling of the snowstorm "purga," the howls of wolves and the roar of breaking, frozen trees.

One night, the winter peered deeply into our eyes. There was heavy snow all night long, the wind stormed into the chimney, and the forest rustled ominously. Three days of snow continued to fall, and when the storm ceased, it was difficult to open the door, and snow poured over our knees.

Grandpa smiled and sighed heavily: "Oh, it was worse than this once."

I accompanied him in that statement. "I also know these old pains. Sometimes my hunger did not even allow for the deceiving comfort of sleep."

In the end, the gale stopped, and the sun shone upon the covered, immaculately white forest, which glowed enchantingly. Branches of trees cracked and broke under the weight of the snow. How could we get to the town and buy something to eat? The car covered with snow was useless, the road was covered up, impassable, and there appeared to be no plans to clear it. So, we set off on foot, but after trudging only several hundred meters, we gasped heavily like blacksmith bellows, and sweat dripped from our noses. Under these conditions, eight kilometers to Pasym would take us all day. Will we even have enough energy to make it? In some places, the snowdrifts were up to our armpits.

We were looking at each other helplessly when suddenly the old man glanced around diligently and shouted, "*Sroka!* (Magpie!)"

"Where's the magpie?" I snorted with laughter.

"What the hell do we need a bird for? To eat?" Ernest looked at me, scandalized. "No bird," he growled, "but Helmut Sroka. Do you see this house at the edge of the forest? Helmut Sroka lives over there; he is my old acquaintance. I am sure we will be able to eat there."

I had strolled past this house and the farm on the lake, but I had never been there and did not know who lived there.

We crossed a few dozen meters from the road and knocked on the door of the house. A middle-aged lady opened it. Soon, a limping man with only one leg appeared, more or less the lady's age. Ernest greeted him like an old friend, introduced me, and soon we sat in the kitchen over plates full of appetizing pea soup and smoked meat.

"So we have been seriously snowed-in!" the host said after a short moment.

"My daughter hasn't gone to work, and the boys cannot go to school," he breathed deeply.

Daughter, what daughter? I pondered. I had seen several girls and women in the forest during autumn mushrooming. Which one could it be? Soon my doubts were resolved. A young woman came into the kitchen with cups, smiled radiantly at us, filled the mugs with coffee, grinned again, and left the kitchen. I felt that the last flash of her eyes was intended for me.

After a few minutes, as Elżbieta (that was her name) wandered around the kitchen, I managed to assess that she had all the good qualities in the right places with an expert eye in feminine beauty. I had seen her figure with a basket of mushrooms in hand at the edge of the forest several times, but the distance between us was too big to assess. Now fate had given me the opportunity. A model, I thought, shapely, tall, slim, with a lovely head on a long, white neck, decorated with a plaited crown of golden hair. And those eyes! Their flash could ignite a feeling in the heart of every man. Graceful in her movement, and the manner in her voice gave her some unique charm of a mermaid.

The short winter day was coming to an end, and, loaded with donated food from the hospitable hosts, we trudged back to our home. On the spot, I lit a fire on the stove, brewed two cups of tea, put one in front of me, and handed the second to Ernest, although he could not pick himself up from the bunk. He slept like a dead man.

At sunrise, there was a loud knock at the door. I ventured out the window.
"Who is banging so loud?"
The fat forester stood in front of the door with a shotgun over his shoulder.

Seeing me, he exclaimed: "Please, gentlemen, do not leave after dusk into the depths of the forest. Wolves are showing up."

"Wolves—ingenious beasts," Ernest began his story the next morning, "In the daytime, a man seen from afar the beast will bypass, but at night you do not want to confront their eyesight. He will dig into any barn or stall and slaughter all of the livestock," he added. "It's strange," he muttered, "After the First World War, which visited this region, they multiplied enormously, and after the last war, there were also many of them. Why?"

"There were quite a few people who had been 'lost' in the woods at both of these times. Remind yourself," I replied.

"Oh, yes, I remember." He tapped his head. "Those who died in the winter of late 1944 lay sprawled there until the following spring."

Another week and no stranger showed up, nor my workers. The roads were still covered. The main trails were cleared of snow, but no one cared for the pavement to the holiday resort that was deserted in the winter, where, with the forester's family, there were just a few of us. Nobody was worried. We were condemned to be cut off from the rest of the world, but it was not too unpleasant. During the day, we chopped trees for the fire, would put together tasty meals, and in the evenings, we sat at the stove gazing into the flames as Ernest dreamed about his endless stories. He was a living chronicle of those times and their people.

"And what about in 1945? How was it here?" I asked him another time during the evening conversation. Ernest thought about it and reached for his favorite pipe.

"Oh, there were…" he sighed heavily, "…hundreds of thousands of frightened, innocent people, fleeing amid frosts and snowstorms. Many of them remained in the ditches, the Soviets murdered many, they raped the women—no one was given a pardon—and they set fire to houses."

"But you miraculously survived. How?" I asked.

"I stayed," the old man replied, "with my wife and granddaughters. The attempt to escape in such a frost was suicide. The young and healthy had chances, but the children and the old were bound to perish. The Soviets also occupied and burned Szczytno. Here, between Dźwierzuty and Pasym, there were fierce battles. The German Panzergrenadier Division defended hopelessly when the remaining tanks were left without fuel. The main strategy was just to give some time to the crowds of refugees hurling northward into waiting merchant ships. It was the last resort—East Prussia was already cut off from the Reich."

"And how did you manage to survive?" I insisted.

"At my house," the old man sighed, "there was not much to eat. One night, the Russian *soldats* (soldiers) stormed with their weapons in hand, but I, an old, crippled peasant, an old wife, and a few disordered children, were no booty for them. They searched the corners and went. Some dozens of people were less fortunate. We buried them in the collective burials in the cemetery. Part of the city disappeared in smoke," he exhaled heavily.

"They paid you beautifully with revenge for your atrocities," this time, I sighed. "And what your soldiers did in Poland, Russia, and all of the other eastern countries, I will tell you some other time," I added. "The worst of this war was the price of the crimes of their leaders, which fell on the innocent."

We were both lost in thought. We were left in our loneliness for over a week, only saved from starvation by our good-willed neighbors. Every day in the afternoon, I trudged through the drifts to the house at the edge of the forest with a thick stick in hand. I was attracted not only by hunger—because bread, butter, and cheese were now abundant—but rather the desire to meet the charming neighbor. She also liked me very much, pouring me large mugs of warm milk and treating me with fresh, fragrant rye bread.

A week passed, and the blizzard ceased. The bright winter sun peeked out. In its rays, you could see how beautiful Masuria also was in the winter, especially here in Rudziska. High, pine-covered hills, smooth frozen lakes, rusty brown clumps of reeds, the untainted whiteness of the snow, blue skies, and an entrancing, miraculous silence reached the eyes and ears.

Now, finally, the roads were clear, yet, even so, only the employees reached through. Ernest went to visit his wife and shop in the town. The short winter days at work passed quickly, and soon again, darkness and silence reigned over the area. Any rumors about wolves quieted—apparently they had moved to the hunting fields. At nightfall, I took a thick stick in my hand, a flask of milk, and ventured home at the edge of the forest. With time, I realized that I was more and more willing to go there for longer, under any excuse to remain.

One day, I did not find the young hostess at home. The parents told me there was a school teacher's conference, and their daughter was expected to return an hour later than usual. I decided to greet her upon her return, outside. The road by the lake was already cleared, and the snow creaked under my feet. Stars winked in the winter sky, and the silver ball of a moon was completely covering the region with its shimmer.

I was just before the intersection of roads near the town when I spotted a familiar figure.

She also recognized me and was the first one to speak: "Are you going to Pasym for a beer?"

"No, no beer. I was concerned for your wellbeing, not to be eaten by the wolves, so I left, towards you," I replied.

I reached for her arm. She did not resist her hand, so I went on: "The night seems to be made for romantic walks," I mused.

Elżbieta gazed at me, smiling. And that's how it began.

In the evening, I bored Ernest with questions about the girl, about her family, why she was still unmarried, and so on. The old man knew this family from childhood, and he told me about them.

"The girl was born in January 1945," he began the story. "Fate happened that the Ruthenians were already in Pasym when the little one issued the first cry. It was a miracle in the midst of tragedy; her cry completely discouraged the soldats when a few of them intruded the house. Among them were also heartfelt people, so they left the mother with the newborn in peace, which was a rare occasion in those days. Do you know what they used to do with our women?" he asked.

The old man, thanks to the handicap, also managed to get away dry—they spotted his limp and waved their hands. It was worse when the front moved further. What followed were gangs of looters and murderers. They didn't even leave a single thread on people, robbing everything. Near the village of Jedwabne, they were so ruthless that its inhabitants went to the Szczytno town hall barefoot, clad only in old potato sacks.

"Poverty was so severe that we only ate frozen potatoes that had remained in the mounds. It would take a long time to describe it all," Ernest murmured.

"The new authorities do not spoil us either. And how was it in Masuria post-war?" I asked.

The old man looked at me and smiled crookedly: "The first years after the war were the worst," he continued his story. "They forced us to become Polish. They called people to the UB (Security Office) under the pretext of a supposedly unsuspicious 'chat.' But once you got there, you were ordered: "You have a Polish surname, you speak Masurian Polish, so you are a Pole," and a short proposal to sign the declaration followed. Whoever did not want to sign was arrested for a few days, and then they were consistently harassed."

"And you," I asked, "do you feel German or Polish, Ernest?"

He looked at me in amazement.

"You have a purely Polish last name, but your name is German?" I added.

"I am Masurian," he answered, "and I will die Masurian."

The days grew longer and longer, and the Masurian spring was slowly approaching. In mid-April, the long-awaited warm days arrived. One evening, a storm boomed in the west, then it rained all night, and the usual gentle hum of the forest now sounded in a fierce clatter, as if hundreds of trains were running nearby. We did not sleep all night. Every now and again, something would fall heavily in the forest as the gale hit the centuries-old trees.

Everything was quiet in the morning. At dawn, we went out in front of the house; there were a few fallen pine trees on the hills, the remnants of the white sheets of snow had disappeared entirely, and the forest became a delicate mist of greenery. Spring! A time of hard work had come for my workers and me. There was not much time left until the beginning of the season and the arrival of the holiday-makers. Everything had to be ready for that time.

Despite the tiredness in the afternoons, I would jump on the bike after work to greet Elżbieta ahead of the path when she would return from school. We met, greeted, kissed passionately, then I planted the girl on the bicycle frame, and we would explore the local area. Yes, I could feel it; I had fallen in love with Masuria and a Masurian, which became as close to my heart as my motherland, which I lost so many years ago.

Our most frequent visit was the forest on the hill. From the high hill, covered with old pines, you could scout the whole area from the palm of your hand. The beautiful Kalwa Lake, full of islands, bays, and coves, was framed by a dark lace of green forests, and a large horseshoe surrounded the peninsula, on the edge of which stood the "Okrągła Góra"—a former old Prussian fortified settlement. In the distance, the roofs of Pasym flickered, among which the towers of old churches shot up into the sky.

Sometimes, we held our hands for hours in this beautiful, peaceful landscape. The forest on the hill remains forever in my heart. I spent the most beautiful moments of my life there. To this day, I consider it an obligation, at least once a year, to visit that forest and drink water from the spring that flows on the hill.

One day, I had an urgent errand to sort out in Olsztyn. I told Elżbieta about it, and she said that she was also heading in the same direction.

"So let's go together. I will come for you tomorrow morning." I suggested meeting at seven o'clock in the morning. After a short moment, she agreed.

I had a terrible night. Nightmarish dreams plagued my mind. The day will be bad, I thought. I got up earlier than usual, ate breakfast, and sat down in the car. After a while, I stopped at the Sroka house a few moments earlier than we had planned.

The tractor was not in front of the house, so the host must already be in the field. There was complete silence in the yard. I knocked, opened the door to the hall and the smell of smoke hit my nose. I grabbed the door handle to the kitchen, and in the first reflex, I stepped back. A fire burned, and the area was full of smoke. A curtain, which separated the kitchen from the rest of the room, was in flames. Any minute, the fire could jump and spread onto the rest of the room.

I hopped up to the burning curtain, ripped it down, and stepped on it. With bare hands, I threw the burning pots into the yard. Finally, I opened the window and spied into the neighboring room, also filled with smoke. Elżbieta was in there, either asleep or already unconscious. I took her in my arms and brought her to the bench in front of the house. I left her and ran into the house again. The boys slept in the corner room. I opened the window and woke up the little ones. I checked once more whether there was any more fire, and I ran out again to the front of the house. Elżbieta opened her eyes and looked at me, terrified. Her mother, wielding a bucket full of milk, ran over.

"What happened?" she asked.

The case was very simple. Her father had gone to the field, and her mother had gone into the cowshed. Elżbieta poured water into a pot, put in a few sausages, and left it on an electric cooker. There was a lot of time left, so before the sausages boiled, she decided to take a moment for a nap. This moment was apparently quite long because the water in the pot evaporated, and the sausages were instantly aflame. The burning flames lit up and reached the curtain. At just that moment, I showed up—so my premonition of a bad day turned out to be almost true. I had come just in time. If I wasn't punctual on that day, Elżbieta's nap could have ended tragically.

When the old Sroka came back from the field, there was no sign of fire. We had cleaned everything up, and only the smell of smoke, despite the open windows, was felt in the cottage.

After this event, I became ever closer with Elżbieta's parents, and I could now see her each day. Every occasion for a meeting brought delightful smiles. Perhaps it was a strange love; it was not a violent passion like one's first love, but a gentle, light touch of butterfly wings warming the heart. If we were alone, Elżbieta embraced my neck with both hands and cuddled me, and it felt like it could stay like this for hours. During long walks in the woods, we held hands like kindergarteners, and we listened to the singing of the birds, the rustling trees, and the shimmers of a forest brook.

Sometimes, at the girl's request, I sang to her the choruses of my childhood; I wanted to sing my whole soul away. Lullabies, Ukrainian dumkas, dramatic Russian melodies, Polish songs, and even witty tunes from operettas. She liked this song the most; "Sorrow, sorrow for a girl, for green Ukraine, sorrow, sorrow, my heart hurts…"

"You sing it with so much feeling as if you have left someone really special there," she asked one time.

"Yes, I have…" I sighed. "…Her name was Wierą. She saved my life, and I will never see her again."

"How do you know so many of these songs?" she once asked.

"Just hearing them once was enough for me," I replied.

In exchange, Elżbieta told me fairy tales she heard in her childhood, many of which probably had Old Prussian origins.

"You see this hill on the peninsula by the lake? It's Okrągła Góra. There was an ancient Prussian stronghold, where in honor of their gods, they sacrificed blood from prisoners captured during the wars. Once a year, when the night is longest, on the hill, Prussian gods meet, and hundreds of them try to decide how to resurrect the power of their former followers. Yes—" she sighed. "Prusai is a nation that no longer exists. Some of them perished during the fighting, and the rest melted into the mass of settlers—Germans, Poles, and Lithuanians—which the Teutonic Order encouraged to inhabit the lands…"

I was listening to her quiet, melodious voice.

"See this church tower in the lake town? That's Pasym. A legend is also connected with the building of this part of the Evangelical church, as satanic forces tried to destroy its construction. On one of the islands on the lake lived a whole devil family. The devil mama sent her young, handsome son to the town to sow affairs and envy between the inhabitants. The young satan played the role of a fisherman, and helped by the satanic forces, his nets were always full of fish. He fell in love with the beautiful Anna, daughter of the headteacher of the municipal school. The devil made himself liked by the headteacher, with whom he drank beer in one of the city taverns. However, Anna did not like it. She was deterred from the devilishly handsome "fisherman" by the smell of fish and his diabolically beautiful eyes. The devil fell into a frenzy when the girl ridiculed his attempts of seduction. Out of fury, he clawed at a large stone in the forest…

"I'll show you that rock one day—it lies there even today," added Elżbieta. "There are traces of his claws. In love, the devil came up with a new idea. He turned into a monastic knight in a white coat with a black cross and circled the forest for so long until he came across Anna as she picked berries. The girl liked the handsome knight and made an appointment with him. However, this affair ended tragically for her. Someone spotted the couple in love and reported them to the mayor. The mayor, who was also a judge, arrested the girl, put her in a pigsty—which served as custody—and set the date of the hearing. Anna stood before the court, accused of flirting with the devil. The witnesses were the devotees rejected by the girl, and because in those days, such matters were treated with serious punishment, they sentenced her to death. The unfortunate girl was burned at the stake in the middle of the town square."

A moment of silence came up. We glanced at each other.

"You know," I said finally, "there might be a lot of truth in this legend about human nature. The devil could have just been a knight from the Szczytno crew, and all the rest could be made up from jealous devotees of Anna. Does any devil surround ourselves?" I looked around. Unfortunately, the devil did circle.

Elżbieta told me about many such fairy tales and legends. I decided that there is a grain of truth in each of them—a combination of human experiences and dreams.

Such were the carefree pleasant days of spring and summer. Finally, autumn stained the leaves, but nothing changed between us. Joyful, tender meetings and affectionate partings, until tomorrow. Increasingly, I thought anxiously about what would happen when the work in Rudziska ended. Unfortunately, fate yet again decided for me.

One day, Elżbieta came to me with red eyes, full of tears. She was silent, and her hands were trembling as if she was feverish.

"What happened? Speak!" I asked uneasily. "You are not sick, are you?"

"Worse. We're leaving for beyond the Oder," she managed at last, hiding her face in her hands.

"When?" I asked after a moment of silence.

"In a month," she looked at me with watery eyes. Thunder shook between us.

"Stay with me," I suggested. "We'll get married."

"But the whole family will be so far away from me. I'm so attached to them. My crippled father, my ill mother, and those two boys—they all need care. I cannot leave them. Let's get married, and you can come with us," she suggested. "My parents will agree for sure. They like you."

Unfortunately, that option was out of the question. My daughter was expecting another child in Warsaw, and I did not want to change my homeland for the third time. Towards the Germans, despite having good friends among them and knowing many people, their language, customs, and having an appreciation for their diligence and solidity, I still felt a deep, remaining hurt in my heart after what I had witnessed them doing in the east all those years prior.

Our following meetings were sorrowful. Each of us had our own thoughts. The words would not come out of our lips, often left knotted in the throat. Only the squeezing of our hands was more intense.

I spoke to her father. We sat in front of the house and peered at the beautiful Masurian autumn. In front of us, down below, surrounded by a colorful ring of woods, the emerald sheet shone over the lake. Autumn is a rich palette of colors, a noise of wild geese and a clang of cranes in the abyss of sky, all saying farewell to the departing summer. We both watched the picture for a long and silent moment.

I spent the day of their departure in Warsaw. Far away in a large city, among the busyness of people, I wanted to lose my grief and longing. Being close to her when they were leaving was too difficult for me and impossible to live with, so it felt like a good way of escaping the pain of love.

A few days later, I returned to Rudzisk. The house on the hill stood empty and abandoned. For a long time, until dark, I wandered along familiar paths. Our "Forest on the Hill" was quiet and speechless; the last leaves had fallen from the trees. I said goodbye to Ernest and took a look at the familiar landscape so close to my heart for a final time. I got in the car and stepped on the gas. My heart stayed there forever.

PART V

Summation

Prince Czetwertyński

Wandering my thoughts somewhere afar, I forgot that the road was narrow and slippery. I woke up in the surgical ward at the hospital.

The medical diagnosis was serious. Damage to my spine's vertebrae, a complicated left-hand fracture, and general bruises on my head and legs. I was expected to be immobilized for a long time, wrapped in a plastered corset and a stiffened cast for my left arm. I had become a bandaged puppet.

"How long will I have to stay in bed?"

"You were lucky," said the surgeon who looked after me. "We can't say the same about your car, though—they took it for scrap," he added.

"What is the prognosis of my recovery, and what shall I expect afterward?" I asked in a hopeless tone.

"We will find out. Your hand is a complicated fracture, but it should heal after a good few weeks; however, the case is worse with your spine—if it goes well, you will walk back home, but if not, you will have a lifetime in the wheelchair," he sighed.

Dark thoughts banged all over my aching head. By nature an optimist, I could not stand the fact that fate had inflicted two heavy blows in such a short time. A lost lover and an accident that had completely changed my entire life so far. It was pretty uncertain whether or not I would be able to work hard and earn well any longer. The car had gone to hell, but that was the least of my troubles. The insurance would return most of its value plus a bonus, so it would be possible to buy a new one. The only question is if I will buy a car or instead a wheelchair, I thought with self-irony. We will see.

If I can walk, I will look around for a different job and find myself a nice apartment, I decided. Anyway, it will be "what God will give me," as my God-fearing mother used to say.

The second variant, disability and wheelchair, I had not yet devised, according to my rule: "I will worry about tomorrow, tomorrow."

Long, dull, monotonous days, interrupted only by medical visits or the changing of dressing, continued to flow. I looked out the window into the cool, pale winter sky. Sometimes I conversed with a couple of the other broken men, like me, in the room. But talking to them was not incredibly interesting, and I still had long weeks of rest ahead of me, so I began to think about what to do to kill the hospital boredom. My thoughts more and more often fled into the past.

One particular day, I discovered that my right hand was relatively healthy. The doctor allowed me to half-sit in the bed—so I could write! A charming young nurse informed my daughter about my accident and bought me a paper and pen.

I wrote to her, and then I pulled up the bucket from my well of memory. But how deep can I go? We'll see, I thought. At school, I had learned the whole poem of the *Pan Tadeusz* (The Last Foray of Lithuania) effortlessly. I used to swallow volumes of Polish, then Russian, Ukrainian, and finally German literature, so something must still be in my head.

I decided to painstakingly bite into my past. Then to my surprise, I could remember the many events from the distant past, from childhood and adolescence, recalling them better than what had happened a week ago, or even yesterday! When I closed my eyes, I vividly spotted some events as if in a mirror—and there were many interesting, tragic, and even unbelievable events. After all, I had lived in a time that completely rewrote the course of the history of our world. I thought that whoever would read my experiences would have the opportunity to understand the logic of the events of these times.

In ancient times and the Middle Ages, cholera, plague, typhus, and other dangerous, contagious diseases plagued humanity. In the twentieth century, our world was attacked with a more severe plague—nationalism. At the expense of the devastation of Europe, immeasurable suffering, and the deaths of over fifty million people, this scourge has been mastered by the effort and goodwill of people—but has it been completely destroyed?

This is something which still smolders in places, and you never know what winds will rekindle this blight.

I had plenty of time for memories and thoughts. I could only write very little because, after an hour of sitting, my spine ached mercilessly.

One day, my daughter from Warsaw visited me. Smiling and content, her life was going well. A lovely husband, a pretty daughter, an apartment, good wages at the editorial office of one of the most popular newspapers—these were at the top of a young woman's achievements in those days.

As she was leaving, she handed me a letter.

It was a strange letter. It was written to my previous address, sent from London, and my last name was a little misspelled as if the sender did not remember it very well or was not sure about it. The letter had wandered for a long time—it had been opened and checked several times, or censored, which was standard practice. The content of that letter initially surprised me, then amused me, finally forcing me into a deep questioning of how the strange, winding roads of human fate meet.

I read it several times; attached was a document on chalk paper, handwritten in wonderful calligraphic letters, documented in Poznań, dated December 14, 1938. It was a will, in which Prince Michał Czetwertyński—the owner of the Obarów estate in the Równe powiat—donates a land estate consisting of a manor, adjoining farm buildings, and eight hundred hectares of arable land to his son Grzegorz Czetwertyński. At the bottom of the document was the prince's signature, along with the stamp and signature of the Poznań notary. The heir of the estate, Prince Grzegorz Czetwertyński, in the long written letter of beautiful Polish, explained to me the whole of this mysterious case.

This prince was the owner and manager of the Obarów estate, devastated during the wars in the years of 1914-1920. The palace was rebuilt, and Prince Michał and his family lived there. My father and mother worked on this property soon after that.

In 1930, the Polish authorities investigated that the estate of Obarów, up until the January Uprising (1863-64), used to belong to a different noble family. As a reward for their participation in the uprising of that time, the estate was confiscated by the tsarist authorities and handed over for the lordship of Prince Michał's grandfather. However, according to his and my father's version, the estate was put up for auction and was purchased. The dispute over the estate lasted from 1921 to 1930. When eventually the Polish authorities took over the estate of Obarów, an agricultural school was organized in the palace. During Soviet governance, they managed a Sovkhoz (State-Owned Farm).

"Why am I writing this letter?" my unknown cousin wrote. "Our father, Prince Michał, despite the loss of all goods in Wołyń, firmly believed that the time would come when this property would return once again to his family. His faith was based on the fact that in his long life (he lived eighty-two years), he saw and experienced many authorities and regimes—and many of them would rise and fall. Living for many years in Great Britain, he got to know the country's political system very well, deciding that the constitutional monarchy is the best and most enduring system. The different hues of democracy are just a game of interests of various social parties, groups, and cliques, which take advantage of temporary access to power. The old prince believed that sooner or later, there would be a rise of a constitutional monarchy that would ensure the regaining of lost property and prosperity of the nation. The king, tsar, or other hereditary ruler would be the father of his people. I was the only son of my father. You were the other," Grzegorz wrote, "although from an illegitimate bed. Today that does not play any role, and anyway, history likes to repeat in circles—as the old proverb says—so maybe you or your posterity will regain some of the lost possessions. I am more than a dozen years your elder, so I have not got much life left. I am going to die without any children, so you will be the last of the family.

"Be well, brother," the letter ended, "and may God bless you."—signed by Grzegorz Czetwertyński.

I read this letter several times. In the end, I decided it was just like the "Netherlands," a famous donation from Zagłoba to the Swedish king in the times of the Deluge. The noble titles were already abolished by the law of the Polish parliament in 1922. The property in Wołyń was not in my interest at all. I was grateful to Grzegorz that he had let me unravel the mystery of my origins. But that was just history.

My stay in the hospital was coming to an end. My hand was still in plaster, and the spinal column issue turned out to just be a mild injury. After three weeks of lying down, I returned to a vertical position, and I had to think about the future. Spring had come. I not only was able to sit up vertically in the bed, but I even managed to start walking, initially along the corridor, then I visited the other areas of the hospital.

In the days of visits, the hospital was bustling and noisy. A farmer neighboring me, from somewhere nearby, had half of a village visiting him. It was busy and crowded, just like at a market. I wandered in front of the building. There was also a whole crowd of visitors sitting on the benches in front of the hospital. I felt forgotten and abandoned, but I could not demand my daughter visit me after her second child's birth. I did not look at any faces; I did not know anyone here.

I walked along the alley once, twice, when suddenly I felt somebody else's eyes on me. I turned back, and a very familiar person met my gaze. These were the eyes of a blonde who once jumped into the bus on a frosty winter morning, and because I repeatedly stared at her, I missed my stop. I walked past again, and our eyes met for a second reunion. Yes, it was her! We knew each other well, we had met, then she traveled to somewhere far away in Poland, and our contact ended.

A mountain will never meet another mountain, but a human will always meet another human, says an old proverb. Was it a happy coincidence or one more disappointment? I questioned. After a moment, I went to her and introduced myself.

"I recognized you straight away," she confirmed. "What a lucky thing! What are you doing here? Who got you in such a state?" She covered me with a hail of questions, looking at my dressings.

"Oh, it's a trifle, just a small collision," I assured with a crooked smile on my face. "In a week or two, it will all be over."

We sat on the bench until the evening. Many years had passed since our last encounter. Apparently, this was how it was supposed to be before two halves of the apple meet, which according to another Indian proverb, describes a pair of people in love who will always finally meet. We told ourselves everything that was to be said. I knew that Stasia didn't lie, and, to my surprise, we agreed that we were meant to be together. Stasia was free, and I was divorced, so nothing happened to prevent our marriage.

My fate continued in an interesting way. The travel agency in Olsztyn recruited me as a guide for foreign trips. These were most often German-speaking so-called *"nostalgiefahrten"*—nostalgic journeys of people who had fled before the approaching front during the war. Now, they wanted to see the familiar sites. I understood them; after all, I also dreamed about my family's Wołyń.

And that's when I also wrote this book.

Polak, chociaż stąd między narodami słynny,
Że bardziej niźli życie kocha kraj rodzinny,
Gotów zawżdy rzucić go, puścić się w kraj świata,
W nędzy i poniewierce przeżyć długie lata,
Walcząc z ludźmi i z losem, póki mu śród burzy
Przyświeca ta nadzieja, że Ojczyźnie służy.

(The Pole is known to love his native land
more than his life—that has become his role,
prepared to leave at his country's command,
to wander the earth, to struggle with fate,
homeless and destitute, far from Poland.
He'll live till this tyranny will abate,
apart, in hope, to serve his fatherland.)

Adam Mickiewicz, from the *Pan Tadeusz*

A note: In the time of the partisan partition of the Polish-Lithuanian Commonwealth, the Polish nobility living in the former Eastern Borderlands were then referred to as Ruthenian nobles. Hence the title of the book, "The Polish Prince."

THE END

Coat of Arms of the Czetwertyński Family

Attribution: Bastian
License: Commons: GNU Free Documentation License, version 1.2

Epilogue

Before he peacefully passed away in November 2018, I was lucky enough to see my great-grandfather in Masuria. I was able to hear him talk firsthand about the same experiences that you read in this book and feel the raw emotion behind his words. Although I hadn't even read more than a couple inaccurately Google-translated chapters at that time, I told him of my aspirations for his story and how I hoped to make it a success for his legacy.

Through the process of putting together Zbyszek's memoirs, I have attempted to keep them as historically accurate as possible. There may be some of his memories that could have occurred a little differently, it may be true that he changed the names of certain people in the book for anonymity, and there are specific interpretations that may have explained the story slightly differently than he initially wrote, but I am sure you have gotten a profound grasp into what actually happened in the twentieth century—and just how it is relevant with the current geopolitical climate in Eastern Europe today.

As my great-grandfather said in his final thoughts many decades ago, even though the effort and goodwill of people mastered the scourge of nationalism after that war, it doesn't mean that it has been eradicated. That is why having the awareness of experiences like Zbyszek's own are so useful to both current and future generations: to learn from the past, for the purpose of creating a better world.

Finally, I would like to thank you for reading what his story has become. *Na zdar*, Zbyszek!

- Polo Altynski-Ross

Additional Photographs

These are real portraits and pictures of Zbyszek and his family:

Zbyszek with his mother (Wladyslawa) and his father (Ignac)

Photos of Solely Zbyszek

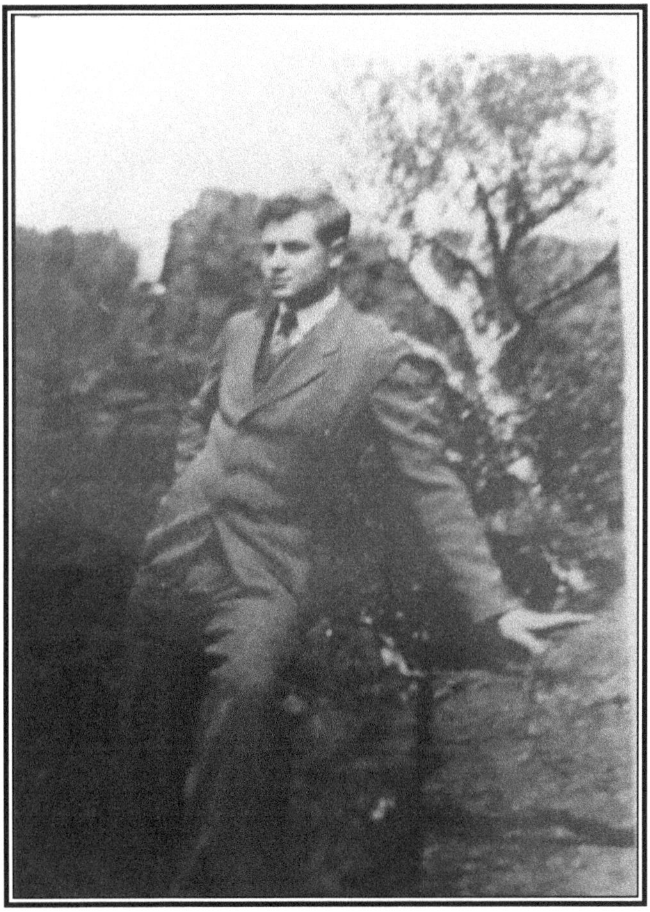

Photos of Zbyszek and Polo's great-grandmother (Lucyna)

Photos of Zbyszek, Lucyna, and Polo's grandmother, Iwona (middle)

Visiting Zbyszek, June 2018

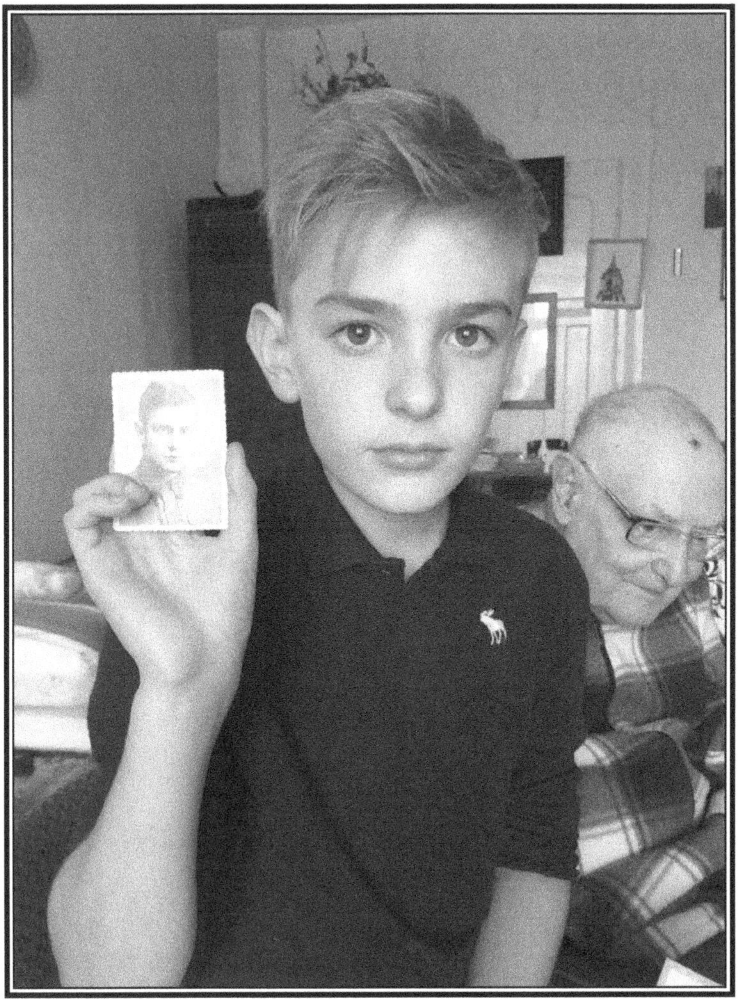

Bibliography

Note about illustration images in this book:

Most, if not all, illustrations contain information from the USHMM encyclopedia of illustrations showing Europe throughout and after WWII. Some images may share similar style characteristics, but none of the maps are direct copies. For assurance, permission has been given to utilize information provided by the museum. Any other information came from a variety of publicly available sources that are verifiable through a quick online search.

Here is a catalog of maps from USHMM for your reference:
"A-Z: Maps." *United States Holocaust Memorial Museum*, https://encyclopedia.ushmm.org/en/a-z/map?query=%2A%3A%2A.

Here are citations for the footnotes throughout the story:
Armstrong, John (January 1990). Ukrainian Nationalism (3rd ed.). Ukrainian Academic Press. ISBN 978-0-87287-755-9. *(Footnote #28)*

Andrzej Paczkowski (2000). Pół wieku dziejów Polski 1939–1989 [Half a Century of the History of Poland 1939–1989]. Warsaw: Wydawnictwo Naukowe PWN. ISBN 978-83-01-14487-6. *(Footnote #46)*

Burds, Jeffrey. *Holocaust in Rovno: The Massacre at Sosenki Forest, November 1941*. Palgrave Pivot, 2014. *(Footnote #17)*

Coynash, Halya. "Volyn 1943: In Remembrance." *Kharkiv Human Rights Protection Group*, 10 July 2013, khpg.org/en/1372801590. *(Footnote #31)*

Dawsey, Jason. "Apocalypse in Dresden, February 1945." *The National WWII Museum | New Orleans*, Feb. 12, 2020, www.nationalww2museum.org/war/articles/apocalypse-dresden-february-1945. *(Footnote #39)*

"Invasion of the Soviet Union, June 1941." *United States Holocaust Memorial Museum*, June 11, 2021, encyclopedia.ushmm.org/content/en/article/invasion-of-the-soviet-union-june-1941. *(Footnote #12)*

Noble, L. "Operation Valkyrie 1944." *Cambridge University Library*, 2014, www.lib.cam.ac.uk/collections/departments/germanic-collections/about-collections/spotlight-archive/operation-valkyrie. *(Footnote #37)*

Popowycz, Jennifer. "The 1941 NKVD Prison Massacres in Western Ukraine." *The National WWII Museum | New Orleans*, The National World War Two Museum, June 6, 2021, https://www.nationalww2museum.org/war/articles/1941-nkvd-prison-massacres-western-ukraine. *(Footnote #13)*

"Stuka | German Aircraft." *Encyclopedia Britannica*, July 20, 1998, www.britannica.com/technology/Stuka. *(Footnote #8)*

Simkin, John. "Erich Koch." *Spartacus Educational*, Sept. 1997, https://spartacus-educational.com/GERkoch.htm. *(Footnote #16)*

Simkin, John. "Communist Secret Police: NKVD." *Spartacus Educational*, 1997, spartacus-educational.com/RUSnkvd.htm. *(Footnote #9)*

Snyder, Timothy. "The Causes of Ukrainian-Polish Ethnic Cleansing 1943." *Past & Present*, vol. 179, no. 1, 2003, pp. 197–234. *Crossref*, doi: 10.1093/past/179.1.197. *(Footnote #32 & 33)*

The Editors of Encyclopedia Britannica, including Ray, Michael. "Berlin Wall | Definition, Length, & Facts." *Encyclopedia Britannica*, 2021, www.britannica.com/topic/Berlin-Wall. *(Footnote #49)*

"Treblinka." *Holocaust Encyclopedia*, United States Holocaust Memorial Museum, Washington, DC, Mar. 3, 2021, encyclopedia.ushmm.org/content/en/article/treblinka. *(Footnote #45)*

"The WWII Polish Deportations – Still an Untold Story." *Polish at Heart*, Mar. 17, 2021, polishatheart.com/the-wwii-polish-deportations-still-an-untold-story. *(Footnote #10)*

Wesolowsky, Tony. "The Vlasov Army: Nazi Sympathizers Or WWII Freedom Fighters?" *Radio Free Europe/Radio Liberty*, Dec. 9, 2019, www.rferl.org/a/the-vlasov-army-nazi-sympathizers-or-ww-ii-freedom-fighters-/30313961.html. *(Footnotes #42 & 43)*

"Warsaw Uprising | Polish History." *Encyclopedia Britannica*, The Editors of Encyclopedia Britannica, July 20, 1998, www.britannica.com/event/Warsaw-Uprising. *(Footnote #44)*

Yurkevich, Myroslav. "Organization of Ukrainian Nationalists." *Internet Encyclopedia of Ukraine*, 1993, www.encyclopediaofukraine.com/display.asp?linkpath=pages%5CO%5CR%5COrganizationofUkrainianNationalists.htm. *(Footnote #23)*

Yaniv, Volodymyr. "Bandera, Stepan." *Internet Encyclopedia of Ukraine*, 2004, www.encyclopediaofukraine.com/display.asp?linkpath=pages%5CB%5CA%5CBanderaStepan.htm. *(Footnote #27)*